Role-Playing for Learning:
Enhancing Skills in Doctrinal Courses

By Yael Efron & Nellie Munin

Role-Playing for Learning: Enhancing Skills in Doctrinal Courses
Published by DRI Press, an imprint of the Dispute
Resolution Institute at Mitchell Hamline School of Law

Dispute Resolution Institute
Mitchell Hamline School of Law
875 Summit Ave, St Paul, MN 55105
© 2025 DRI Press. All rights reserved.
Printed in the United States of America.
ISBN-13: 978-1-7349562-8-3

Mitchell Hamline School of Law in Saint Paul, Minnesota has been educating lawyers for more than 100 years and remains committed to innovation in responding to the changing legal market. Mitchell Hamline offers a rich curriculum in advocacy and problem solving. The law school's Dispute Resolution Institute, consistently ranked in the top dispute resolution programs by *U.S. News & World Report*, is committed to advancing the theory and practice of conflict resolution, nationally and internationally, through scholarship and applied practice projects. DRI offers more than 30 dispute resolution courses each year along with two certificate options. In 2025, DRI Press launched a Skills Series as part of the DRI Laboratory for Advancing Dispute Resolution Skills Teaching https://mitchellhamline.edu/dri-skills-lab/

Cover design by Karin Preus/Acorn Design.

Contents

Foreword	5
Introduction	7
PART 1 – Role-Plays	
International Business Law	15
Globalization and the Law - Theoretical Background	17
The role-plays	
The Coffee Venture	23
Colonel Chicken Goes Abroad	39
International Trade Law	55
Introduction to International Trade Law	57
The role-plays	
Selling the Dead Sea?	59
Let There be Gas!	67
The United Currency Wars	83
Taxation and Tax Law	91
Teaching Tax Law as a Social Instrument	93
The role-plays	
Tax Obedience in COVID-19 Times	97
Sweet Surrender	101
Tax on Disposables	111
Harmful tax competition: to participate or not to participate?	121
Resident or Non-Resident? A Tax Policy Dilemma	127
Public International Law	131
The Challenge of Teaching Public International Law (PIL) and How Role-Plays Can Assist	133
The role-plays	
Converging!	137
Little Golano	187
Flashpoint Syria	193
PART 2 – Teacher's Manual	215
Conducting and Debriefing Educational Simulation Games/Noam Ebner	217
The Editors	237
Acknowledgements	239
Bibliography	241

Foreword

The Importance of Experiential Learning to The Development of Skills: From Knowledge-Based Instruction to Understanding-Based Instruction / Gideon Taran[*]

The digital world in which we live provides the general public with access to endless knowledge resources that were once the preserve of only a few. This challenges the traditional knowledge-based approach to education, gradually leading to a transition from knowledge-based instruction to understanding-based instruction.

The concept of "understanding," although familiar to everyone involved in learning and teaching, is not simple. Studies that have sought to research the nature of understanding by means of its expression among students have found that students perceive understanding as the ability to appreciate the nature of the knowledge, the ability to identify the meaning and the importance of information, and the ability to link new information to personal and professional experiences. Understanding is expressed in the sense of cohesion and connectivity between bodies of knowledge that enables flexibility in adapting them to changing needs and goals. We can learn from this that understanding is locked in the existing knowledge structure of the learner and in the thought processes they can perform with and about it. When the learner has complex knowledge structures, the learner can operate with flexibility in new and different situations from those for which the knowledge structures were built: to think, analyze, improvise, and invent. Understanding, therefore, is "the ability to think and act flexibly with what one knows."[1] These thinking processes are referred to by Perkins as "comprehension performance."[1]

Since the structure of knowledge is hidden and exists in the human brain, tracing understanding is accomplished through the thinking processes that the learner performs using their knowledge. A student's understanding at a specific point in time should be assessed by asking them to perform an action that requires the activation of their understanding: using knowledge in different contexts/levels; transferring knowledge to new situations; performing a variety of thinking actions on a specific topic such

---

[*] Gideon Taran is a pedagogy expert, holding a bachelor's degree (with honors) in geography and history and a master's degree in political science. He served as vice president for pedagogy in several schools and led complex and groundbreaking development processes in the fields of education, teaching, and learning. He initiated, developed, and implemented evaluation systems that serve the decision-making and pedagogical design processes. Taran founded a company for the development, design, and guidance of pedagogical processes educational systems. He served as a lecturer in the Department of Education at the Western Galilee Academic College and as head of the Teaching Quality Unit at the Zefat Academic College. He is leading groundbreaking development processes of programs for pedagogical renewal and designing updated educational models for the challenges of the time.

[1] DAVID PERKINS, TEACHING FOR UNDERSTANDING (1998) at 40.

[2] *Ibid.*

as explaining, presenting evidence, giving examples, generalizing, problem-solving, argument building, creating analogies, and representing it in a new way. Essentially, the performance of understanding is the embodiment of understanding. The above-listed activities deviate from the norm and require non-routine responses based on understanding. As such, they always require a certain cognitive effort. A student's response to a task that requires understanding not only indicates their current level of understanding but also promotes it. The significance of this is that, based on the performance of understanding that rises in complexity, it is possible to advance the student's level of understanding.

Transference is the ability to expand what we have learned from one context to new contexts. There is a distinction between near transference and distant transference. Near transference occurs in situations that are similar in their characteristics to the original learning situation and occurs through an unconscious, automatic activation of patterns that were well practiced. Distant transference, on the other hand, occurs in situations that differ from the original learning situation in many characteristics. It depends on a deep and thoughtful simplification of the learning context to principles that can be applied in different contexts. The less similarity between the characteristics, the farther the transference. The farther the transference, the more it requires the application of previous knowledge while learning and acquiring new knowledge and integrating the old with the new. Therefore, the performances that express distant transference deepen and expand understanding.

The learning process itself, through which this understanding develops, is a process that relies on the cognitive and emotional involvement of the student who is learning. Although learning occurs spontaneously in each person during their life experiences, learning that results in understanding is not satisfied with random occurrences, and it requires the active, mindful, and directed involvement of the learner. This involvement requires the student to obtain personal knowledge based on the community knowledge (in our case, the legal community) while participating as an apprentice in various legal communities and in self-regulation of learning processes with long-term intentions. Participation in role-playing games leads to involvement that has great value to the student.

The contributions of this book to the transition from knowledge-based instruction to understanding-based instruction are twofold. First, it offers practical and accessible tools to foster understanding. This spares instructors the need to "reinvent the wheel" and equips them with the necessary materials, analysis, and feedback for this purpose. Second, it allows for a choice, not only between diverse learning materials but also between different pedagogical goals - from encouraging participation and increasing motivation to deepening and integrating complex knowledge. This is done by highlighting and detailing the range of possibilities for feedback and analysis of the exercises offered in it.

For the adventurous who are willing to break away from familiar routines and try innovative teaching methods, a life-changing experience is guaranteed. Once you try, you won't understand how it was possible to teach without role-playing games.

Introduction

Role-Playing in a Multicultural Learning Environment – Benefits and Challenges

Educators have consistently strived to make theoretical concepts tangible. Teachers across various subjects and educational settings grapple with the challenge of communicating abstract ideas to diverse audiences while aiming to ignite curiosity and sustain engagement. Frequently, we seek didactic tools that bridge the gap between theory and practical application. This need becomes even more pronounced in intricate learning environments, such as multicultural or worldview-diverse classrooms.[1] This book wishes to provide opportunities for positive experiences in such settings. We offer our insight into the method of role-playing in various law courses in a highly diverse class.

Our experience is embedded in the law school of Zefat Academic College (ZAC), located in the north of Israel. The school was established in 2007 to serve the region's unique and varied population. The law school's students are of all religions, ethnic groups, social statuses, and ages.[2] ZAC is one of two law schools established in Israel out of a declared political goal of strengthening Israel's peripheral regions.[3] The remarkable diversity of students within the ZAC Law School's classes presents an exceptional research prospect. It enables the investigation of legal education and pedagogy in a multicultural context, where varying viewpoints, perspectives, and cultural backgrounds frequently disrupt conventional teaching methods. The diversity challenge is further amplified due to stringent budget limitations and the administrative and academic regulations imposed by the Commission of Higher Education on public institutions like ZAC.[4]

---

[1] While classes globally typically exhibit some diversity—such as variations in students' gender, age, social status, and race—multicultural classes at ZAC extend beyond these factors. In addition to the existing diversities, ZAC's multicultural classes comprise students from distinct cultural backgrounds who, despite ongoing political conflict, must share the same physical space and engage with one another daily. The ultimate aim of multiculturalism is to cultivate connections and promote acceptance among these diverse cultures. Charles Taylor, *The Politics of Recognition*, MULTICULTURALISM: EXAMINING THE POLITICS OF RECOGNITION 25-73 (Amy Gutman, ed., 1994)

[2] The student body at ZAC comprised during the examined years approximately sixty percent Jews, who make up the majority group in Israel generally. The other forty percent comprises diverse minority groups, such as Muslims, Christians, Druze, and Circassians. All ethnic groups in class are highly diverse themselves and are comprised of students of all ages—from eighteen-year-olds fresh out of high school to retired elderly citizens. Yael Efron & Yaron Silverstein, *Legal Education as a Means for Social Ethnic and Inter-Ethnic Change: The Case of Arab Law Students in Zefat College*, 19 Hamishpat [ColMan L. Rev.] 331, 336 (2014) (Isr.).

[3] ISRAELI HIGHER EDUCATION COMMISSION, COMPILATION OF MAIN RESOL.: 2002-2007 (Mar. 2007) (Isr.), http://bit.ly/45rYtv8.pdf

[4] ISRAELI HIGHER EDUCATION COMMISSION, COMPILATION OF MAIN RESOL. (May 1997) (Isr.).

Coming from underprivileged communities, many students perceive their legal degree as a means for social mobility and their future legal practice as potential financial relief.[5] Therefore, the pedagogical choices at ZAC Law School attempt to combine professional training with a wider humanistic, theoretical grounding as suggested in the scholarship.[6]

Teaching at this law school necessitates faculty members to create distinctive teaching methods to address these challenges. These approaches should employ clear language that resonates with all students while also emphasizing common ground and cultural awareness. Importantly, this must be accomplished without compromising the rigorous educational standards. During class discussions on moral and legal dilemmas, the discourse frequently mirrors cultural variations and emotional responses to current events within the student groups.[7] The ZAC Law School functions as a dynamic testing ground for creating innovative teaching tools to address these requirements. This book introduces a pedagogical instrument that was developed and put into practice to tackle these challenges. Role-playing has been effectively integrated into various courses at the ZAC Law School for several years.

Utilizing Role-Playing as an Educational Tool in Diverse Learning Environments
Experiential Learning in Legal Education

Since its inception, legal academia worldwide has grappled with fundamental questions about the optimal approach to teaching and learning law. What constitutes essential content for law schools? Who should be responsible for imparting legal knowledge, and how should it be done? While legal systems vary, a common dilemma arises in discussions about law school curricula. This pivotal question—though often framed as a dilemma—is whether the legal academy's primary role should be vocational training.[8] Many scholars assume that the role of the legal academy is mainly associated with reviewing, challenging, and criticizing the law and legal culture.[9] Surveying legal curricula suggests that law schools are generally aligned with the more theoretical approach.[10] However, the expectation and the assumption of the legislature, the bar, the bench, and the students themselves are that the academic studies of legal trainees prepare them for practice.[11] This is due to the direct link between the process

---

[5] Yael Efron & Yaron Silverstein, *Law Students as Agents of Change*, 6 MAASEY MISHPAT 105, 110 (2014)(Isr.). On academic studies as a resource for empowerment of underprivileged communities, see Efron & Silverstein, supra note 4, at 340.

[6] AUSTIN SARAT, MATTHEW ANDERSON & CATHRINE O. FRANK, LAW AND THE HUMANITIES: AN INTRODUCTION (2009).

[7] For student reflections on the clashes between their ethnic culture and their newly acquired legal values, see Efron & Silverstein, supra note 4, at 355-56.

[8] For a review of some of the literature and a comparative discussion on these questions, see Yael Efron, Legal Education in Israel: Where Is It Headed?, 9 ALEI MISHPAT [Law Review of the Academic Center of Law & Business] 45 (2010) (Isr.).

[9] David Sugarman, Beyond Ignorance and Complacency: Robert Stevens, Journey Through Lawyers and the Courts, 16 INT'L J. OF LEGAL PROF. 10 (2009).

[10] This observation is discussed in Efron, supra note 10, at 64-68 and also in John Lande & Jean R. Sternlight, *The Potential Contribution of ADR to an Integrated Curriculum: Preparing Law Students for Real World Lawyering*, 25 OHIO ST. J. ON DISP. RESOL. 247, 251–52 (2010).

[11] Id.

of academic legal education and the accreditation process for legal licensure.[12] Those who advocate for a more skill-oriented curriculum also do so on the claim that law schools should focus on adequate preparation for practice as part of their social responsibilities.[13]

With that said, it is pretty uncommon today to view the theory–vs.–practice divide as a dichotomy.[14] Although a theoretical approach dominates legal education, many opportunities for experiential learning are offered in the form of legal clinics, moot court competitions, and practical workshops. Today, the well-accepted view of legal education is that "good theory is practical, and that good practice is informed by theory."[15] Recent years seem to have brought about changes in the legal academy's perspective regarding the importance of practical teaching and experiential learning.[16]

Furthermore, technology has always affected the legal curriculum.[17] Nowadays, the introduction of Artificial Intelligence tools for research and writing demands a novel approach to the role of the legal academy. A focus on knowledge acquisition or writing skills cannot suffice. New search engines can easily and quickly find information and innovative technologies can now draft documents, summarize judicial decisions and scholarship, extract and compare arguments, and much more.[18] Therefore, future lawyers must be equipped with a different skillset than before. Such skills should include fluency in both traditional and innovative technologies, interpersonal skills that are irreplaceable by machines, and, most importantly, resilience - the ability to adapt to rapidly changing circumstances.[19] By simply reiterating what they learned from their own law professors, professors cannot teach law students to successfully adapt.

New law school didactics seek to break through the traditions of teaching law by offering experiential opportunities for students to practice independent legal research, enhance rhetorical capabilities, and perfect their oral and written expression.[20] These methods not only target the acquisition of skills but also aim to promote values such as professional ethics, collegiality, acknowledgment of others, and empathy to distress.[21] The legal pedagogy should include the development of interpersonal communication and emotional intelligence as an integral part of lawyering skills.[22] Given the unique makeup of the student body at ZAC, special attention is also drawn to the promotion of intercultural literacy and

---

[12] A JD serves as the first professional law degree required to practice law in the United States. Similarly, an academic degree is required in most global jurisdictions.

[13] Stephen Wizner, The Law School Clinic: Legal Education in the Interests of Justice, 70 FORDHAM L. REV. 1929, 1934 (2002).

[14] Yael Efron, *Clinical Legal Education in Israel*, in CLINICAL LEGAL EDUCATION IN ASIA: ACCESSING JUSTICE FOR THE UNDERPRIVILEGED 91, 95 (Shuvro Prosun Sarker ed., 2015) (hereinafter: Efron, 2015); Yael Efron, What is Learned in Clinical Learning? 29 CLINICAL LAW REVIEW 259, 299 (2023) (hereinafter: Efron, 2023).

[15] Wizner, *supra* note 15, at 1932.

[16] Efron 2023, *supra* note 16, at 264-65.

[17] Yael Efron, *The Pentalectic Sphere as Means for Questioning Legal Education - Towards a Paradigm Shift*, 9 ARIZONA SUMMIT LAW REVIEW 285, 363-68 (2016).

[18] As an example of many such tools, see https://ailawyer.pro/

[19] RICHARD SUSSKIND, TOMORROW'S LAWYERS: AN INTRODUCTION TO YOUR FUTURE (2017).

[20] John Lande & Jean R. Sternlight, The Potential Contribution of ADR to an Integrated Curriculum: Preparing Law Students for Real World Lawyering, 25(1) OHIO ST. J. ON DIS. RESOL. 247, 261 (2010).

[21] See Wizner, *supra* note 15.

[22] Leonard L. Riskin, The Contemplative Lawyer: On the Potential Contributions of Mindfulness Meditation to Law Students, Lawyers, and their Clients, 7 HARV. NEGOT. L. REV. 1, 17 (2002).

sensitivity.[23] This may also be relevant to other law schools, especially those serving students from un-derprivileged backgrounds.

Role-playing, in which students are assigned a role and expected to act out a given scenario, is a useful example of an experiential technique for teaching and learning. Its use has been documented and studied for more than half a century.[24] The literature exposes the shortcomings as well as the advantages of role-playing as a method for learning theoretical concepts and enhancing professional skills and competencies.

While several studies indicate that role-playing is not much more effective for acquiring knowledge than lecture and case-study methods, there are other well-established advantages to role-playing. The majority of studies found that role-playing significantly increased students' interest in the content they were learning, helped them retain it for a longer period and in greater detail, and helped them develop a positive attitude and reduce their worry about the subject.[25] Role-playing not only brings theory to life and offers students the chance to put theory into practice; it does so in an enjoyable and accommodating manner.

However, educators who employ role-plays as teaching tools must keep in mind that the legal system is based on social needs and functions in a social environment.[26] As a result, culture significantly impacts pedagogy and curriculum design. Individual cultures have an impact on a variety of legal education-related factors, such as learning preferences,[27] involvement in particular didactics,[28] and desire to study law.[29] Research on learning capacities indicates that there are, in fact, differences based on culture.[30] The collective cultural characteristics displayed by every student in the class may not always constitute the law school culture. It differs from the individual's societal culture, at times even contradicting it.[31] When the culture of the law school and a particular learner's (or teacher's) cultural background contradict, educational tensions are created.

Role-playing is an effective way to resolve many conflicts in the classroom. However, adopting the identity of another person may be viewed as insulting in particular social contexts. A group with a

---

[23] Phyllis E. Bernard, *Finding Common Ground in the Soil of Culture*, in RETHINKING NEGOTIATION TEACHING: INNOVATIONS FOR CONTEXT AND CULTURES 29 (Christopher Honeyman, James Coben & Giuseppe De Palo eds., 2009). On challenges and benefits of learning law in a multicultural environment, see also Efron & Silverstein, *supra* note 4, at 344.

[24] For an extensive review of this literature, see Daniel Druckman & Noam Ebner, *Onstage or Behind the Scenes? Relative Learning Benefits of Simulation Role-Play and Design*, 39(4) SIMULATION AND GAMING 465, 467 (2008).

[25] Id.

[26] See Menachem Mautner, *Three Approaches to Law and Culture*, 96 CORNELL L. REV. 839 (2011).

[27] See examples of culturally categorized learning styles in Kimberlee K. Kovach, *Culture, Cognition and Learning Preferences*, in RETHINKING NEGOTIATION, *supra* note 22, at 343, 348-49.

[28] Nadja Alexander & Michelle LeBaron, *Death of the Role-Play*, RETHINKING NEGOTIATION TEACHING: INNOVATIONS FOR CONTEXT AND CULTURES (Christopher Honeyman, James Coben & Giuseppe De Palo eds., 2009), at 179, 182-84.

[29] Efron & Silverstein, *supra* note 4, at 355.

[30] Empirical data clearly support the notion that one's culture directly affects learning preferences. See Glauco De Vita, *Learning Styles, Culture and Inclusive Interaction in the Multicultural Classroom: A Business and Management Perspective*, 38(2) INNOVATIONS EDUC. & TEACHING INT'L 165 (2001).

[31] Efron, *supra* note 19 at 326-33.

strong noninterference ethic can occasionally feel it is improper and intrusive to "play" someone else.[32] Therefore, it is important to use role-plays with awareness in multicultural settings. The foundation of experiential learning is the idea that for each student's experiences to hold significance, they must be grounded in reality. The topics covered in the exercises and simulations should be ones that the students are likely to encounter.[33] When context is artificial, knowledge and skills may be similarly artificial, thus reducing the likelihood of the transfer of skills into real situations.[34] Simulations based on pseudo-reality may overcome these obstacles. The pseudo-reality simulation design method developed by Ebner and Efron[35] has successfully engaged students from diverse backgrounds in role-playing. The reason students are happy to engage in a fictional scenario is that the method of pseudo-reality allows them to detach themselves emotionally from their own lives yet stay in a context of familiar fact patterns and dilemmas with which they are well-acquainted.

This book contains a number of role-plays that can be edited to fit various needs. Each one is self-contained. Some of the role-plays in this book are detailed and well-developed and have been tested in an academic setting. Some allow the teacher or students to add significant details. Some of the role-plays contained herein are accompanied by a brief introduction to a specific area of law. For others, knowledge of an area of law is either assumed or unnecessary. Generally, these role-plays cite to Israeli law but your country's law can be substituted.

All the role-plays in this book are intended to provide an in-depth experiential learning opportunity. The Teachers' Manual at the back of the book details how they can be used, and provides information about set-up, timing, and debriefing.

Although we did not conduct our role-playing experience as a scientific experiment, we value the need to share the knowledge we accumulated in the process with other educators and thus invite our colleagues into our experiences.

There are significant scientific flaws in drawing broad generalizations from sporadic test instances. We want to emphasize that this book does not recommend transferring our findings, since we are aware of potential criticisms in this regard. Conversely, by presenting our personal experience, which largely confirms conclusions that have been established in academic research, we hope to inspire colleagues to investigate the topics that have been explored here.[36] Our objective in this book is to enrich our shared understanding and practice and perhaps even inspire fellow researchers to pursue contradicting conclusions in different settings.[37]

We hope that you will enjoy reading the book and invite you to play along!

Nellie Munin and Yael Efron, 2025

---

[32] Alexander & LeBaron, *supra* note 30, at 182.
[33] Kovach, *supra* note 29, at 346.
[34] Alexander & LeBaron, *supra* note 30, at 184.
[35] Noam Ebner & Yael Efron, Using Tomorrow's Headlines for Today's Training: Creating PseudoReality in Conflict Resolution Simulation-Games, 21(3) HARV. NEGOT. J. 377 (2005).
[36] For the relevance of case study methodology, see Roger Gomm, Martyn Hammersley & Peter Foster, *Case Study and Generalization*, in CASE STUDY METHOD: KEY ISSUES, KEY TEXTS 98 (Roger Gomm, Martyn Hammersley & Peter Foster, eds., 2000).
[37] Phil Hodkinson & Heather Hodkinson, The Strengths and Limitations of Case Study Research 11 (Dec. 5, 2001) (unpublished paper), https://www.academia.edu/31677978/The_Strengths_and_Limitations_of_Case_Study_Research. The authors argue that the findings of case studies are traditionally held scientifically sound, if they are grounded in theory, until contradicted by a different case study.

PART 1
Role-Plays

International Business Law

Globalization and the Law - Theoretical Background

Across history, narratives abound of individuals departing their familiar abodes to venture into distant lands, immersing themselves in foreign cultures. These sagas trace back to antiquity, with echoes resonating even within the sacred texts of the Bible. Fueled by an insatiable curiosity, these intrepid expeditions persist to this day, bolstered by technological innovations that facilitate mobility and seamless communication.[1] Throughout history, numerous expeditions have been driven by economic or political motives, often sponsored by states to undertake costly journeys to distant lands. In the contemporary era, advancements in transportation have significantly lowered expenses, making such voyages more prevalent and accessible. These expeditions not only facilitate cultural tourism but also foster intercultural exchange. Remarkably, the media, internet, and telecommunications enable cross-cultural exposure and dialogue, even without physically embarking on these journeys.

Meanwhile, law, as a reflection of our reality, remains a dynamic framework perpetually adapting to the evolving landscape of human behavior. The educational process — just as the law[2] — operates in a social setting and is justified by social needs. The development of the individual learner is a product of the learner's society and culture.[3] Therefore, culture must play a crucial role in curricular design and pedagogy. Law studies must follow and reflect such developments.[4] As the world becomes a village, legal frameworks provide rules for engaging in international transactions, disputes, and resolution mechanisms.

Globalization also leads to increased interactions between diverse cultures. These interactions significantly influence the fundamental nature and context of both international and national legal norms, as well as the dynamics of legal procedures. This impact extends to various aspects, including negotiations, dispute resolution, and even the daily practices of legal professionals. Like the law, culture is the

---

[1] Noam Ebner, *Negotiation is Changing*, J. Disp. Resol. (2017).
[2] Menachem Mautner, *Three Approaches to Law and Culture*, 96 Cornell L. Rev. 839 (2010).
[3] Graham Ferris, *The Legal Educational Continuum That Is Visible Through A Glass Dewey* 43 The Law Teacher 102 (2009).
[4] Yael Efron, *The Pentalectic Sphere as Means for Questioning Legal Education - Towards a Paradigm Shift*, 9 Arizona Summit Law Review 285, 327 (2016).

logic by which we give order to the world.[5] This reality prompts a question that has been widely debated in scholarly literature: To what extent does legal education address these phenomena?

The existing body of literature delineates various pedagogical endeavors aimed at nurturing students' cultural sensitivities. However, it is noteworthy that these efforts have only become more prevalent within the realm of legal studies in recent times.[6] There is still a need for a comprehensive approach regarding the most effective methods. Various constraints (e.g., economic, time, etc.) seem to undermine potential initiatives to include this issue in law school curricula.

Our role-plays in this chapter attempt to meet the challenge of effectively preparing law students for globalized business and legal practices. In one of these role-plays, "The Coffee Venture," we brought the global world into class literally and not just figuratively. This interactive international business negotiations role-play was offered in a course that was taught by five instructors from three countries (Canada, China, and Israel). This anecdotal experience reaffirms findings that are well-established in academic literature. We encourage our colleagues to follow suit and explore for themselves the many benefits of this and the other role-plays in this chapter.

As a means of a theoretical background for these role-plays, we use the terms "sensitivity," "competency," "fluency," and "intelligence" interchangeably with regard to cultural and intercultural knowledge, skills, and values. We chose to do so despite literature that differentiates these terms since these concepts are not the focus of this book.[7]

---

[5] Susan Bryant & Jean Koh Peters, *The Five Habits of Cross Cultural Lawyering*, RACE, CULTURE, PSYCHOLOGY AND LAW 47-62 (Kimberly Barrett and William George eds., 2005).

[6] Piomelli Ascanio, *Cross-Cultural Lawyering by the Book: The Latest Clinical Texts and a Sketch of a Future Agenda* 4 HASTINGS RACE AND POVERTY JOURNAL 131 (2006); Bryant & Peters, *id*; Jan L. Jacobowitz, *Lawyers Beware! You Are What You Post---The Case for Integrating Cultural Competency, Legal Ethics, and Social Media*, 4 SCIENCE & TECHNOLOGY L. REV. 541(2014); Antoinette Sedillo López, *Making and Breaking Habits: Teaching (and Learning) Cultural Context, Self-Awareness, and intercultural Communication Through Case Supervision in a Client-Service Legal Clinic*, 28 WASHINGTON UNIVERSITY JOURNAL OF LAW AND POLICY 37 (2008); Marci Seville, *Chinese Soup, Good Horses, and Other Narratives: Practicing Cross-Cultural Competence before We Preach*, VULNERABLE POPULATIONS AND TRANSFORMATIVE LAW TEACHING: A CRITICAL READER 277 (Society of American Law Teachers, 2011); Laurel S. Terry, *U.S. Legal Ethics: The Coming of Age of Global and Comparative Perspectives*, 4 WASHINGTON UNIVERSITY GLOBAL STUDIES LAW REVIEW 463 (2005); Paul R. Tremblay, *Interviewing and Counseling Across Cultures: Heuristics and Biases*, 9 CLINICAL L. REV. 373 (2002); Carina Weng, *Multicultural Lawyering: Teaching Psychology To Develop Cultural Self-awareness*, 11 CLINICAL LAW REVIEW 369 (2005).

[7] For discussions on these concepts, see P. CHRISTOPHER EARLEY & SOON ANG, CULTURAL INTELLIGENCE: INDIVIDUAL INTERACTIONS ACROSS CULTURES (2003); and Mark Hungerford Salisbury, *The Effect of Study Abroad on Intercultural Competence Among Undergraduate College Students*, PH.D. DISSERTATION, UNIVERSITY OF IOWA (2011), available at: https://iro.uiowa.edu/esploro/outputs/doctoral/The-effect-of-study-abroad-on/9983777141002771?institution=01IOWA_INST.

Why Globalization Is Crucial to Legal Studies

The literature recognizes the effects of globalization on global business conduct,[8] the essence of law, legal process, and legal education. In essence, global regulation has been and continues to be crafted to uphold fundamental norms and principles within the ever-evolving context of our interconnected "global village." These norms span diverse domains, including human rights, labor rights, gender rights, intellectual property rights, competition, environmental protection, international trade and investments, financial transactions, agriculture, and maritime law. Knowledge and deep understanding of these norms and their cultural roots[9] are important for law students to engage in both international law and domestic law effectively.[10] As a consequence of globalization, numerous national legal systems draw inspiration from, or are pragmatically influenced by, international regulations. In legal practice, even attorneys specializing in domestic law routinely represent clients with backgrounds and experiences that are vastly different from their own, and the fact of these differences can impede understanding, communication, and, ultimately, effective representation."[11]

As recognized in the literature, the basic lawyer-client exchange could sometimes be described as an intercultural one, even if the individuals involved have some cultural variables in common. The culture of the legal profession evidences its own values, history, procedures, etc.[12] Relationships with clients may require: "… [an] awareness of power and role issues including who has expertise and what sort of expertise is required to solve problems; diversity in legal systems and the role of law; and, in some instances, awareness of avenues for avoiding the law's application."[13] Certain cases may require learning about legal processes in other countries. Thus, "all businesses and their lawyers must think globally, even if they operate only domestically."[14] Silver states: "Just as e-mail, texting, Facebook, and tweets are part of the lexicon and skill-set for the current generation of law graduates, and have remarkably changed patterns of work over the last twenty-five years, so will tomorrow's lawyers be required to understand

---

[8] Ian S. Mutchnick, Cherly A. Moyer & David T. Stern, *Expanding the Boundaries of Medical Education: Evidence for Cross-Cultural Exchanges*, 78 ACADEMIC MEDICINE S1 (2003); Sherry Sullivan & Howard S. Tu, *Developing Globally Competent Students: A Review and Recommendations*, 19 JOURNAL OF MANAGEMENT EDUCATION 473 (1995).

[9] Hofstede (1984) identifies specific dimensions of value systems in 40 countries that affect human thinking, organizations, and institutions. Hofstede shows how countries may be divided into cultural areas. GEERT HOFSTEDE, CULTURE'S CONSEQUENCES: INTERNATIONAL DIFFERENCES IN WORK RELATED VALUES (1984). Further discussion on the role of culture-dependent models of leadership in business management is provided in ROBERT J. HOUSE, PAUL J. HANGES, MANSOUR JAVIDAN, PETER W. DORFMAN & VIPIN GUPTA, CULTURE, LEADERSHIP, AND ORGANIZATIONS: THE GLOBE STUDY OF 62 SOCIETIES (2004).

[10] Carole Silver, *Getting Real About Globalization and Legal Education: Potential and Perspectives for the U.S.*, 24 STANFORD LAW AND POLICY REVIEW 457 (2013).

[11] Debra Chopp, *Addressing Cultural Bias in the Legal Profession*, 41 N.Y.U. Rev. L. & Soc. Change 367, 367 (2017)

[12] Jacobowitz *supra* 6, at 8.

[13] Silver *supra* 10, at 461.

[14] Martini & Susler *supra* 11.

how to work in a globally diverse environment...as well as in contexts shaped by globalization."[15][16] The necessary skills lawyers need to exercise in a global environment may differ from one case to another. "Despite the differences, in each case lawyers must acquire intercultural skills that allow them to develop relationships, strategies for effective communication, and approaches to managing uncertainty that characterize global encounters."[17]

In the context of business management, Earley and Ang summarize these qualifications using the term cultural intelligence, which is composed of three facets: 1) cognition (the ability to develop patterns from cultural cues), 2) motivation (the desire and ability to engage others), and 3) behavior (the capacity to act in accordance with cognition and motivation).[18]

In recent years, there has been a growing fear of the social and economic implications of massive global waves of immigration motivated by economic, social, and political reasons. The recognition that the ripple effects of financial and economic crises are amplified by globalization underscores the emergence of nationalist sentiments, xenophobia, and a proclivity toward insular thinking. These notions, unfortunately, erode the positive facets of globalization, including cross-cultural interactions. In many countries, intolerance towards diverse ethnic groups, religions, or cultural groups has grown, risking the stability of communities and global societies.[19] Alternatively, exposure to other cultures may enhance and reinforce mutual cultural sensitivity, dismantling superstition, suspicion, and even hatred and potential violence inflamed by cultural ignorance and fear of the unknown "other." These factors may play a decisive role in legal processes involving negotiations, cooperation, and legal interpretation, which may further "require sensitivity to ambiguity resulting from language and cultural differences."[20]

Raising awareness about other cultures to enhance the development of cultural sensitivity and tolerance (both domestically and internationally) is, thus, of major educational importance, particularly in law studies.[21] In the United States, for example, a Carnegie Foundation report issued by Sullivan and colleagues addresses the need for legal education that instills ethical and social values in practitioners. The report contends that "despite progress in making legal ethics a part of the curriculum, law schools

---

[15] Silver *supra* 10, at 457-458.

[16] A survey conducted in 2009 among Philadelphia, Pennsylvania (U.S.A.) bar members indicated that 3 the majority (67.5%) of members encountered issues that required them to know something about foreign and/or international law. See Suzan DeJarnatt & Mark Rahdert, *Preparing for Globalized Law Practice: The Need to Include International and Comparative Law in the Legal Writing Curriculum*, 17 THE JOURNAL OF THE LEGAL WRITING INSTITUTE 1, 7-9 (2011).

[17] Silver *supra* 10, at 495.

[18] Earley & Ang *supra* 7.

[19] This has been reinforced by the refugee crisis, particularly in Europe. See for example, Heather Horn, *Is Eastern Europe Any More Xenophobic Than Western Europe?: Investigating a Stereotype of the Refugee Crisis*, THE ATLANTIC (2015), available at: https://tinyurl.com/4psa335x; Gianni Pittella, *Populism, Racism and Xenophobia Have Infected Europe*, EURACTIVE (2016), available at: https://tinyurl.com/mr2jy2am

[20] Silver *supra* 10, at 461.

[21] The role of culture in the emergence of conflicts and the competencies required for the management of such disputes is discussed in MICHELLE LeBARON, BRIDGING CULTURAL CONFLICTS: A NEW APPROACH TO A CHANGING WORLD (2003) and MICHELLE LeBARON & VENASHRY PILLAY, CONFLICT ACROSS CULTURE: A UNIQUE EXPERIENCE OF BRIDGING DIFFERENCES (2006).

rarely pay consistent attention to the social and cultural contexts of legal institutions.[22] To meet this challenge, the Carnegie Foundation report particularly recommends using "well-elaborated case studies" and pedagogical creativity.[23]

Challenges to Fostering "Cultural Intelligence" in Legal Education

While the literature generally acknowledges the importance of fostering "cultural intelligence" of law students in a global world, some obstacles that may challenge this process include:

1) The need for analysis of the impact of globalization processes on the very structure of legal education and the role of education in maintaining professional values and competency levels.[24]

2) Many existing international or intercultural programs offered by academic institutions suffer from weak or unsystematic conceptualization and assessment of success.[25]

3) Cultural intelligence acquisition is a long process of learning by doing.[26] Thus, due to various constraints (e.g., time, cost, etc.), law school curricula can, at best, only trigger such processes by raising student awareness of their importance, which offers them limited experiential opportunities.

4) Experiential learning tends to invoke objection from experienced practitioners who had not been educated in such a manner. This might be attributed to a fear of competition with newly educated lawyers that may force them to update their skills or perish.[27]

5) Law teachers must be well-informed of influential factors attributed to globalization as it relates to law in order to teach these legal matters in their courses effectively.[28] Those who are not knowledgeable may form yet another source of resistance.

We assert that incorporating intercultural experiences into law school curricula should be embraced. In addressing these challenges, pragmatic considerations involve devising effective strategies to equip

---

[22] William M. Sullivan, Anne Colby, Judith Welch Wegner, Lloyd Bond & Lee S. Shulman, Educating Lawyers: Preparation for the Profession of Law (2007), at 11.

[23] *Ibid.*

[24] James Faulconbridge & Daniel Muzino, *Legal Education, Globalization and Cultures of Professional Practice*, 21 Georgetown Journal of Legal Ethics 1335 (2009).

[25] Janeiro Fábregas, María G., Ricardo López Fabre & José Pablo Nuño de la Parra, *Building Intercultural Competence Through Intercultural Competency Certification of Undergraduate Students*, 10 Journal of International Education Research 15 (2014).

[26] David C. Thomas & Kerr C. Inkson, Cultural Intelligence: Surviving and Thriving in the Global Village (2017).

[27] *Translating and the Law: Legal Language*, The Economist (2012), available at: https://www.economist.com/business/2012/11/10/legal-language

[28] Thus, in 2012, the theme of the annual meeting of the Association of American Law Schools was "Global Engagement and the Legal Academy," recognizing the challenges of teaching students to interact with lawyers educated in other countries and to "develop cultural competencies for practice" Association of American Law Schools, *Presidential Workshop on Globalizing the Curriculum at the 2013 AALS Annual Meeting*, AALS News: A Quarterly Publication of the Association of American Law Schools (2012), available at: https://www.aals.org/app/uploads/2020/09/AALSNewsNovember2012Triennial.pdf .

students for functioning in a global context. Depending on specific circumstances, proponents argue that spending time abroad can enhance individuals' ability to work effectively in a global environment and foster intercultural competence[29] and cross-cultural sensitivity (i.e., knowledge, awareness, and acceptance of other cultures).[30] Nevertheless, this option is not feasible for all students due to financial and personal constraints. Attempts to overcome these obstacles may take the form of creating a global atmosphere on national campuses and/or at law schools by hosting international students. Some believe that such interaction may reduce prejudice,[31] raise intercultural sensitivity and awareness,[32] and enhance effective learning of international matters.[33] Such achievements would depend on meaningful interaction between native and international students, necessitating "intentional choreography." This entails "ensuring that the contact among students, both qualitatively and quantitatively, is appropriate to facilitate learning."[34] For example, domestic and international students attending the same courses on the same campus may facilitate meaningful interactions.[35] However, many campuses cannot afford to host international students for various reasons (e.g., cost, space constraints, shortage of multilingual teachers, ability to offer courses to foreign students that address specific credentials, etc.).

We believe that the role-plays in this chapter can help overcome some of these challenges. If students or faculty from abroad visit your campus, you can utilize these games as an enjoyable learning experience, infusing legal and business learning materials with positive global interactions. Even without international students or faculty, the role-plays will still provide an opportunity to understand some of the issues that may arise in international matters.

---

[29] See Mark Hungerford Salisbury, *The Effect of Study Abroad on Intercultural Competence Among Undergraduate College Students*, PH.D. DISSERTATION, UNIVERSITY OF IOWA 23-33 (2011), available at: https://iro.uiowa.edu/esploro/outputs/doctoral/The-effect-of-study-abroad-on/9983777141002771?institution=01IOWA_INST for the significance of intercultural competence. It seems to be commonly agreed that this concept "applies the notion of competence to describe the successful engagement or collaboration toward a single or shared set of goals between individuals or groups who do not share the same cultural origins or background" (at 26) and involves "cognitive, intrapersonal, and interpersonal capacities required of intercultural competence, including openness to diversity, racial tolerance, respect for racial and ethnic differences, cultural knowledge, multicultural understanding, increased interracial comfort, international understanding, and pluralistic orientation" (at 33).

[30] Amanda Kubokawa, *Positive Psychology and Cultural Sensitivity: A Review of the Literature*, 1 GRADUATE JOURNAL OF COUNSELING PSYCHOLOGY 130 (2009); Charles M. Vance, *The Personal Quest for Building Global Competence: A Taxonomy of Self-Initiating Career Path Strategies for Gaining Business Experience Abroad*, 40 JOURNAL OF WORLD BUSINESS 374 (2005).

[31] Thomas Pettigrew, Linda R. Tropp, Ulrich Wagner & Oliver Christ, *Recent Advances in Intergroup Contact Theory*, 35 INTERNATIONAL JOURNAL OF INTERCULTURAL RELATIONS 271, 277 (2011).

[32] Madhav Sharma & Loren B. Jung, *How Cross-Cultural Social Participation Affects the International Attitudes of U.S. Students*, 9 INTERNATIONAL JOURNAL OF INTERCULTURAL RELATIONS 377, 381-2 (1985).

[33] Rebecca Lindsey Parsons, *The Effects of an Internationalized University Experience on Domestic Students in the United States and Australia*, 14 JOURNAL OF STUDIES IN INTERNATIONAL EDUCATION 313 (2010).

[34] Betty Leask, *Using Formal and Informal Curricula to Improve Interactions Between Home and International Students*, 13 JOURNAL OF STUDIES IN INTERNATIONAL EDUCATION 205, 219 (2009).

[35] Silver *supra* 10, at 475-486.

The Coffee Venture Role-Play[1]

A Multi-Stage Plot

This role-play sets an example for the Multi-Stage Simulation didactic method.[2] This method consists of a rolling plot with different modular stages played by participants throughout the course. Through this method, all the "negotiating venues"[3] are covered under one story line. In each session of the course, a new development in the storyline is used to illustrate and practically apply the issues presented. In certain segments of the course, the role-play is used as an introduction to a discussion on a particular practice or theory. In other cases, the role-play is used to apply a theory previously taught.[4] Each phase of this multi-stage simulation is methodically debriefed.[5] The debriefing aspect is the basis for the next item on the course syllabus. The specific fact pattern for the role-play is included after the description of its actual use in class at ZAC.

The consecutive stages of the role-play start with setting the "pseudo-reality" scenario.[6] The plot contains general details that are shared by both parties, as well as confidential information delivered

---

[1] This exercise was developed by Nellie Munin & Yael Efron. It was conducted at ZAC with five instructors from three different countries (Canada, China and Israel) who collaborate in fostering cultural fluency in a multicultural undergraduate class that consisted of twenty students (nine Jews and eleven Arabs). Instructors utilized this course to introduce the twenty students to Chinese business culture, with which they were not familiar. A more detailed account of this course can be found in Yael Efron & Nellie Munin, *International Business Negotiations in a Global World: Cultural Sensitivity in Multicultural Law Classes*, PEDAGOGICAL APPROACHES TO INTERCULTURAL COMPETENCE DEVELOPMENT 31-66 (Christine E. Poteau, ed., Cambridge Scholars Publishing, 2020).

[2] John Lande, *Suggestions for Using Multi-Stage Simulations in Law School Courses*, UNIVERSITY OF MISSOURI SCHOOL OF LAW LEGAL STUDIES, RESEARCH PAPER NO. 2013-08: 1-7 (2014).

[3] JEANNE M. BRETT, NEGOTIATION GLOBALLY 2-4 (2nd ed., 2007).

[4] In his guest lecture at ZAC law school on May 13, 2013, Former Chief Justice Aharon Barak described Israel as a "living laboratory of international norms." For his description of the Israeli legal system see Aharon Barak, *Some Reflections on the Israeli Legal System and Its Judiciary*, 6(1) Electronic J. Comp. L. (Apr. 2002). For the notion of Israel as a "laboratory" for legal norms, see also Daphne Barak-Erez, *The National Security Constitution and the Israeli Condition*, ISRAELI CONSTITUTIONAL LAW IN THE MAKING 429-444 (Gideon Sapir, Daphne Barak-Erez and Aharon Barak, eds., 2013).

[5] For a discussion on the method used to debrief the class and implement the role-play activity, see Ellen E. Deason, Yael Efron, Ranse Howell, Sanda Kaufman, Joel Lee, & Sharon Press, *Debriefing the Debrief*, EDUCATING NEGOTIATORS FOR A CONNECTED WORLD 301-332 (Rethinking Negotiation Teaching Series, volume 4, Christopher Honeyman, James Coben, and Andrew Wei-Min Lee eds., 2013) available at: https://open.mitchellhamline.edu/dri_press/4/.

[6] For a discussion on the "pseudo-reality" method for creating simulation storylines, see Noam Ebner & Yael Efron, *Using Tomorrow's Headlines for Today's Training: Creating PseudoReality in Conflict Resolution Simulation-Games*, 21(3) HARV. NEGOT. J. 377 (2005). Available at: http://ssrn.com/abstract=1292594.

discretely to each party in accordance with the specific role assigned to them. The case storyline is designed specifically around legal, economic, and social dilemmas covered in the course. The dilemmas reviewed in the course resemble real life dilemmas encountered by business professionals globally and by the students in their daily lives. Example dilemmas from the course that can be presented in intercultural contexts include theories and skills for inter-group and intra-group business negotiations, business interests, and shareholder constraints, interpretation and implementation of commercial transactions, and alternative dispute resolution systems in international business settings with a focus on negotiation, mediation, and arbitration.

The Authors' Experience

This role-play, involving creating a joint venture with a Chinese entity, was used by us to teach an intensive course that lasted two consecutive weeks, with a total of six sessions (four academic hours per session). Usually, each session started with a theoretical instructional component illustrated by short exercises, followed by active role-playing that was directly related to the lesson. As the negotiations drew to a close, participants were tasked with devising a pragmatic solution to the elements of the hypothetical dilemma that had been introduced and agreed upon by all parties. This resolution was intended to be derived by applying the theoretical principles imparted during earlier course sessions.

Following the "pseudo-reality" scenario phase, the students were split into two groups, each comprising ten students. These students assumed specific roles within the fictional narrative. Groups were intentionally created to comprise individuals of diverse ages, genders, and ethnic, cultural, and religious backgrounds. Within each group, an appointed member served as a coordinator, responsible for organizing the group's preparatory work and acting as a liaison with the instructors. As the exercise unfolded, time constraints and the complexity of the case prompted the groups to identify the critical issues at hand. Subsequently, the groups further subdivided into sub-groups of five students each, representing both business partners. Each sub-group grappled with a contentious issue, aiming to reach a mutually agreed-upon solution within a specified timeframe.

Later, each of the negotiating teams convened to consolidate its position, providing a succinct summary. Following this, the teams reconvened in a plenary session for inter-group negotiations. As the allotted time elapsed, the instructors facilitated a comprehensive debrief involving the entire class. In this collaborative endeavor, the professor of the international business law course evaluated the legal dimensions of the negotiation and resolution, while the dispute resolution instructors scrutinized the procedural aspects.

Cultural Implications of the Imaginary Plot

The groups' approaches towards the contract and Chinese law presented a case reflecting two phases in the business relationship between the two groups of different cultures: Israeli and Chinese. Thus, for example, Israelis are presumed to have an informal approach to business-doing while Chinese are presumed to prefer a more formal approach. Generally, Israelis are characterized by an ambition to obtain quick results, while Chinese business culture may entail a longer negotiation process to gradually build trust and strengthen relationships.[7]

The initial phase focuses on acquaintance, trust building, and the gradual advancement toward a contract for establishing a joint venture in China. At this stage, cultural differences influence the parties' observations, their impression of the potential partner, their vision regarding the engineering or planning of the joint venture (and its future operation), and, of course, the desired legal structure for this venture. This phase reveals different approaches to the acquaintance process, as well as the rhythm and dynamics of the negotiations. Choosing to conduct the negotiations in a third country (India) aims to facilitate mutual acquaintance in a foreign location "midway." This approach may lead to various plausible effects. For instance, it might contribute to an additional cultural burden, thus forming an extra source of stress for the parties. On the other hand, it may offer a new terrain waiting to be culturally explored by both parties, providing opportunities for social bonding intervals between negotiation sessions.

The second phase of the multi-stage simulation unfolds after the parties have established the contract and commenced its implementation. During this phase, pragmatic challenges arise due to the parties' distinct cultural backgrounds. These cultural differences significantly impact how the parties interpret the contract and perceive their legal obligations. Moreover, these differences influence the groups' assessment of the legal strategies they can employ to fulfill their mutual contractual duties.

Notably, the encounter between Israeli and Chinese cultures proves intriguing, as both nations are renowned for their creative interpretations of contracts. Typically, these inventive interpretations aim to favor the interpreter. However, this divergence in approaches intensifies the conflicts, posing a significant hurdle during the initial establishment of the mutual business. Following a thorough analysis and acknowledgment of this challenge, the parties must now navigate how to leverage their creative approaches to bridge their conflicting interests in the second phase of negotiations.

In our class, the "creative" approach also adversely affected the groups' assessment in establishing a margin of maneuver strategy according to the models introduced to students by Professor Andrew Wei-Min Lee (an expert in Chinese law). Lee's role included instruction and student discussions through video conferences. His instruction included critical and modern approaches to Chinese law (and enforcement authorities) that address diverse issues, including bribes and tax evasion. He also warned the students that such conduct may now be severely punishable, risking the future of their joint venture altogether. Involving an instructor with such legal and cultural expertise offered the class an in-depth view of the situation as it would have played out in real life, contributing both to their knowledge and to the activity's authenticity. If possible, such an addition to the introduction to the role-play is highly recommended.

---

[7] For more information on Chinese business culture, see John L. Graham & N. Mark Lam, *The Chinese Negotiation*, HARVARD BUSINESS REVIEW (2003), available at: https://hbr.org/2003/10/the-chinese-negotiation?autocomplete=true; Zhenzhong Ma & Alfred Jaeger, *Getting to Yes in China: Exploring Personality Effects in Chinese Negotiation Styles*, 14 GROUP DECISION AND NEGOTIATION 415 (2005), available at: https://doi.org/10.1007/s10726-005-1403-3. For information on Israeli business culture, see IOR, ISRAELI WORLDVIEW (2018), available at: https://www.iorworld.com/resources/israel/.

Business Interests

The case revolves around distinct business interests held by the two parties. As a foundational step in both negotiation phases, each group needs to ascertain these interests. At the outset of the negotiations, both parties harbor concealed motivations that serve as incentives for their commitment to this joint venture. For instance, each company grapples with either domestic or global competition, posing a threat to its future profitability and, conceivably, its very survival. In line with research[8] on global negotiations and strategies, this activity aims to engage the other party in an effort to try to expose these unique motivations and apply them in negotiations. To that extent, the parties meticulously strategize their approaches, considering when to deploy specific arguments and tactics. Decisions revolve around the timing of introducing relevant points (if at all). Additionally, the parties engage in discussions about the boundaries of compromise. Pragmatically, they test their assumptions during the role-play, all in pursuit of achieving the optimal outcome for the party they represent.[9] The students come to a profound realization: negotiation techniques and decisions are significantly influenced by culture.

In our class at ZAC, as the day's intensive negotiations drew to a close, discussions centered on power division between the joint venture partners. These deliberations proved exhausting and frustrating. Each party fiercely vied for control over the joint venture. Interestingly, the students expressed their frustration, reflecting on their earlier stages of negotiation. They had assumed that trust had been established and constructive relationships forged, anticipating smooth progress. However, the reality proved more intricate and challenging. Through analysis and exchanges, they realized that negotiations are never a linear process. Specifically, they learned that they could endure ups and downs and that different emotions may be experienced through different stages. However, the collision between the Israeli cultural tendency to strive to a quick solution or a sequential time management approach[10] and the Chinese cultural tendency to progress slowly, resulted in a tiring and frustrating negotiation experience for the partners in their effort to achieve results that better serve their interests (a synchronous time management approach). This substantially reinforced the crisis in the negotiation process.

During the second phase of the exercise, the parties had to assess what would have been most beneficial to each of them. This entailed determining whether to terminate or continue the contract. The case was engineered to ensure that both parties would opt for the latter option. This choice forced them to negotiate again, looking for the best way to settle the dispute. In cultural terms, this is the more difficult path because, as the plot unfolds, negotiations reveal that some of the issues that prevented the implementation of the contract are, in fact, cultural drawbacks or misunderstandings.

Furthermore, the trust painstakingly established between the parties during the initial phase might have suffered partial or complete erosion in the second phase due to evolving events and cultural misinterpretations. Consequently, rebuilding trust became imperative to sustain cooperative efforts. The strategies employed to restore mutual confidence also depended on the distinct cultural backgrounds. For instance, the "Israelis" demonstrated heightened attention and respect for the hierarchy of decision-making within the Chinese party and authorities. Conversely, the "Chinese" endeavored to be more

---

[8] Jeanne M. Brett, Negotiation Globally 10-11 (2nd ed., 2007).
[9] Ibid, at 11-16.
[10] Fons Trompenaars & Charles Hampden-Turner Riding the Waves of Culture: Understanding Diversity in Global Business (3rd ed., 2012).

attuned to the "Israeli" expectations for swift decision-making. During this phase, the instructors seized the opportunity to explore alternative dispute resolution frameworks with the students, including mediation and arbitration.

Instructors stressed that the choice of dispute settlement framework is, to a great extent, culture dependent. For example, in Israel, approaching courts to solve a dispute is most common. Nevertheless, alternative frameworks have gained more attention in recent years due to overloading within the court system. China seems to be moving in the opposite direction. For instance, historically,[11] the business community preferred to avoid the courts since Chinese courts used to deal mainly with criminal processes as laws changed constantly and many of the judges did not have a legal education. Lee informed the students that this tendency is gradually changing as the rule of law improves, becomes more systematic, and is applied by judges, particularly in major cities functioning as international business centers, such as Beijing and Shanghai. However, foreign business individuals fearing that Chinese courts may be biased towards Chinese parties may still opt for arbitration tribunals involving domestic and foreign arbitrators, such as those operating in Hong Kong and Singapore.

Finally, the groups participated in a mediation based on the same set of facts underlying the imaginary dispute presented by the role-play. Students who had taken a mediation course in previous years or were trained as mediators served as the mediators in this dispute. The students learned that this form of dispute resolution mechanism also requires cultural sensitivity to lead the parties to a mutually agreed upon solution. The role-play in this chapter does not go into detail regarding the mediation process, as the purpose of this book is to use role-plays to teach doctrinal topics, rather than pure dispute resolution skills. There are plenty of complementary resources for dispute resolution and mediation teaching.

Alternative Costs

Both phases of the role-play carried significant economic implications. In the initial phase, choosing not to strike a deal could have exposed both partners to the risk of complete defeat by their respective competitors. In the subsequent phase, failure to reach an agreement might have signaled the demise of the joint venture, leading to investment losses. Importantly, the perception of failure varied across cultures, resulting in distinct consequences for each partner. Generally, failure is viewed as an essential learning experience in Israeli culture.[12] In Chinese culture, failure is not an option.[13] In the specific scenario, the project's location in China could have potentially led to greater public exposure for the Chinese partner (and its potential failure), in contrast to the Israeli partner, which operated from a remote location. Consequently, the interplay of this circumstance with the cultural significance attached to failure in Chinese culture may have placed considerable pressure on the Chinese partner.

---

[11] For further discussion on litigation, mediation, and arbitration options for foreign 23 investors in China, see Jerome A. Cohen, *Settling International Business Disputes with China: Then and Now*, 47 CORNELL INTERNATIONAL LAW JOURNAL 555 (2014). Available at: http://www.lawschool.cornell.edu/research/ILJ/upload/Cohen-final.pdf

[12] Osnat Lautman, *The Positive Attitude Toward Failure in the Culture of Israeli Innovation*, OLM CONSULTING (2016), available at: https://olm-consulting.com/positive-attitude-toward-failure-culture-israeli-innovation/

[13] Deborah Lau, *The Chinese Tradition Trap – Failure is Not an Option*, REPROGRAMMING DIRECTIVE (2010). https://deborahlau.com/2010/04/chinese-tradition-trap/

Legal Context

The role-play exercise incorporated legal standards, encompassing fundamental principles from diverse areas of law relevant to the countries studied in the course. These areas included contract, corporate, tax, private international, and criminal law. Throughout the course, students received pertinent written materials to apply legal norms and principles during the role-play. Additionally, their Skype meeting with Professor Lee provided a unique chance to assess how cultural disparities manifest in the respective legal frameworks of both China and Israel.

Global Aspects of Lawyering

The role-play encompasses global elements relevant both to legal substance and legal process. It exposes the students to a foreign legal system. It encourages them to conduct a comparative study of both legal systems involved (Israeli and Chinese) while searching for common denominators that could serve as a basis for a mutual deal. It also exposes the students to cultural differences that may affect the legal rules each system opts for in the process. The need to become familiar with foreign and international legal norms and negotiation techniques serves as an incentive to apply the course's theoretical principles. Finally, through this exercise, students experience the effects of cultural differences and the importance of cultural sensitivity to the formation and implementation of international business transactions.

As previously noted, the legal process exposes the students to different approaches to negotiation and implementation to establish an agreement across cultures and legal structures. It further exposes them to various approaches emanating from, inter alia, cultural differences to reach a settlement in a dispute. The role-play offers students an opportunity to experience negotiation dynamics to close a deal that seems attractive to both parties and to seek resolutions to disputes. Regarding the latter, the exercise offers students an opportunity to examine the effectiveness of a rule-oriented approach compared to an interest-based approach to dispute resolution, based on compromise and collaboration. It illustrates the importance of a pragmatic win-win approach to dispute resolution and its advantage over a win-lose approach to ensure long-term sustainability. A common language that is not the mother tongue of any of the parties is used to level the playing field. Finally, students can enjoy the cultural perspectives of their diverse instructors.

Cultural Conflicts Around Values

Cultural conflicts are well reflected by the simulation. As Molinsky[14] reports, cultural conflict may occur when individuals face difficulties when norms for appropriate behavior in a newly encountered culture conflict with their native cultural values and beliefs. In our experience, the cultural conflicts were particularly prominent during the groups' reference to the legal dilemma that entailed deciding whether to disguise the coffee as tea to receive tax benefits but were also present in other circumstances. For instance, one circumstance that created a cultural conflict included resolving the question of whether monetary persuasion – or rather bribe – would help to prevent the government's requirement of reim-

---

[14] Andrew Molinsky, *A Situational Approach for Assessing and Teaching Acculturation*, 34 JOURNAL OF MANAGEMENT EDUCATION 723 (2010).

bursing the grant or the potential workers' lawsuit or whether the reimbursement deadline should be extended.

Use With Caution!
Portraying a Different Culture
Although the participants acting as "Chinese" professionals engaged in preparatory research on Chinese business culture and were instructed by a professor whose expertise includes business and negotiations in Chinese culture, they expressed some concerns and frustration with acting in the role-play in such capacities. As previous research indicates, this presents a weakness of this experience.[15] This type of difficulty can be resolved if, in reference to the current study, a Chinese group of students played the "Chinese" group in the negotiations[16] via video-conferencing technology.

Time frame
We engaged in this role-play over two consecutive weeks, with the goal centered around long-term relationship-building. The purpose was to help students evaluate the interests of each party and find compromises that would safeguard their most critical concerns. The fact that both parties invested money, time, and effort further underscored their mutual commitment to the project. Long-term relationships allowed the participants to develop intercultural sensitivity and establish mutual trust.

However, it's essential to acknowledge that unbridged cultural differences could have an adverse impact on these relationships. Additionally, given that the role-play unfolded over a mere two-week period, there might be limitations in fully developing long-term connections among the fictional parties. Nevertheless, this potential drawback could be mitigated to some extent by the students' existing long-term relationships.

English
Coinciding with cultural differences, the use of English (a foreign language for both parties) may have reinforced misunderstandings and undermined the common business project. Although language mistakes are difficult to avoid, they are seldom deal-breakers.[17] Therefore, we believe that the opportunity to practice their English in a business-like setting helped build students' confidence and motivation.

---

[15] Nadja Alexander & Michelle LeBaron, *Death of the Role-Play*, RETHINKING NEGOTIATION TEACHING: INNOVATIONS FOR CONTEXT AND CULTURES (Christopher Honeyman, James Coben & Giuseppe De Palo eds., 2009).

[16] This tactic was used by business professors de Figueiredo and Mauri (2012), who assigned domestic and international students on teams to tackle a problem referring to the home country of the latter. Thus, domestic students needed foreign students' background knowledge (both in terms of their language and their knowledge about their home country). In the context of law studies in a global world, it is essential that law instruction include opportunities for students to interact with counterparts fluent in other languages to help overcome mutual communication obstacles. See Carole Silver, *Getting Real About Globalization and Legal Education: Potential and Perspectives for the U.S.*, 24 STANFORD LAW AND POLICY REVIEW 457, 491 (2013). The "Colonel Chicken" role-play in this book employs the same tactic.

[17] JEANNE M. BRETT SUPRA 8, AT 25. (2nd ed., 2007).

Group Collaborations and a Musician's Experience

At the end of the course, we had the rare opportunity to enjoy an extra session given by Professor Rena Sharon, a Canadian music professor and internationally acclaimed pianist. In her session, Professor Sharon explained and illustrated how small groups of musicians playing chamber music without a conductor negotiate to interpret a musical piece. The musical examples used in the course introduced students to different interpretations of musical pieces based on personal interpretation, which, to some extent, depended on the interpreter's cultural background. From a perspective far removed from legal studies, this remarkable session gave our students insights into the widespread applicability of negotiation principles taught in the course. Additionally, it underscored the universal impact of cultural differences on interpretation and, consequently, the achievement of shared objectives. The role of arts as a means of managing conflicts and promoting resolution is becoming increasingly prevalent in literature.[18] If you can host an artist in your class to discuss how the arts inform conflict resolution – do not hesitate!

---

[18] ANDREW FLOYER ACLAND, CARRIE L MACLEOD, AND MICHELLE LEBARON, THE CHOREOGRAPHY OF RESOLUTION: CONFLICT, MOVEMENT, AND NEUROSCIENCE (2013).

THE COFFEE VENTURE[*]

Background Information for the Role-Play

The Chinese market is a potential market of 1.4 billion consumers, making it an attractive challenge for producers globally. While traditionally the Chinese people prefer tea, their interest in coffee has grown in recent years.

Idit is an Israeli company that owns a coffee factory in the city of Zefat. Established in the 1950s, this factory used to enjoy governmental financial support. This support stopped in recent years, while competition with new coffee brands in the local market grew. This competition diminished Idit's market share and profits. Idit is interested in relocating its factory to China, to enjoy both cheap labor and potential access to a huge market. Idit management believes that this is the right time to penetrate a newly developing market.

Idit contacts a Chinese company, Yang Fe, which specializes in worker recruitment and placement in foreign plants established in China.

According to Chinese law, foreign investors must establish joint ventures with local partners to enjoy tax benefits and other incentives accorded by the Chinese government to foreign direct investments. Thus, the two companies are negotiating the establishment of such a joint venture, named Yang Id. According to their business plan, Idit will construct the plant and bring it to the operational phase, while Yang Fe will supply the workers and be responsible for all the necessary interactions with the local government, to ensure that the benefits offered by it will be given to Yang Id.

The parties decide to meet in the geographic middle, India, to negotiate the contract.

In the negotiations, the parties must consider the following facts:

1) The estimated cost of plant construction is $1 million. Subject to the conditions set forth by Chinese law, the Chinese government is supposed to finance $200,000 out of this sum as a grant. An additional $500,000 will be given as a loan, but if Yang Id will only hire Chinese production staff for 10 years, this sum will also turn into a grant and the loan will be forgiven.

2) Under intense pressure from tea producers, the Chinese government imposed a 40% purchase tax on coffee. The tax has to be paid by the producers, at the factory gate (before marketing to stores), but, in actuality, is added to the price paid by the consumer, thus substantially raising the price of coffee and harming its potential competitiveness compared to tea. As a pre-condition for the contract conclusion, Yang Fe, aware of this difficulty, requires Idit to agree that the coffee leaving the factory will be packed in packages on which the word 'tea' is written, instead of 'coffee' (an illegal transaction).

---

[*] This exercise was developed by Nellie Munin & Yael Efron.

3) The Chinese share of financial investment requires a determination of the rate of Chinese participation in the joint venture's establishment costs. The manner of payment is not yet established between the parties (over time? At once? If the Chinese financial contribution starts only when construction is complete, do they have to pay some 'price' for this delayed payment?).

Phase 1

Instructions to Idit Team

Idit has no choice but to close the factory in Zefat. Many of the factory's neighbors are suing Idit for the smell and pollution caused by the factory. Idit tried for a long time to look for an alternative location for the factory in Israel, but the costs involved in such relocation are very high. In fact, they threaten the financial balance of Idit, which is already competing in a more and more competitive market. On the other hand, rumors about the possible closure of the factory have already caused strikes and demonstrations by its workers, who approached the media as well as politicians to try to prevent this result. Idit owns some other plants in Israel, but will not be able to offer jobs to the workers from the Zefat plant.

Idit's negotiators know that without a Chinese partner, they will not be entitled to the benefits offered by the Chinese government and, accordingly, will not be able to afford to establish a factory in China.

Idit's bargaining position relies on a new patent-based technology owned by it. This technology allows Idit to preserve coffee's taste and flavor for longer periods than its competitors, while producing coffee for substantially cheaper.

Idit's negotiation team includes its General Manager, Chief Engineer, CFO, and legal advisors.

Phase 1

Instructions to Yang Fe Team

Yang Fe receives a substantial financial bonus from the Chinese government every time it succeeds in placing Chinese workers at a foreign investor's plant in China (thus contributing to the reduction of high unemployment rates there). Recently, Yang Fe expended a great deal of time and effort on negotiations with potential foreign direct investors who turned out to be unable to satisfactorily complete the deals. The owners are afraid that the Chinese government may deprive them of their expected bonus, which is necessary to balance their great expenses.

Therefore, Yang Fe is negotiating simultaneously with another company from Costa Rica. This company enjoys a comparative advantage in terms of access to raw materials (i.e., the coffee beans) grown in Costa Rica. This fact is of particular importance in light of the shrinking global supply of coffee beans due to a mysterious epidemic for which there is still no known cure.

At the same time, Yang Fe is aware of the comparative advantage of Idit in the global market due to its unique patent. In addition, Yang Fe estimates that it would be easier to convince Israelis than Costa Ricans to hire 'foreign' (i.e. Chinese) workers, assessing that due to the high rate of foreign employees in the Israeli market, Israeli mentality may be more open to this option.

Yang Fe's negotiation team includes its General Manager, Chief Engineer, CFO, and legal advisors.

Phase 2
Founders' shares – general instructions to both parties

The newly established Yang Id company is intended to be co-owned by Yang Fe and Idit. Founders' shares of this company incorporate voting rights as well as rights to profits. Naturally, each of the two partners is interested in having more influence than the other in the decision-making process regarding the operation of this company. Likewise, each wants to enjoy the greatest share possible of profits. However, while a 50-50 division of profits may be considered, a 50-50 division of voting rights may completely freeze any activity of Yang Id. Thus, the parties must decide on a mutually acceptable formula, considering that it is necessary to determine which party will have privileged voting rights which would allow it to make a final decision in cases of controversy.

1) Should the party with privileged voting rights have them in all cases or only in specific circumstances? If only in specific circumstances, which ones? Should a list of cardinal issues be excluded, where no party would prevail even if freezing would be the result? If certain issues are excluded from privileged voting rights, which issues?

2) Can the party giving-up the privileged rights be 'compensated' in terms of profits' share, and, if so, under which formula?

Each party should take into account its weaknesses when assessing whether it can afford no agreement on these issues, leading to failure of the negotiations. Each party should also determine what compromises it would be willing to make to avoid a failure of negotiations.

Phase 3
Controversy over implementation of the contract – instructions to both parties

The parties entered into a contract under which:

- Idit undertook a commitment to complete the construction of the new plant within one year.

Yang Fe committed to supply 80 workers as soon as the plant is ready for operation. For that purpose, Yang Fe contracted with 80 workers, specifying the date when work starts. The contract was introduced to the Chinese government, and Yang Fe won the bonus promised.

In fact, Idit does not successfully complete the plant construction within one year due to the following reasons:

- The issuance of building licenses by Beijing municipality is delayed by six months due to negligent action by Yang Fe, which was responsible for all connections with local authorities.

- A delay of another month was caused by Idit's refusal to pay for raw materials necessary for construction before the licenses were issued.

Upon learning about the delay, the Chinese government requires Yang Fe to return the bonus while the workers are practically unemployed. Yang Fe knows that in the meantime, due to a modification of the relevant Chinese law, the bonus sum will be cut in half. Thus, when the workers finally start to work for the joint venture, Yang Fe will be only entitled to half of the initially anticipated bonus sum.

Negotiate a dispute settlement.

Phase 4
Mediation

Mediators are invited to assist in resolving the dispute between the parties.

For the purpose of this book, the instructions for mediators are excluded. There are plenty of complementary resources available for teaching mediation and other dispute resolution skills.

According to the facts introduced, discussion in this debriefing phase could include the following aspects:

- Cultural differences and their effect on negotiations.
- Power dynamics.
- The challenges of commercial negotiation.
- Political interests.
- Lobbying.
- Coalitions of interests.
- Alternative/competing transactions.
- The state of the market.
- The financial state of the parties.

"Colonel Chicken Goes Abroad"[1]

As mentioned earlier, one of the shortcomings of role-plays that depict cultural differences is the difficulties students may encounter in portraying someone from a different culture.[2] In this negotiation, that challenge was eliminated by students portraying characters of their own cultural identity. This negotiation exercise was conducted completely online as an inter-school international experience for Israeli and American students. Prior to its beginning, the students were informed of the expectations from them during and after the negotiations. We are including the exact instructions the students received, with the hope that instructors adapt them to their needs. Because these are the exact instructions used in the past, at the very least dates, times, and locations will need to be changed to adapt them for future use.

Each instructor decided for their own group whether and how to prepare and evaluate their students.

---

[1] This simulation is derived, with permission of the author, from problem 9.1 (pp. 776-77) in Folsom, Gordon and Spanogle, INTERNATIONAL BUSINESS TRANSACTIONS: A PROBLEM ORIENTED COURSEBOOK, 5TH EDITION (West Group 2002). Simulation created by James Coben and Giuseppe De Palo for "Making and Saving Deals in the Global Business Environment," a joint venture of Hamline University School of Law and the University of Rome "La Sapienza" (Summer Study Abroad 2003). Professor Ken Fox of Hamline University Business School and Yael Efron of Zefat Academic College School of Law adapted the scenario in 2024 to fit an American-Israeli business venture.

[2] Nadja Alexander & Michelle LeBaron, *Death of the Role-Play*, RETHINKING NEGOTIATION TEACHING: INNOVATIONS FOR CONTEXT AND CULTURES (Christopher Honeyman, James Coben & Giuseppe De Palo eds., 2009).

"Colonel Chicken Goes Abroad"

General Instructions
Background

You have been selected to participate in an online negotiation exercise that will be conducted by students from two universities, namely, Hamline University in St. Paul, Minnesota, and Zefat Academic College in Zefat, Israel.

The exercise involves a simulated commercial negotiation between a major U.S. fast food company ("Colonel Chicken"), and a potential Middle East franchisee ("BB Israel") seeking to open a franchise in Zefat. For purposes of the negotiation, Hamline teams represent the U.S. franchisor, and Zefat teams represent the Israeli franchisee.

For purposes of this exercise, please assume the following:

- **Both sides are extremely interested in reaching an agreement to establish a franchise of the U.S. fast food company in the Middle East.**

- Each side will be very unhappy if you do not successfully complete the negotiation

- Each side will be very unhappy if you do not satisfy the interests they have communicated to you in their confidential documents

- However, both sides also have certain constraints or limitations that are detailed in your respective confidential instructions. **The challenge for you is to try to get the best possible deal within the time given that will satisfy most, if not all, the interests of your client.**

- Since this is a commercial negotiation, you are expected to keep your language and manner respectful, cordial, and professional at all times.

This exercise aims to have all participants experience a realistic, cross-cultural commercial negotiation, much like the ones you will likely encounter when you go on to practice law or business in your respective countries. Please be mindful that this is intended to provide a meaningful learning experience for everyone, and that the success of this exercise depends on your full cooperation and strict compliance with the guidelines and timetable set forth below.

Technical Instructions

All negotiations will be conducted via email using a common email account, which will be provided by your instructors. The negotiation period will start on [*fill in the date and hour*] and end on [*fill in the date and hour*]. Please refrain from sending anything to your negotiation counterpart before the negotiation period starts or after it ends. The teams might not require the full number of days to conclude the negotiation.

Considering that participants will be in different time zones, we will use Greenwich Mean Time (GMT) as the common time zone reference in order to avoid any confusion regarding schedules.

- Israel (Zefat) will be 2 hours ahead of GMT
- St. Paul (Hamline) will be 6 hours behind GMT

Once the negotiation begins, students should monitor their emails, and when they receive a new email, they should **reply to at least confirm they have received the email as soon as they are able.** If they can give a substantive response immediately, that is fine. However, if they need more time to prepare a substantive response, they should tell their counterpart by what day/time the counterpart can expect to receive their substantive response. This way, both sides can plan their time and not worry about when to expect a substantive response. It is the responsibility of all participants to determine what time that would be in their respective time zones, and to adhere strictly to the negotiation schedule.

As soon as possible after the negotiating window opens, **the franchisor (Hamline) will commence the negotiation by sending an email to the franchisee (ZAC teams).** The parties will then continue their negotiations until they are able to reach agreement or until the exercise concludes.

In order to avoid confusion, please **do not use team designations. Instead, please simply refer to yourselves as "counsel for franchisor" or "counsel for franchisee" as the case may be.**

In order for the negotiation to proceed smoothly, it is important to remember that there should only be one "thread" or conversation that takes place the whole time. To ensure this, counsel for the franchisor must start the negotiation, and the counsel for the franchisee must then respond to their posting by clicking the "reply" button and typing their response. Then, counsel for the franchisor must respond by also clicking the "reply" button, typing in their own response, and so forth.

Under no circumstance should the parties initiate separate conversations by composing new emails to the other side. If this happens, the negotiation would become very confusing and difficult to track. The idea is for the parties to simply keep replying to each other and, in the process, have one continuous email record of their negotiation. At the conclusion of the exercise, you will be asked to forward the final negotiation email to the organizers, which should, ideally, contain the complete record of the negotiation and answer a few questions that are designed to help you review your performance.

Preparation

Upon receipt of these instructions, you will also receive a copy of the general information and your confidential instructions. The key to any successful negotiation is extensive preparation, and the goal for all participants is to secure the best possible deal that would meet the needs of their client. Thus, you are strongly urged to take some time to plan (whether individually or as a team) long before the exercise begins on how you intend to conduct the negotiations, what your negotiating strategy would be, what your client's interests and objectives are, and what ideas or options you might want to propose to the other side. In preparing for the negotiation, it would also be helpful for you to try to anticipate the other side's own needs and objectives and think about how you might want to respond if the other party expresses these needs during the negotiation.

Negotiation Strategy

All participants are free to decide what their negotiating strategy would be. However, please bear in mind that your counterpart will be in a different time zone and may not be available online during the times that you are. Thus, in order to have a structured and fruitful discussion, it is highly advisable for you and your counterpart to agree, soon after the negotiation commences, on a framework for your negotiation. This might include matters such as negotiating schedules, length of time within which to expect responses, common agenda for the negotiations, list of issues to be resolved, and other procedural items that need to be clarified and agreed upon before you move on to the substantive negotiations. Otherwise, you might encounter the unpleasant and frustrating situation where you will be repeatedly checking your email, not knowing when the other party intends to respond.

Assessment

Each instructor shared with their students the requirements for self-reflection and assessment for students' preparation and reflection of the exercise.

Good luck on your upcoming negotiation!

"Colonel Chicken Goes Abroad"[1]

General Information for All Parties

Colonel Chicken Inc. is a Texas fast food franchising corporation. More than 70 years ago, the company founder, Colonel Ulysses F. Chicken, first gave the world a taste of his most famous creation – Original Recipe Skinless Fried Chicken. The recipe features a blend of 10 herbs and 3 spices – noted on all company advertising and signage as "The Colonel's 13 secrets." Today, security precautions protecting the recipe would make even James Bond proud. One company blends a formulation that represents only part of the recipe. Another spice company blends the remainder. A computer processing system is used to safeguard and standardize the blending of the products, but neither company has the complete recipe.

Colonel Chicken has successfully established over 100 franchises in the United States. The company uses a formula called "seven-point non-conventional franchising" (lovingly referred to as the "SNCF" by all employees, including its legal counsel). The SNCF requirements are:

1) Careful selection and ownership of the site by the company and required use of the site by the franchisee;

2) mandatory franchisee use of secret recipes, special patented cooking equipment, and purchases of chicken from a list of designated sources;

3) extensive cooperative English language advertising programs;

4) aggressive protection of its trademarks, COLONEL CHICKEN (TM), CHICKEN-LICKEN-GOOD (TM), and THE COLONEL'S 13 SECRETS (TM) which appear in red, white, and blue against an outline of the boundaries of the State of Texas;

5) active supervision of quality controls maintained by its franchisees in accordance with Colonel Chicken's copyrighted instruction manual;

6) exclusive use of "Western" building design which draws upon the company's Texas heritage; and

7) strongly "recommended" prices.

Colonel Chicken has never opened a franchise abroad; however, the company's marketing division is convinced that the time has come to expand to the Middle East. The first franchise is under negotiation

---

[1] This simulation is derived, with permission of the authors, from problem 9.1 (pp. 776-77) in Folsom, Gordon and Spanogle, INTERNATIONAL BUSINESS TRANSACTIONS: A PROBLEM ORIENTED COURSEBOOK, 5TH EDITION (West Group 2002). Simulation created by James Coben and Giuseppe De Palo for "Making and Saving Deals in the Global Business Environment," a joint venture of Hamline University School of Law and the University of Rome "La Sapienza" (Summer Study Abroad 2003).

with an Israeli group of investors – BB Israel, which has preliminarily identified a property for the site of the first restaurant in the newly developed student-dormitory area near Zefat Academic College campus. Counsels are negotiating online to work on four sections of the Franchise Agreement: 1) Franchise Payment; 2) Royalties and Advertising Contribution; 3) Signs; and 4) Menu and Service. An initial draft of the franchise agreement, prepared by counsel for Colonel Chicken, has been exchanged between the parties in anticipation of the online negotiation.

The relevant sections are reproduced in the following document.

FRANCHISE PAYMENT

SERVICES BY COLONEL CHICKEN (THE "COMPANY" OR "FRANCHISOR")

A. *Franchise Payment.* The Company acknowledges payment to it by Franchisee of the total sum of $500,000, consisting of $200,000 as and for a franchise fee; $150,000 for initial assistance essential to Franchisee consisting of the training and the services detailed at Paragraph B, subparagraphs 2, 3 and 4 below; and $150,000 for a grand opening advertising fund. Franchisee acknowledges that the grant of the franchise constitutes the sole consideration for the payment of the franchise fee and that said sum shall be fully earned by Company upon execution and delivery hereof.

B. *Services by Company.* Company agrees, during the term of this Franchise Agreement, to use its best efforts to maintain the high reputation of the Colonel Chicken franchised restaurants ("Franchised Restaurants") and in connection therewith to make available to Franchisee:

1) Initial standard specifications and plans for the building, equipment, furnishings, decor, layout, and signs identified with Franchised Restaurants, together with advice and consultation concerning them.

2) A pre-opening training program conducted at Company's training school and at a Franchised Restaurant.

3) Opening promotion programs conducted under the direction of Company's Marketing Department.

4) The Company's confidential standard business policies and operations data instruction manuals (hereinafter collectively called "Manual"), a copy of which is (or will be) delivered and loaned to Franchisee for the term hereof.

5) Such special recipe techniques, food preparation instructions, new restaurant services, and other operational developments as may from time to time be developed by the Company and deemed by it to be helpful in the operation of Franchised Restaurants.

6) A standardized accounting, cost control, and portion control system.

ROYALTIES AND ADVERTISING CONTRIBUTION

A. *Royalties*. Franchisee agrees in consideration of Company's licensing its use of the names "Colonel Chicken," "Chicken-Licken-Good," and "The Colonel's 13 Secrets," together with such other trademarks and service marks as may be authorized for use by Company, to pay a monthly royalty in the amount of five (5) percent of Franchisee's gross sales. Royalties shall be paid on or before the tenth (10th) day of each month and shall be based upon sales for the preceding calendar month.

B. *Advertising and Sales Promotion*. The Franchisee agrees, as partial consideration for the grant of this franchise, to pay to Company a monthly advertising and sales promotion contribution. This sum shall be equal to five (5) percent of Franchisee's gross sales. The advertising and sales promotion contribution shall be paid on or before the tenth (10th) day of each month and shall be based upon Franchisee's gross sales for the preceding calendar month. The advertising and sales promotion contribution shall be expended by Company at its discretion for advertising and sales promotion both in Franchisee's market area and on a national basis, except for that portion used for creative and production costs of advertising and sales promotion elements and for those market research expenditures which are directly related to the development and evaluation of the effectiveness of advertising and sales promotion.

STANDARDS AND UNIFORMITY OF OPERATION

A. *Signs*. Franchisee agrees to display Company's names and trademarks at the premises, in the manner authorized by Company. Franchisee agrees to maintain and display signs reflecting the current image of Company. The color, size, design, and location of said signs shall be as specified by Company. Franchisee shall not place additional signs or posters on the premises without Company's written consent.

B. *Menu and Service*. Franchisee agrees to serve the menu items specified by Company, to follow all specifications and formulas of Company as to contents and weight of unit products served, and to sell no other food or drink item or any other merchandise of any kind without the prior written approval of Company. Franchisee agrees that all food and drink items will be served in containers bearing accurate reproductions of the Company's service marks and trademarks. Such imprinted items shall be purchased by Franchisee through Company or through a supplier or manufacturer approved in writing by Company. Franchisee shall remain open for business from 11:00 A.M. to 10:00 P.M. daily unless Company consents to other hours or days at the request of Franchisee.

"Colonel Chicken Goes Abroad"

Confidential Information – Counsel for Colonel Chicken ("Franchisor" or "Company")

Since that time 70 years ago when the Colonel (now deceased) first concocted his secret recipe, millions of people across the United States have come to love his one-of-a-kind chicken, homestyle side dishes, and hot and fresh biscuits. The company still takes pride in doing things the Colonel's way, utilizing only the highest quality ingredients, innovative recipes, and time-tested cooking methods. Now the time has come to go international and bring that same high quality to additional millions abroad. You have been instructed to "bring home" a deal. Your client wants the red, white, and blue Colonel Chicken logo prominently displayed near the newly developed Zefat Academic College student dormitory.

You and your negotiating counterpart from BB Israel have agreed in advance that the contract will be binding only when all sections have been fully negotiated, reviewed by counsel, and signed by corporate officers. Four issues are up for discussion today.

Franchise Payment

The draft you prepared contains the standard franchise fees ($500,000) used in the United States:

$200,000 - Franchise fee
$150,000 – Initial Services provided by the Company to the Franchisee
$150,000 – Grand Opening Advertising Fund

This formula has worked extremely well in the United States for the last few years, and you see little reason to change it here. Anything less than a total $500,000 franchise payment would make you suspicious that BB Israel is undercapitalized. However, you are open to negotiating how the money is allocated between the three categories of expenses comprising the franchise payment (fee; initial services; advertising), so long as the franchise fee and payment for initial services is at least $300,000 combined (in other words, you could choose to allow BB Israel to dedicate up to $200,000 of its $500,000 Franchise Payment to the grand opening advertising fund <u>if absolutely necessary</u> to make the deal).

Royalties and Advertising

Most franchises in the United States pay a 3.5% royalty rate and contribute 4% of gross sales toward advertising and sales promotion. Management is comfortable with similar rates for this Middle Eastern venture. In fact, notwithstanding your draft proposal asking for 5% on both issues, you have authorization to go as low as a 3% royalty rate, and a 3.5% contribution to advertising. What you cannot do is to surrender control of advertising completely to the franchisee. The SNCF specifically emphasizes centralized approaches to advertising, and you must continue this commitment.

Signs

The SNCF is stronger nowhere than on signage – a key to the entire franchise operation. The red, white, and blue map of Texas, as well as the Company trademarks, are a critical part of franchise success. You do not anticipate any problems here. "The Colonel's 13 Secrets" is just like the golden arches of McDonald's. It simply would not be Colonel Chicken without emphasizing the recipe's 10 secret herbs and 3 secret spices. Likewise, Colonel Chicken without Texas is unthinkable. Surely, it is in everyone's best interests to build on a strong track record.

Menu and Service

You have heard from some colleagues in the fast-food business that Israeli franchisees often want permission to serve alcohol. Much as you would like to agree, this is simply not possible. The Colonel was a strong supporter of prohibition in his younger days. Indeed, his will decreed that Colonel Chicken restaurants would never sell alcohol. So long as his wife Catlin remains on the board of directors, a deal approving the sale of alcohol will never be approved. You are concerned that this is a deal breaker. Perhaps there are some creative solutions. For one thing, you are relatively certain that Catlin (and the more passive members of the board under her control) will not object to alcohol being brought onto the premises from elsewhere – after all, they may be teetotalers, but they are also pretty darn accomplished capitalists.

Another relevant issue is the commonly desired Kosher and Halal approval in Israel. The Israeli authorities have very rigid regulations as to who is entitled to be certified as Kosher/Halal. You anticipate that such certification will be a strong demand from your counterpart. However, how can you convince Israeli authorities that the Colonel's 13 secrets contain only Kosher/Halal ingredients without revealing the safely guarded recipe? There is simply no chance that the Board will approve surrendering the most safely kept secret of the Company and the source of its pride! You fear that this might be a deal breaker, so a creative idea must be generated.

"Colonel Chicken Goes Abroad"

Confidential Information – Counsel for Franchisee

BB Israel is convinced that obtaining this franchise will be a huge economic success. You are optimistic that agreements can be reached on all four issues set for discussion on Tuesday. However, you are interested in impressing on your American counterparts that BB Israel will need more overall control than permitted in the first draft of the franchise agreement. Colonel Chicken may have succeeded for 70 years in the United States, but its "seven-point non-conventional franchising" (SNCF) is by no means a recipe for success here in Israel. Indeed, you will need to find a polite way to let your American counterparts know that the acronym SNCF means nothing here in Israel, and using acronyms in Latin characters is likely to alienate Hebrew speakers, especially in a traditional city like Zefat! The bottom line is that you know the Israeli market and want to persuade your American colleagues to recognize your contribution to success.

Franchise Payment

You can live with the proposed $500,000 in total expense but would prefer to allocate the numbers differently. You know the Israeli market and believe that a much more substantial marketing campaign is necessary than that being proposed. Accordingly, you want the franchise payment to be broken down as follows:

$150,000 – Franchise fee
$100,000 – Initial Services provided by the Company to the Franchisee.
$250,000 – Grand Opening Advertising Fund

From your perspective, anything less than a $250,000 commitment to initial advertising will seriously compromise the project from the outset. <u>If absolutely necessary</u> to close the deal, you can agree to an advertising contribution as low as $200,000 but you will not be happy.

Royalties and Advertising

The proposed 5% rates for royalties and advertising are far in excess of what you expected. Comparable rates for similar franchises in Israel are usually 3% (and sometimes even a little less, due to the different accounting standards). You will try to negotiate the lowest possible rates you can, but in no event higher than 3% (royalty) and 3.5% (advertising). Moreover, you will only agree to pay a 3.5% advertising rate if you can negotiate at least equal power in controlling the advertising decisions. Without a track record of success in international operations, you have no confidence that Colonel Chicken will make prudent decisions.

Signs

There is one major problem with the company's signage – the number 13. Many Israelis regard this number as an omen of bad luck. Why not use 10 or 18? Both are associated with good luck. After all, it is a secret recipe – no one will know. Bottom line from your perspective: if the number 13 is on the signs, it will have an adverse effect on sales. You would also like to discuss how critical the map of Texas is to the overall signage. Very few Israelis will even recognize it as the map of Texas, and maps generally are a source of conflict in the Middle East. From your perspective, the trademark terms (Colonel Chicken and Chicken-Licken-Good) are the important things, not color schemes or state outlines.

Menu and Service

Two issues are absolutely critical. You want permission to serve wine and beer. And your menu must be Kosher and Halal. You expect difficulty negotiating both points.

With respect to the first issue, the majority of potential customers will be students looking for a place to relax at the end of long day of study. You read somewhere that Colonel Chicken was a supporter of prohibition in the 1930s and his last will and testament actually decreed that none of his restaurants would ever serve alcohol. You are guardedly optimistic that the company will not apply this limitation to its Israeli franchisees. If it does, it could be disastrous for your success. Luckily, the site you are investigating near the student dormitory would allow you to have a common seating area with another restaurant establishment. If worse comes to worst, perhaps you could arrange for your customers to purchase wine and beer from the neighboring business. Hardly ideal, but it might be workable.

The second issue is much more problematic. The majority of potential customers, both the college students at the dormitory and the families residing in the Galilee, the geographic area of the college, observe Kosher or Halal diets. No serious food business could survive without such certification. But with the recipe being so secretly protected, how can you convince the Israeli authorities to issue the Kosher/Halal certificate? You must negotiate a method to prove clearly that all ingredients in the recipe are Kosher and Halal.

International Trade Law

Introduction to International Trade Law

The two following role-plays differ from the previous ones by illustrating international transactions between a government and a foreign private entity, which might be supported by its own government.

Each role-play focuses on the dilemma underlying the handling by a state of a unique resource. Each involves strategic considerations weighed against other potentially conflicting considerations. In *Selling the Dead Sea*, the issue revolves around the need for foreign investments to finance the expensive rehabilitation of a unique natural resource. *Let There be Gas* illustrates the business and political considerations that exist in the complex relationships in the Mediterranean region.

Risk management plays a decisive role in such scenarios since the risks involved concern not only a single business but may affect entire nations and regions. In many cases, third international parties (like other states or international organizations) might be involved in the negotiations or in the exercise of such transactions. In these cases, their positions should be considered in the course of the negotiations because they might affect the results.

Apart from the cultural differences affecting any international or inter-cultural negotiations, negotiations of the kind illustrated below may involve national conflicting feelings based on a history that may have involved mutual hostilities between the parties. In such cases, trust-building[1] would play a major role in the negotiations and in the transaction's success, particularly if the transaction implies long-term cooperation between former rival nations. Third parties may play a decisive role in this context as well.

Later in this chapter, we present a "Prisoner's Dilemma" game. "Prisoner's Dilemma" games aim to illustrate a conflict of interests between parties. They are based on a well-known scenario. In that original scenario, two prisoners were jailed and are interrogated. If no one reveals any detail, they will both be safe and released from jail for lack of evidence. Naturally, the police want to tempt at least one of them to talk. The police promise each prisoner that if they are the one who will talk, they will be saved on the account of the other prisoner, who will be incriminated. With no way to communicate, each prisoner cannot ensure that the other will not talk first and incriminate them. There is also the potential that, eventually, both will talk and incriminate each other.

A similar risk underlines scenarios involving other conflicts of interests. In the context of this chapter, the conflicts addressed are public international law conflicts, between states. A group of states agrees to certain rules aiming at ensuring a fair balance of interests. However, due to conflicting interests, each state has a temptation to mislead the other party, allegedly playing by the agreed upon mutual "rules

---

[1] See, e.g., Nellie Munin (2023). *With a Little Help of my Friends - Examining the Logic behind Israel-Jordan-UAE Water for Electricity Deal.*

of the game," while in fact deviating from them to enhance its own interests at the expense of the other party.

The game illustrates that such a strategy could be effective if the deviation from the rules is minor. However, as the scope of deviation augments and the other party opts for a similar strategy (deviating from the agreed rules), all parties lose.

Since political alliances between states sometimes involve asymmetric participants, namely strong countries and weaker countries, a potential loss may have a greater effect on the latter than on the former. This is another point for discussion and consideration during the game.

Our experience of playing these games in various countries shows that different groups react to the challenges set forth by the games with unique approaches. In some cases, the players tend to gamble, attempting to win the whole jackpot, while in others they demonstrate a more cautious and responsible approach. We've come to learn that the different approaches to the game do not seem to represent any cultural differences but rather mainly represent the different characters of the playing individuals.

Selling the Dead Sea?[*]

General Information

The Dead Sea – the lowest point on earth – is considered a national resource and a sought-after international tourist attraction. Sadly, the Dead Sea is shrinking and receding – a fact that causes severe ecological problems such as sinkholes – due in part to the activities of the "Dead Sea Works" company, which received an exclusive franchise from the state of Israel to extract salt from the dead sea and sell it at a profit, under the Dead Sea Concession Law-1961. In the past few years, there have been ideas of how the Dead Sea could be restored. At one point "the water canal project" was being considered, among other things. This project entailed transferring water from the Mediterranean Sea to the Dead Sea by canal. The option of transferring water from the Red Sea to the Dead Sea was also considered. However, neither idea was realized due to technical, ecological, and financial challenges. Attempts by the Israeli government to incentivize the "Dead Sea Works" company themselves to rehabilitate the environmental damage they caused did not bear fruit.

In light of the Abraham Accords, a company from the United Arab Emirates heard that the franchise of the "Dead Sea Works" company is due to expire in the coming years, and the Israeli government is considering whether to renew it. The Emirati company proposes to purchase the concession to extract salt from the Dead Sea waters from the Israeli government, after the concession of the "Dead Sea Works" expires. In exchange for the concession, the company offers to launch a joint initiative with the Jordanian salt industry on the other side of the Dead Sea, to jointly rehabilitate the area and turn it into a thriving international tourist attraction on both sides.

The company is willing to invest hundreds of millions of dollars in the rehabilitation of the area, with the condition that the State of Israel will grant it an exclusive and non-reversible concession to extract salt from the Dead Sea. If the State of Israel opposes, the company is willing to compromise on a concession for 100 years.

The parties gathering to discuss the proposal:
Group 1: The Emirati company (backed by the United Arab Emirates government).
Group 2: The Israeli Ministry of Economy.
Group 3: The Israeli Ministry of Foreign Affairs.
Group 4: The Israeli Ministry of Tourism.

---

[*] This role-play was developed by Nellie Munin and Yael Efron (2023) and successfully played at the international trade workshop at Zefat Academic College's law school.

As part of the discussion, the parties are asked to address, among other things, the following points:

A. Is the Dead Sea salt extraction industry a strategic industry?

B. If so, does the strategic aspect derive from its location or its essence?

C. If so, to what extent should this consideration be weighed against other considerations?

D. The impact of the transaction on the local market:

   a. Is the industry that will be created strategic? What will be its strategic weight compared to the Dead Sea salt extraction industry?

   b. Will the move lead to job losses or to the creation of jobs?

   c. Is there relevance to short-term considerations (existing industry) versus long-term considerations (promises that in the best-case scenario may take time to materialize)?

   d. Can something be done for employees who lose their jobs to provide them with a professional transition to new industries and thus ensure their source of livelihood? How can the government assist with this?

   e. Does implementing the proposal have the potential to reduce the concentration of power and increase competition in the salt and tourism markets? How will this affect prices? Is it appropriate to encourage this or should local production be protected at all costs?

F. Is it appropriate to put an industry or a certain area (such as the relatively unpopulated Dead Sea area) at risk in order to generate income that will benefit another region (in this case, the central part of Israel)?

G. Will accepting the proposal create a "honey trap"[1] for Israel? If so, in what sense, and what is the weight of this consideration compared to other considerations?

H. How can an economic initiative be leveraged to strengthen peace relations and normalization in the region? What is the theoretical literature's approach to this? How can this idea be expressed in a proposed solution?

---

[1] A 'honey trap' means potential exposure of a country (in this case, Israel) that is economically dependent on another country (in this case, the UAE) to political pressure by the latter. For further explanation see: Nellie Munin (2020). Do The New Peace Agreements Between Israel and the Gulf States Set a "Honey Trap" for Israel? Bratislava Law Review, 4(2), 95-110.

Basic bibliography for the exercise:

Brodie, Tomer (2010). It will sell you space, the golden field: State sovereignty and international economic law. https://www.idi.org.il/parliaments/7751/8170 [Hebrew]

Munin, Nellie, *Do The New Peace Agreements Between Israel and the Gulf States Set a "Honey Trap" for Israel?* Bratislava Law Review, 4(2), 95-110, 2020.

Press Barnathan, G. (2006). *The Neglected Dimension of Commercial Liberalism: Economic Cooperation and Transition of Peace.* JOURNAL OF PEACE RESEARCH, vol. 43(3), 261-278.

The exercise's schedule and outline:

1) Set a date for submitting the written arguments to the instructors.

2) Set a date for classroom negotiations.

3) Classroom negotiations between the groups should last at least 45 minutes. Negotiators should attempt to reach a transaction outline by that time.

4) Give the groups at least 30 minutes to present the agreements reached and/or points of disagreements between the participants.

5) Leave at least 20 minutes for exercise debrief and summary.

6) For further instructions and/or ideas regarding the exercise's setting, please consult part 2 of this book.

Instructions - Group 1: The United Arab Emirates company (backed by the government of the United Arab Emirates)

As a governmental company, you are driven not only by the interest of creating profits for the corporation's owners and shareholders but also by the drive to promote the interests of the Emirati government. You and your government are aware of the strategic importance of the Dead Sea to Israel, both economically and geographically, in that it borders Jordan and the Palestinian Authority. You believe that in such a sensitive place it is better to have an objective and mitigating foreign factor that can leverage political clashes between these three parties to its benefit, both politically and economically.

The United Arab Emirates (UAE) aims to present itself to the world as an advanced nation that promotes peace and works towards it and even demonstrates better achievements than "traditional" powers such as the United States, the European Union, and Russia. While these countries have experienced notable failures in maintaining global peace, China is currently benefiting from these failures. There is no reason that the UAE should not benefit from at least an equivalent status, if not more.

To achieve this, you are prepared to invest hundreds of millions of dollars to gain control of the Dead Sea factories. This control will enable you to encourage the countries surrounding the Dead Sea to invest money in developing the area, and you will benefit from the fruits of these investments, returning part of your own investment, if not all of it. Your vision includes, among other things, hotels, water parks, spa resorts based on the unique minerals of the area, several casino centers, and, in short, turning the place into the healthy Las Vegas of the Middle East. Through this vision, you promise the State of Israel that you will create many job opportunities in this area currently stricken by unemployment. This will attract hundreds of thousands of settlers to the area and ease the burden and pressure in the center of the country, which suffers from traffic density, parking, and housing shortage. You are willing to assure the Israeli government that the funds generated by the regional project will enable it to invest in solving these problems.

The economic control in the development of the region will also give you significant political power compared to other players. The United Arab Emirates was the first to identify the economic and political potential of the Abraham Accords, and, as the UAE has managed to get its hands on the holdings of the Israeli "Delek" company in the gas reservoirs discovered in the Mediterranean Sea, you are confident that before others understand what you are doing, the factory will already be in your hands. Therefore, in addition to persuading the Israeli government to transfer and grant the concession to you, there is paramount importance to you in absolute secrecy of the negotiation and granting process. It is clear to you that if the potential transaction becomes known to other wealthy parties, such as Chinese companies, you may lose your advantage.

Instructions - Group 2: Representatives of the Israeli Ministry of Economy

You, like all Israeli government representatives, are aware of the strategic importance of the Dead Sea to Israel, both economically and geographically, in that it borders Jordan and the Palestinian Authority. You are aware of the limitations to the development potential of the region. They emanate from security rivalries with these neighboring countries. Hence, there is immense pressure, primarily from the Israeli Minister of Economy, but also from the residents and businesses in the area, to give a chance to the idea that, in such a sensitive place, it might be best to have an objective and mitigating foreign factor that might be able to assist in promoting the area economically.

You have put in a lot of effort in negotiations regarding the Abraham Accords (AA) and your success thus far encourages you. You can see that, currently, the United Arab Emirates is the most active partner of the four AA partners, and you are impressed by their goodwill and by the enormous business potential that the relationship with the UAE offers to Israeli industry as a whole. You understand that the UAE has an interest in this project and, due to the importance of Israel's relationship with the UAE, you do not want to upset or disappoint its government. You are also attracted by the hundreds of millions of dollars that the Emiratis offer, as well as the fact that they are willing to contribute to the rehabilitation of the Dead Sea region, which you do not see any other practical way of achieving in the near future.

It is clear to you that if, God forbid, the ecological disaster that has been predicted for some time actually occurs, and a sinkhole swallows up the entire hotel area, it will end the tourism industry there. Such an event would cause irreversible damage that will worsen the situation in this already struggling and impoverished region, and from there it is a short road to an economic blow to the entire state of Israel. Needless to say, such a huge sinkhole could also endanger agriculture in the area and even affect the use of the main road (Route 90) as a tourist route leading to areas in the south of Israel (the Arava and Eilat).

Furthermore, the Emiratis' visionary plan to turn the place into "the Las Vegas of the Middle East," creating many jobs in this area, may yield a lot of money that could be used to address problems in the center of Israel, and this is very appealing to you. You hope that creating jobs and establishing settlements will ease the burden of traffic, parking, and housing in the center of the country and will attract to this peripheral area well-established populations that will strengthen the region both economically and in terms of compliance with laws and regulations.

You are aware of the risk involved in entrusting a strategic industry to foreign hands, but you estimate that the chance of success is greater than the risk. In any case, the State of Israel cannot fund such a project from its budget. Thus, perhaps it is preferable to entrust the fate of the area to a partner who is interested in establishing its economic status in the area, and who will be investing all its energy in it, rather than taking a risk with other partners who may be interested in the project (such as China, the United States, or the European Union) but have scattered their investments in a way that does not promise any preference to the Dead Sea area.

Instructions – Group 3: Representatives of the Israeli Ministry of Foreign Affairs

You, like all Israeli government representatives, are aware of the strategic importance of the Dead Sea to Israel, both economically and geographically, in that it borders Jordan and the Palestinian Authority. You are aware of the limitations to the development potential of the region. They emanate from security rivalries with these neighboring countries. Hence, there is immense pressure, primarily from the Israeli Minister of Economy, but also from the residents and businesses in the area, to give a chance to the idea that, in such a sensitive place, it might best to have an objective and mitigating foreign factor that might be able to assist in promoting the area economically.

You have put in a lot of effort in negotiations regarding the Abraham Accords (AA) and your success thus far encourages you. You can see that, currently, the United Arab Emirates is the most active partner of the four AA partners, and you are impressed by their goodwill and by the enormous business potential that the relationship with the UAE offers to Israeli industry as a whole. You understand that the UAE is interested in this project and, due to the importance of the relationship with the UAE to you, you do not want to upset or disappoint its government.

However, you are concerned that the substantial economic impact over the development in the region will also give significant political power to the United Arab Emirates compared to the other players. You are concerned that they will reach a point where they can dictate to the State of Israel how to conduct itself in the region, while holding the joint ventures captive to their political desires. There is no guarantee that the UAE's influence on the Palestinian Aauthority and Jordan will be aligned with the interests of the State of Israel. In such a case, you are concerned that the State of Israel might lose its hold on the important and unique strategic asset, the Dead Sea, along with all that entails. The distance between the Dead Sea and Jerusalem, and specifically the distance between the Dead Sea and the Temple Mount, is less than an hour's drive away, and only a few minutes by flight. You must ensure that Israel does not lose control!

Instructions – Group 4: Representatives of the Israeli Ministry of Tourism.

You, like all Israeli government representatives, are aware of the strategic importance of the Dead Sea to Israel, both economically and geographically, in that it borders Jordan and the Palestinian Authority. You are aware of the limitations on the ability to develop the region's tourism due to security concerns with these neighboring countries, and this greatly frustrates you because it is an exclusive tourism asset: the lowest point on earth, a unique natural asset, rich in rare minerals with proven medicinal properties. You would like to see many more hotels, many more tourists, and a flourishing tourism industry with shops and attractions such as sailing and developed medical tourism in this area. You would like to see the establishment of an airport nearby where low-cost flights could operate and bring in a tourist airlift to the area, especially during the cold winter months when there is a high demand for warm destinations. Therefore, you definitely want to give a chance to the idea that in such a sensitive place, it might best to have an objective and mitigating foreign factor that might be able to assist in promoting the area economically.

You draw inspiration from the Abraham Accords, and you want to fulfill their tremendous tourism potential. Your challenge is to ensure that not only outbound tourism to Dubai and Morocco takes place, but also inbound tourism to Israel. You can envision the possibility of tourists from Europe, the United States, Russia, and the Far East arriving to enjoy the region and combining it with a visit to other neighboring countries. There is an opportunity here to present Israel as a vibrant and unique leisure destination, and perhaps tourists who come to the Dead Sea will expand their visit to other tourist attractions in Israel. In addition, you are aware that one of the difficulties in marketing Israeli tourism is its high prices, and you hope that creating such a place, with many hotels and attractions, will perhaps lead to increased competition in the industry and resulting lower prices.

You can see that, currently, the United Arab Emirates are the most active partners of the Abraham Accords, and you are impressed by their goodwill and by the enormous business potential that the relationship with the UAE offers to Israeli tourism: potential for wealthy tourists and wealthy investors. You are also attracted by the hundreds of millions of dollars that the Emiratis offer, as well as the fact that they are willing to contribute to the rehabilitation of the Dead Sea region, which you do not see any other practical way of achieving in the near future. It is clear to you that if, God forbid, the ecological disaster that has been predicted for some time actually occurs, and a sinkhole swallows up the entire hotel area, it will end the tourism industry there. Such a sinkhole would cause irreversible damage that will worsen the situation in this already struggling and impoverished region. From there it is a short road to an economic blow to the entire state of Israel. Needless to say, such a huge sinkhole could also affect the use of the main road (Route 90) leading to the southern area of the Arava and to Eilat and make it dangerous to use as a tourist route. On the other hand, the Emiratis visionary plan to turn the place into "the Las Vegas of the Middle East," creating many jobs in this area, is very appealing to you.

You are aware of the risk involved in entrusting a strategic industry to foreign hands, but you estimate that the chance of success is greater than the risk. In any case, Israel cannot fund such a project from its budget, and perhaps it is preferable to entrust the fate of the area to a partner who is interested in establishing its economic status in the area and willing to invest all its energy in it due to a sense of obligation to Israel and its neighboring Arab countries. This is unlike a Chinese partner, for example, who will have a sense of obligation to its own interests and to itself alone.

Let There be Gas!*

General Information

Over the years Israel has been considered as a low-quarry country. This was true until Israel discovered gas reservoirs in its territorial waters that could supply the country's needs for years to come.

The state of Israel quickly learned it could not rest on its laurels.

To produce the natural gas and locate additional gas fields, Israel relies on the assistance of private investors willing to bear the high cost involved in these processes. To motivate these investors, Israel grants them vast tax benefits, which have already been criticized by the public.

In addition to these issues, the countries bordering the state of Israel are also interested in Israel's gas reservoirs – and they are trying to appropriate part of this natural treasure for themselves.

Luckily for Israel, the timing of the discovery of the gas reservoirs could not have been better: the whole world is currently dealing with the cumulative repercussions of pollution - from factories, cars, airplanes, and other sources - that increase the greenhouse effect. The warnings of expert international environmentalists, previously regarded as unsupported theories, are becoming a reality in a world in which the weather is more and more extreme, leading to many natural disasters around the globe. These natural disasters have brought even the most skeptical countries to the understanding that green energy sources, like solar energy and natural gas must replace the contaminating fuels (kerosene, mazut, coal, diesel). Furthermore, the growing isolation, both on the political level and on the security level, of countries like Iran and Russia that are rich in these types of fuels is causing dependence on such countries to be a constant threat to the independence of many countries. So, the demand for natural gas is increasing all over the world, and a country that can supply it can expect considerable profit.

Luckily for Israel, not many countries own natural gas reservoirs. In contrast, the world-wide demand for natural gas is considerable and still growing. The shortage of this resource has been particularly exacerbated recently because two of the world's largest suppliers of it, Russia and Ukraine, have been at war with each other.

In light of the large amounts of gas that have been discovered, Israel realized that it could afford to sell gas to other countries. This would serve Israel financially and improve the country's international status.

Sadly, Israel cannot sell its natural gas without the cooperation of other countries, for two reasons. First, it does not have the funds required to lay the foundation (the unique pipeline) to transfer the gas to

---

*This role-play was developed by Nellie Munin and yael Efron (2022) and exercised successfully in the international trade workshop at the law school of Zefat Academic College.

other countries. Second, for the project to be more profitable, Israel would like to sell the gas to countries with which it does not have diplomatic relations.

Many countries have approached Israel, requesting to collaborate on this project. Israel has chosen to begin negotiations with several of them: Jordan and Egypt (the bordering countries with peace agreements with Israel) and Greece and Cyprus (the two European Union countries geographically closest to Israel). Due to the legal structure of the EU and the way it functions, the EU, as a separate legal entity, will take part in the negotiations.

Turkey sees itself as a natural ally to this alliance because it has been considered for many years now as an EU candidate (despite this seeming more tenuous in the past few years, Turkey still hopes that this promise will be kept) and also because Turkey is considered a very powerful country in the region, given that it straddles the East and West. In light of the Turkish leaders' behavior in the past few years, the rest of the partners to this alliance are ambivalent about including Turkey and have yet to take a final position regarding this question.

All parties meet in a neutral country – Sweden – to begin the negotiations.

The first stage of the negotiations will focus on 2 main issues:

1) The manner of contribution to the gas pipeline project by each party. The parties can suggest contributing:

    - The gas;

    - Money to build the pipeline that will be used in order to distribute the gas to other countries and the infrastructure needed for it;

    - Manpower to carry out the building of the pipeline on site;

    - Raw materials and necessary products to build the infrastructure;

    - Professional expertise to build the pipeline and the infrastructure, and to operate them;

    - Commitment to purchase a certain amount of gas per year;

    - Marketing capability, including diplomatic relations with countries that can be potential customers;

    - The diplomatic ability to prevent disturbance to the progress of the project by hostile bodies or competitors.

Each party will elaborate as to what it can and is willing to contribute to the project, and each side will proportionately price the profits (in percentages) that it expects in return. **In the class discussion, all parties will have to reach an agreement about these issues.**

2) Should Turkey be invited to take part in the project? This question has political and diplomatic aspects as well as financial aspects (Turkey's participation will come at a cost to the profits of the rest of the parties). Every country must formulate its position on this issue while considering all its interest (not limited to this project alone). **In the class discussion, the countries will have to reach an agreement regarding the question of involving Turkey in the project and, if so, to what degree?**

Basic bibliography for the exercise:

Gabriel Mitchel, *The Eastern Mediterranean Gas Forum: Cooperation in the Shadow of Competition* (2020). https://tinyurl.com/2k3a6meh

Ehud Eran *FES Southern Perspective: Israel's Strategic Interests in the Eastern Mediterranean* (2021). http://library.fes.de/pdf-files/bueros/israel/17835.pdf

Eduard Soler, *The EU and Eastern Mediterranean: How to Deal with Turkey* (2021). https://www.cidob.org/en/publications/eu-and-eastern-mediterranean-how-deal-turkey

The exercise's schedule and outline:

1) Decide whether to role-play only the first part, or both parts of the simulation.[1]
2) Set a date (or separate dates) for submitting the written arguments for each part to the instructors.
3) Set a date (or a separate date for each part) for classroom negotiations.
4) Classroom negotiations between the groups should last at least 45 minutes. During that time, negotiators should attempt to reach an agreed-upon solution.
5) Give the groups at least 30 minutes to present the agreements reached and/or points of disagreement between the participants.
6) Leave at least 20 minutes for exercise debrief and summary.
7) For further instructions and/or ideas regarding the exercise's setting, please consult part 2 of this book.

---

[1] For more on the features, benefits, and challenges of multistage negotiations, see: John Lande, *Suggestions for Using Multi-Stage Simulations in Law School Courses*, University of Missouri School of Law Legal Studies, Research Paper No. 2013-08: 1-7 (2014).

Stage A: the negotiation – who will take part in producing and transporting the gas and in what way

Individual instructions for the Egypt and Jordan Group

Egypt and Jordan understand that the situation in the Middle East has changed with the conclusion of the Abraham Accords. They follow the growing cooperation between Israel and the United Arab Emirates and Morocco with wide eyes, aware of this cooperation's financial and political potential.

After maintaining "cold" peace with Israel for years due to their support of the Palestinian people, the new reality has Egypt and Jordan reconsidering their steps. Both countries are not in very good financial states, which worsened due to the COVID-19 pandemic. In both countries, the people have historically been engaged in criticism of and complaint about the authorities and in activism against government actions with which they disagree. Leaders of both countries know that, in the cruel surroundings in which they live, financial instability can quickly escalate into political unrest, and this instability, in turn, can provoke violent or hostile forces to try to take over the country. Syria and Lebanon are concerning examples of this possibility.

Both countries are concerned about being left off the new regional "playing field" and are willing to change their normal patterns of conduct in order to take part in the new regional "rules of the game." They will not give up their Declarative Support of the Palestinians, but at the same time they will do all they can in order to not miss the opportunity presented by taking part in the gas project. Taking part in this project can ensure an influx of money from those who will invest in it, like the European Union, and also ensure a significant share of the profits. They will negotiate for their countries so that the project creates workplaces for their citizens. Participation in the project might also reduce the increasing public criticism of the high rate of poverty and unemployment in their counties.

They are interested in navigating the negotiations in a way that positions them as the linking factor between the source of the gas – Israel – and the final customers – countries with whom Israel does not have diplomatic relations. This way they will have control over both sides of the equation and both sides will depend on them. This will also improve their international status and put them in a new and better position for negotiating with all countries that will take part in the project, as well as in other trade areas.

These countries can also offer infrastructure benefits:

Egypt has big liquefaction facilities on its shores that can transform the gas into liquid to transport it in pipes to distant destinations. Egypt also has a standing cooperation agreement with Turkey regarding gas, worth 4 billion dollars. Jordan has an existing gas pipeline and a connection with Syria that can transport the Israeli gas to Turkey and connect to its pipelines that lead to Europe.

Although Turkey also has ties with countries with whom Israel does not have diplomatic relations, Turkey has repeatedly proven that, when it comes to Israel, it cannot be trusted. On the contrary, under President Erdogan's leadership over the past few years, the relationship and financial cooperation between the two countries has suffered. On one hand, Egypt and Jordan have an interest in reminding Israel that leaning on Turkey's support in the project might be detrimental. On the other hand, Egypt and Jordan have financial interests when it comes to Turkey, and they cannot allow themselves to ignore its regional power and ties with countries like Russia and Syria.

Stage A: the negotiation - who will take part in producing and transporting the gas and in what way

Individual instructions for the Greece and Cyprus Group

In the past few years, Greece and Cyprus have suffered from a relatively insignificant status in the European Union: they are two small countries located on the geographic edge of the EU. What they have in common is that, at the time of its formation, the EU was reluctant about each of them joining. In Greece's case, this was due to the unstable financial condition. In Cyprus's case, this was due to the political condition that after the civil war that occurred in the '70s, the country remained split into Greek and Turkish parts. The rift among the citizens of Cyprus is so deep that the EU's threats that it might cause Cyprus to be denied as a member did not help to resolve it, and Cyprus became an EU member despite the continuing split.

The growing European need for natural gas as a source of energy, on the one hand, and the war between Russia and Ukraine, two main energy suppliers to Europe, on the other hand, provide Greece and Cyprus with an opportunity to prove to Europe how important they are as the "gate to Europe" despite their economic and political conditions.

Their geographic proximity to Israel and the gas reservoirs in the Mediterranean Sea created this opportunity for them and they are not going to let it slip away. For Israel, they are important because they can affect the decision-making process in the EU and convince the EU to support the project financially. For the EU, they are important because the pipeline will have to cross their countries to run its course to the depth of the continent. In addition, they have tight connections with Israel, including in tourism, security, and more, in spite of the fact that the EU as a whole has had a more tense relationship with Israel over the past few years, because the Israeli-Palestinian conflict resolution process has lagged.

Greece and Cyprus hope that taking part in the gas pipeline project will create income and employment opportunities that will elevate their economies and diversify them.

They are very pleased that Israel turned to them first for cooperation, and not to Turkey. They will do anything they can to leave Turkey out, due to the negative history between them. Up to this point, they have managed to keep Turkey out of the EU. They do not trust Turkey and they are concerned that Turkey will take over the project and point the pipes her way, a strategy that will leave Greece and Cyprus out. They fear Turkey can offer cheap manpower and lower expenses, especially in light of the Turkish lira's dismal state and Turkish connections to Russia and Syria.

They are aware that Turkey has connections to countries with which Israel does not have diplomatic relations. However, they are counting on the fact that Turkey has proven to Israel in the past that Israel can't trust its support. On the contrary, under President Erdogan's leadership over the past few years, the relationship between Turkey and Israel, and their economic cooperation, has suffered and been mostly disappointing. Greece and Cyprus do not want to get on Turkey's bad side because they do not know if they might need Turkey in the future or if the EU will decide to accept it as a member. Still, they are interested in reminding Israel that leaning on Turkey for support of the project might be "betting on the wrong horse."

Greece and Cyprus are aware that if they cooperate fully with the European Union, it would be possible to combine the European pipeline and the Turkish pipeline to transport gas to Europe in a manner that would make the project significantly cheaper. With that being said, the conflict between

Greece, Cyprus, and Turkey includes the question of who has control over the "economic waters" of the Mediterranean Sea that the pipes run through. Until the dispute over who controls what part of the Mediterranean Sea is resolved, this cooperation will not be possible, but it might be possible to use Turkey's interest in being included in the pipeline project as incentive for resolving this conflict once and for all.

Stage A: the negotiation - who will take part in producing and transporting the gas and in what way

Individual instructions for the Israel Group

Israel urgently needs the gas profits. These profits will aid Israel in improving its financial state and its diplomatic status.

From a financial point of view

These profits will contribute to covering the deficit created by four governmental elections and the current crisis and to funding a series of important looming public expenditures.

Israel knows for certain that to make the gas profits, it must collaborate with other countries.

To obtain the money and the technical expertise needed to fund and lay the infrastructure (the pipeline) to transfer the gas to other countries, Israel is aiming towards the European Union, the largest trade bloc in the world. Because, in the past few years, the EU has conditioned many financial collaborations with Israel on solving the Israeli-Palestinian conflict, Israel has decided to turn to the two EU countries that are geographically closest to it: Greece and Cyprus. Israel hopes that these countries will understand the benefits this project will bring their way, in strengthening their economies, and in fostering their relations with the rest of the EU countries and with Turkey, such that they will agree to collaborate with no harsh terms while also convincing the EU to take part.

To market to countries with which Israel does not have diplomatic relations, Israel has decided to join forces with its neighboring countries, with whom it has "cold" peace agreements, Egypt and Jordan. Israel is taking advantage of the fact that these countries are concerned that the signing and implementing of the Abraham Accords, gradually creating a "new Middle East," means they may be left behind. Although Turkey also has connections with countries with which Israel doesn't have diplomatic relations, Turkey has proven itself unreliable to Israel when it comes to its support. Under the leadership of President Erdogan, the relationship and financial cooperation between the countries have suffered mostly setbacks and disappointments. For Israel, leaning on Turkey's support might be betting on the wrong horse. On the other hand, Israel is well aware of the fact that, after the United States reversed its promise of financial support in the Biden administration, the best and fastest way to transport gas to Europe is through connecting to the Jordanian pipeline and connecting it through Syria to the Turkish infrastructure.

From the political-strategic point of view

Israel hopes that its control over the gas in which many countries have an interest will provide an opportunity to create closer connections and stronger regional alliances with its neighbouring countries. The hope is that this control will strengthen Israel's financial and political status in the world, while leveraging the European gas shortage created by the conflict between Russia and Ukraine to benefit Israel.

Stage A: the negotiation - who will take part in producing and transporting the gas and in what way

Individual instructions for the European Union Group

Over the years, the European Union has taken action regarding the Middle East with a sense of financial and political superiority. According to the traditional idea of spreading the "normative power," the EU tried to offer the Middle East different levels of financial aid – as "carrots" – hoping that it would create the basis for allowing the EU to intervene in Middle Eastern political matters. This, in turn, would enable the EU to dictate the EU leadership model, one that has prevented war in Europe for over 70 years, in the Middle East.

The European Union has not succeeded in materializing this vision. The signing of the Abraham Accords – initiated and sponsored by the United States – broke through the existing model, took root in the area, and offered new financial options that opened the door to new political opportunities as well. The European Union found itself at a crossroads and had to reconsider its approach.

In addition, Russia, which has cut off the supply of gas to the European Union mid-winter in the past to strong-arm the EU into certain political decisions, continues to threaten this line of action and is now also entangled in a war with Ukraine. This situation endangers the stability of the gas supply to Europe, which depends on it for heating and industry. The European Union understands that it must diversify its sources of energy to secure as many energy resources as possible for the European economy.

The end of American President Trump's first term in 2020 and the weakening of the international standing of the U.S. administration gave the EU hope of rebuilding its relevance in regional political processes. However, to do so, the EU must find a way to "take back" its former political statements that conditioned its willingness to financially support regional collaborations in the area on political progress between Israel and the Palestinian Authority. It must take the diplomatic achievements of Greece and Cyprus and present them as European Union achievements. It must cover up the little success in the Middle East and the desperate need for gas by presenting the agreement as a European contribution to the materializing of the Abraham Accords and the new Middle East.

In the past few years, the European Union has repeatedly rejected the inclusion of Turkey as a member, despite its promises to do so dating back to the 1990s. The international terror attacks the EU suffered in the early 2000s strengthened the opposition to the acceptance of the big Muslim country. President Erdogan, who saw these repeated rejections as humiliating, used them as leverage to strengthen ties with Russia and Syria. This step also strengthened the opposition to accepting Turkey as a member of the EU – even among those who, up to that point, held relatively moderate views on the matter. The European Union understands that including Turkey in the gas pipeline project might improve public opinion of the country's international image and might create a European reliance on Turkey since Europe desperately needs the gas supply. The EU fears Turkey could use this reliance to pressure the EU to accept the country as a member. With that being said, the EU acknowledges Turkey's regional power, and does not want to push Turkey too far by ignoring it or disrespecting it more than it already has. The EU will not hesitate to remind Israel that, although Turkey has ties with countries with which Israel does not have diplomatic relationships (which theoretically might be of use to Israel in regard to the gas project), Turkey has proven more than once that Israel can't rely on its support. Quite the contrary, under President Erdogan's leadership in the past few years, the financial collaborations, and the general relationship between the two countries have gone mostly downhill. The EU might remind Israel of its tumultuous relationship with Turkey just to try to distract Israel's attention from the disappointments it has endured in its relations with the EU itself.

The European Union understands the financial and political importance of resolving the conflict between Greece, Cyprus, and Turkey over the "financial waters" in the Mediterranean Sea, and the EU is interested in doing all that it can to use the current situation as leverage for that purpose.

Stage A: the negotiation – who will take part in producing and transporting the gas and in what way

Individual instructions for the Turkey Group

Turkey's failure to manage it internally and in its diplomatic relations with the West, combined with a deep financial crisis of the crash of the Turkish Lira, brought Turkey to a new and unprecedented low.

In the past few years, Erdogan, the President of Turkey, has chosen to change his strategy from one that aimed to cooperate with the West and join the European Union to one that joins forces with Russia, Syria, and other countries considered hostile by the Western world. Turkey is now paying this policy's financial and political price.

Despite Erdogan's hostile political expressions against the West, he is not blind to the financial and political significance of the signing of the Abraham Accords and the discovery of gas reservoirs in the Middle East – and the regional developments that follow these events. President Erdogan understands that if Turkey doesn't rush into action, she will be left behind and excluded from the fruits of the upcoming financial initiatives that are developing in the Middle East, resulting in economic and political isolation for Turkey.

Erdogan is trying to find a way to get off the tree he climbed. He made an effort: He invited the Israeli President to visit Turkey and even stated clearly in his welcoming speech that Turkey is interested in participating in the gas production and pipeline project.

Turkey knows there are countries taking part in the project that are hostile towards it and that some, like Greece, Cyprus, the EU, and even Israel, are suspicious due to negative past experiences with Turkey. Turkey understands that these countries will try to prevent its participation in the gas project, but still hopes that its economic capabilities, professional knowledge, and unique political connections that can be utilized for the project will tilt the scales in its direction. Turkey's connections with the countries with which Israel does not have diplomatic relationships have significant economic value. Turkey will do all it can to ensure its place in the project, even if it means enduring some humiliation. It must benefit from the discovery of the gas reservoirs, use the Turkish capabilities to grow in power in the region, and rebuild and strengthen its relationship with the European Union. It cannot stay on the sidelines of regional processes. If possible, Turkey should try to dilute the achievements and the rise in regional power of Greece and Cyprus. It should project to all participants that it cannot be ignored – and to the EU that it is trustworthy, so that, maybe, in the future its membership in the EU will be considered positively.

Turkey has an existing gas pipeline infrastructure that can be used to transport the gas, which is a better option than building a new pipeline at a very high cost. Turkey is counting on the fact that, after the Biden administration went back on the U.S promise to contribute to the funding towards the building of a new gas pipeline (a promise that was made by the first Trump administration), the European Union will find it difficult to come up with the funds to build the new line. Suffering from a bad financial state, Turkey hopes the EU and the rest of the partners to the gas pipeline project will be reduced to including Turkey to use their existing pipeline so that they can transport the gas to Europe.

Turkey knows that if it cooperated fully with the European Union then it would be possible to combine the European pipeline and the Turkish pipeline to transport gas to Europe in a manner that would make the project significantly cheaper. However, the conflict between Greece, Cyprus, and Turkey includes the question of who controls the "economic waters" of the Mediterranean Sea that the pipes run through. Until the dispute over who controls what part of the Mediterranean Sea is resolved, this cooperation will not be possible. On the other hand, it might be possible to use the pipeline project as incentive for resolving this conflict.

Stage B: The conflict with Turkey

Due to Turkey's dissatisfaction with its role in the agreement that it and the rest of the partaking countries have reached regarding the gas project, Turkey's President Erdogan declared that there is now conflict between Turkey and any countries that may sabotage the alliance. Turkey's interest is still in joining this alliance (and not in preventing it) since preventing the alliance would not benefit Turkey – so Turkey must tread lightly and be cautious. Conflict resolution experts have been invited to take part in the conference in Sweden to assist the countries in reaching agreements.

Israel's Interests:

Israel's interest is to maintain the alliance. On the one hand, Israel is concerned about Turkey's unstable position and about the possibility of it harming the project. On the other hand, Israel is aware that using the Turkish pipeline will be very cost effective and will also speed up the timetable for seeing profits from the project. Israel does not want to upset Turkey because it does not want to create regional escalation. Israel is aware that Turkey is a popular destination for Israeli tourists as well as an important import source of many products. The countries have connections in many trade branches, as well as personal and cultural connections. Israel would like to maintain the health of this relationship and, if possible, improve it. Israel can't ignore the political ties between Turkey and countries like Russia, Syria, and the Palestinian Authority, and it would prefer that Turkey play a calming role in the region as opposed to a provoking role. Turkey's association with hostile elements is liable to harm Israel both economically and from the point of view of its security.

Stage B: The conflict with Turkey

Due to Turkey's dissatisfaction with its role in the agreement that it and the rest of the partaking countries have reached regarding the gas project, Turkey's President Erdogan declared that there is now conflict between Turkey and any countries that may sabotage the alliance. Turkey's interest is still in joining this alliance (and not in preventing it) since preventing the alliance would not benefit Turkey – so Turkey must tread lightly and be cautious. Conflict resolution experts have been invited to take part in the conference in Sweden to assist the countries in reaching agreements.

Egypt and Jordan Interests:

Egypt and Jordan have an ambivalent approach to Turkey. On the one hand, Turkey is a Muslim country. They appreciate its support of the Palestinian struggle and its ability to contribute to the project financially and with expertise. Egypt and Jordan are concerned that excluding Turkey from the project with no hope of collaboration in the future might cause it to associate with unstable forces in the area and beyond in a way that could jeopardize the region's political stability, creating competition that will affect the project's profitability. On the other hand, Turkey's involvement in the project, and the use of the Turkish pipeline in particular, diminishes the importance of Egypt and Jordan to the project, and so for that reason they have incentive to prevent Turkish participation.

Stage B: The conflict with Turkey

Due to Turkey's dissatisfaction with its role in the agreement that it and the rest of the partaking countries have reached regarding the gas project, Turkey's President Erdogan declared that there is now conflict between Turkey and any countries that may sabotage the alliance. Turkey's interest is still in joining this alliance (and not in preventing it) since preventing the alliance would not benefit Turkey – so Turkey must tread lightly and be cautious. Conflict resolution experts have been invited to take part in the conference in Sweden to assist the countries in reaching agreements.

Greece and Cyprus Interests:

Greece and Cyprus will do everything in their power to prevent Turkey from taking part in the project. Turkey is a historic sworn enemy of Greece and Cyprus, and they have no trust in it. They worry that if Turkey joins the project, it will try to diminish their involvement in it as much as possible and that Turkey will also affect the rest of the countries taking part in the project – by positive and negative means – so that those countries will prefer Turkey over Greece and Cyprus. Greece and Cyprus would prefer to avoid connecting their pipeline to the Turkish pipeline at all costs, to prevent their dependency on Turkey. However, their financial states make it difficult for them to counter the Turkish offers in any significant way. The only thing Greece and Cyprus can use as leverage over Turkey is their geographical location at the gate of the continent and their close ties with the EU.

Stage B: The conflict with Turkey

Due to Turkey's dissatisfaction with its role in the agreement that it and the rest of the partaking countries have reached regarding the gas project, Turkey's President Erdogan declared that there is now conflict between Turkey and any countries that may sabotage the alliance. Turkey's interest is still in joining this alliance (and not in preventing it) since preventing the alliance would not benefit Turkey – so Turkey must tread lightly and be cautious. Conflict resolution experts have been invited to take part in the conference in Sweden to assist the countries in reaching agreements.

The European Union's Interests:

The EU understands it cannot ignore Turkey's regional power and that it is better to have Turkey collaborate positively in the project rather than excluding it, which would leave Turkey angry and frustrated. The EU knows that one of the reasons Turkey has made connections with countries that the EU sees as dangerous is its disappointment at not being accepted as an EU member despite the long process it has gone through as a candidate. The EU also understands that there is no chance that this process will be completed anytime in the foreseeable future because many EU member countries oppose the idea. And, so, the EU believes that allowing Turkey to take part in the gas pipeline project is an act that might "calm" it for a while and encourage Turkey to rebuild its ties with the West, instead of strengthening its new connections to countries that are more extreme. The EU assumes that, in terms of the gas pipeline project itself, the more countries that are involved in the project, the better. The EU assumes the project will ensure the supply of gas to Europe and the EU would like to diversify the available alternatives. The EU understands that using the Turkish pipeline will speed up the timeline for building the project's infrastructure and will allow the supply of gas from Israel to reach Europe sooner, which means diminishing dependence on Russia and Ukraine.

The United Currency Wars[*]

'Prisoner's Dilemma' games illustrate conflicts of interest between parties.[1] They are based on a familiar scenario: two prisoners are incarcerated and face interrogation. If neither prisoner divulges any information, they will both go free due to lack of evidence. However, the police aim to coax at least one of them into talking. The promise is that if one prisoner speaks up, they will be spared at the expense of the other, who will be incriminated. With no means of communication, participants cannot ensure that the other won't speak first and implicate them. Ultimately, there is no guarantee that both won't eventually talk, resulting in mutual incrimination.

In scenarios involving conflicting interests, a comparable risk arises. This conflict pertains to disputes between states. A coalition of states establishes specific rules with the goal of achieving a balanced equilibrium of interests. However, due to conflicting agendas, each state faces the temptation to deceive the other party—ostensibly adhering to the agreed-upon 'rules of the game' while subtly deviating from them to advance its own interests at the other party's expense. Such a strategy is effective only as long as the deviation from the rules is minor. However, as the scope of deviation augments, and the other party opts for a similar strategy ("tit-for-tat"), all parties may lose.

This 'Prisoner's Dilemma' game reflects a conflict of interests regarding deviation from financial stability rules that were agreed by the parties (the "Alliance") as a major condition for the establishment of a united currency among them. These rules were dictated by the rich and strong partners to the weaker partners when the Alliance was established, to ensure that the latter would not financially collapse, dragging all the other countries with them. Respecting the stability rules requires strict financial discipline, something all parties find hard to maintain considering strong external and internal pressures. However, deviation from the stability rules would undermine the Alliance, weakening all its parties.

---

[*] The framework for the game is inspired by a well-known Prisoner's Dilemma game developed by Ebner and Winkler and was adapted to the International Trade context by Nellie Munin. For the original game with detailed notes on preparing, conducting and debriefing the game, see: Noam Ebner & Yifat Winkler, *The Pasta Wars: A Prisoner's Dilemma Simulation-Game* Ebner, 40 SIMULATION & GAMING 134 (2008).

[1] The term was coined by ALLBERT W. TUCKER, A TWO-PERSON DILEMMA, presented at the Stanford University Psychology Seminar (1950) but was conceptualized by MERRILL M. FLOOD & MELVIN DRESHER, A STUDY OF RATIONAL BEHAVIOR IN THE CONTEXT OF CONFLICT (RAND Corp., unpublished manuscript, 1950). See WILLIAM POUNDSTONE, PRISONER'S DILEMMA (Anchor Books 1992).

Instructions

Divide the class into four groups and read the instructions together. Give each group a sheet with the instructions, a slip sheet, and a balance sheet.

There should be no communication between the 4 groups. Messages from each group are passed to the instructor each round, using a slip from the slip sheet held by each group.

Each country must decide separately what its policy will be for the next month. They do not know what the other countries will do and will find out only after all slips are handed to the instructor.

The game is played for 3 consecutive rounds (this phase may be shortened to one round in case of time constraints).

Towards the **4th round**: The Alphaville Central Bank (ACB) announces that since the global financial crisis severely hit the Alliance's main global competitor (while the Alliance still manages to keep stable), in the next month any effect of the Members' financial behavior may be doubled. Consequently, the Members decide to send their representatives to a coordination meeting. It should be mentioned that the 30 years of Alliance did not wipe out the bad memories of the allies from hundreds of years of resentment and wars, and their relationships bear mutual suspicion.

Towards the **6th (or 5th) round**: free communication is allowed until the final decision is announced to the instructor. When a decision is given to the instructor, it will not be revealed by the instructor. This is optional.

Towards the **7th (or 6th) round:** the financial crisis that hits Alphaville at last makes market terms, including the options for profit and for loss, much more extreme. According to the Alphaville Central Bank, expected profit or loss may be X4. Due to the obvious potential danger to the Alliance's market, it is further announced that the fine for breaching the stability criteria will be extended proportionally to 400,000 AC per each month of breach. The Members decide to meet again. This is the last meeting – no other meeting will be possible before the 8th round.

After **the last round**, ask each country:
How much did each of you gain/lose?
If there were a ninth round – what would you do?
Would you form a 'coalition' in the future? With whom?

At the end of the game, you can announce that the ACB revealed that all four did not follow the criteria in the recent year. According to the alliance's agreement, each of them should be referred to the Alphavillian Court of Justice (ACJ) and be charged with a fine for each month of breaching the stability criteria. However, reference to the court of each Member is subject to a political decision the three of the four Member states.

Questions for discussion:

- What can be learned from this exercise regarding international trade interests?
- What are some of the similarities and differences you can find when comparing this game to international trade treaties you know?
- Considering your experience from this game and from real-life, if you were to draft

a new international trade treaty, what would you make sure to include in it?

Note: to illustrate the "prisoner's dilemma" a minimum of 4 rounds will do. A longer game depends on time constraints and allows a greater focus on negotiation dynamics.

Background

After hundreds of years of wars and despair, four countries in Alphaville continent decided thirty years ago, to opt for an economic alliance (the "Alliance") which is legally identical to the European Union model. Since then, this Alliance, including four member states ("Member," collectively "Members"), is following the legal developments in the EU, updating its model accordingly. Consequently, when the EU concluded the Maastricht Treaty, establishing the EMU, this Alliance followed and created the AMU, relying on the same set of agreements.

All four countries are AMU members. However, Alpha and Beta share a similar size (big) and economic strength. Gamma and Delta, the other partners, are smaller in size and economically weaker countries that joined the Alliance to enjoy economic support from Alpha and Beta. Alpha and Beta consciously agreed to contribute more money to the joint budget of the Alliance since they were keen to get a political hold in Gamma and Delta to prevent these countries from turning to other influential countries, which are Alpha and Beta's political rivals. Yet another reason was Alpha and Beta's hope to enjoy cheap and interesting investment opportunities in Gamma and Delta.

When the AMU was established, stability criteria identical to the EU's 'Maastricht Criteria' were also established, and each of the four partners legally committed to them. The initiative to establish these criteria was from Alpha and Beta, who were afraid that if for some reason Gamma, Delta, or both become economically unstable, this instability may spillover to Alpha and Beta, endangering their economies.

If the four partners respect the stability criteria, each of them will gain net 100,000 Alphavillian Coronas (AC) per month. If one of them does not respect the criteria, it should be fined by 100,000 (AC) per that month. This sum will be contributed to the Alliance's budget but will only be used to finance further enforcement, so the Members cannot enjoy it for other purposes.

The Conflict

Unfortunately, in recent years all four allies find it difficult to fulfill these criteria and still enjoy incomes due to the global financial crisis. As their financial situation became tough, each of them (separately) concluded that if only one country breached the criteria, it may gain 300,000 AC per month. So, even having to pay a 100,000 AC fine, it will still enjoy a net gain of 200,000 AC. If two countries breach the criteria, each will enjoy a 200,000 AC gain, diminished to 100,000 AC net gain after paying the fine. If three breach the criteria, each will enjoy a 100,000 AC gain, but the fine will totally diminish it, so the net gain will be 0. However, if all the four countries breach the criteria and the financial crisis will hit them severely, each will lose 300,000 AC per month.

Members breaching criteria	Gross Profit	Net profit (after fine payment)	Members obeying criteria	Net profit
0	****	****	4	100,000
1	300,000	200,000	3	100,000
2	200,000	100,000	2	100,000
3	100,000	0	1	100,000
4	****	-300,000	****	****

Currency Wars

Monetary Policy Decision Slip

Month # 1 Country _____ Decision: _____	Month # 2 Country _____ Decision: _____
Month # 3 Country _____ Decision: _____	Month # 4 Country _____ Decision: _____
Month # 5 Country _____ Decision: _____	Month # 6 Country _____ Decision: _____
Month # 7 Country _____ Decision: _____	Month # 8 Country _____ Decision: _____

Profit / Loss Balance Sheet

Month #	Our choice	Members breaching criteria	Members obeying criteria	This Month's Profit / Loss
Total Profit / Loss:				

Taxation and Tax Law

TEACHING TAX LAW AS A SOCIAL INSTRUMENT

Learning the current legal rules is undoubtedly important for law students. It is equally important for them to understand why the law is as it is. Concerns have been voiced around the lack of sufficient understanding or appreciation of the role of law in society.[1] A narrow view of the law as only being about a dispute resolution system underestimates its broader role of affecting human interactions.[2] The courts' interpretation of statutes plays a crucial role in structuring political power,[3] but so does the interpretation taken by the implementing authority, in this case the tax authority. The written law gives the implementation authority room for discretion, and one question underlying the exercise described in this section is whether and to what extent this discretion should be affected by exceptional global circumstances.

As educators, a special responsibility rests on our shoulders. We are charged with the role of bridging an information gap between the law and those who will provide legal services to society after graduation. We are the agents able to uncover the values and interests that created the legal infrastructure both generally and specifically in tax law.[4] Studying the political process allows for direct confrontation with fundamental, sometimes conflicting, values underlying democracy. When students understand the values and policies from which the legislation grew, they will in the future be able to represent the interests of clients and society more broadly, because they see the broad picture.[5]

Furthermore, as legal educators we have an impact on how our students perceive the legal system. By focusing on the justice system's fairness, we can create constituencies that are more informed and motivated to address its challenges.[6] We join the ongoing call for legal education to play a more active role in access to justice issues not only by supporting research but also by integrating those issues into curricular and academic activities.[7]

---

[1] Kellye Y. Testy, *Why Law Matters*, 65 J. LEGAL EDUC. 707, 708 (2016) (in Testy's view, "the role of law in society is insufficiently understood or appreciated and that gap is a harmful one").
[2] *Id.*
[3] Dakota S. Rudesill, Christopher J. Walker & Daniel P. Tokaji, *A Program in Legislation*, 65 J. LEGAL EDUC. 70, 80 (2015).
[4] For example, the taxation of same-sex couples reflects a value-based political process, worthy of class discussion. See Anthony C. Infanti, *Bringing Sexual Orientation and Gender Identity into the Tax Classroom* 59(1) J. LEGAL EDUC. 3, 16 (2009) (stressing the need to present in class discussions a balanced view of how exclusion from the attribution rules can both benefit and harm same sex couples).
[5] *Supra 4* at 80.
[6] Deborah L. Rhode, *Access to Justice: An Agenda for Legal Education and Research*, 62 J. LEGAL EDUC. 531, 532 (2013).
[7] *Ibid* at 545.

Tax payment is a major civil duty in a modern state. In democratic states, the duty to pay tax is determined by legislation, serving as a 'contract' between the government and taxpayers.[8] From a *government* point of view, tax is a major source of state revenue. It finances the government's actions, ensuring stability and facilitating the achievement of policy goals for which the government was elected. Broad tax avoidance undermines governance.

Individuals expect tax revenues to be used by the government to improve the collective and individual welfare. Taxes are the price individuals are willing to pay to the state that will supply them the goods and services they need and expect from an elected government.[9] Legislators can use the tax to re-divide wealth, to improve social justice,[10] or to direct public behavior.[11] Social justice is inevitable to tax law.[12] To a great extent, it determines the public's obedience to tax laws.

Tax obedience is affected by several factors, including the overall tax burden and the ratio between it and income; enforcement effectiveness; and taxpayers' understanding of and identification with tax-paying importance.[13] Two potential justice-informed criteria for determining tax burden may be *a taxpayer's ability to pay*,[14] or the *taxpayer's benefit*.[15]

---

[8] John Locke (1632-1704) believed that rulers' legitimacy derives from the agreement of their subjects to their ruling: RICHARD ASHCRAFT. REVOLUTIONARY POLICY AND LOCKE'S TWO TREATIES OF GOVERNMENT. Princeton: Princeton University Press (1986).

[9] Yoseph Edrey, *Constitutional Limitations on Tax Legislation*, BRIDGING THE SEA 205, 211, 214 (Yoseph Edrey and Marco Greggi, eds. 2010).

[10] David Elkins, *Redistributive Taxation and the Constitutional Protection of Property*, BRIDGING THE SEA 241 (Yoseph Edrey and Marco Greggi, eds. 2010).

[11] Eithan Berglass, *Direct Taxes and Indirect Taxes* 9 BANKING QUARTERLY 36, 60-67 (1970).

[12] ADAM SMITH, AN INQUIRY INTO THE NATURE AND CAUSES OF THE WEALTH OF NATIONS 310-11 (Book V(2), E. Camman ed.; 4th ed., 1925); Yoseph Edrey, *An overall Tax Base in Israel*, 12 MISHPATIM 431 (1983) (*Isr.*); Justice Aharon Barak in CA 165/82 *Kibbutz Hatzor vs. Income Tax Assessor Rehovot*, PD 39(2) 70 (1985) (*Isr.*), in section 5, stressed the importance of interpreting tax laws according to the changing circumstances as well as according to common principles of equality, justice and morals.

[13] Tomaz Lesnik, Davorin Kracun, Timotej Jagric, *Recession and Tax Compliance – The Case of Slovenia*, 25(2) INZINERINE EKONOMIKA-ENGINEERING ECONOMICS, 130, 132 .(2014)

[14] Smith, *supra* note 12.

[15] Edrey, *supra* note 12 at 433.

Tax Obedience in COVID-19 Times
Introduction and Background

Tax payment is a major civic duty in a modern state. Broad tax avoidance undermines governance. Several factors affect tax obedience, including the overall tax burden and the ratio between it and income, enforcement effectiveness, and taxpayers' understanding and identification with tax-paying importance.[16]

In times of severe economic crises, the temptation to avoid tax payments grows. Such an act may involve protest against a government's perceived responsibility for the crisis or its failure to handle it.

The COVID-19 pandemic hit the global economy in early 2020. In Israel, it caused a sharp increase in unemployment, from 3.8% in 2019 to 18.2% in 2020. A total of 75,000 businesses ceased to exist, and others struggled with the aftermath. In the beginning, the International Monetary Fund (IMF) assessed that this crisis could lead to the greatest recession since the 1930s.[17] The World Trade Organization considered it the worst economic crisis since World War II.[18]

Economic crises cause payment – including tax payment – delays. As businesses' economic challenges grow, sometimes leading to insolvency, the odds for tax revenues decrease. Businesses experiencing cash flow difficulties may artificially inflate their expenses to gain VAT refunds, or to avoid tax reports or payment, in order to enjoy the unpaid sums. Despite the risk, some taxpayers may prefer tax avoidance over bankruptcy.[19] Tax avoidance may serve as an alternative 'credit' source for businesses unable to raise credit. In China, some[20] have drawn a correlation between tax avoidance and recession, combined with a credit crunch. Moreover, businesses stressed due to the crisis may accumulate losses. They may use them in future years to diminish their tax charges.[21] While this practice is legal, it decreases tax revenues when they are necessary to pull out of the crisis.

Some believe that tax authorities tend to avoid strict enforcement of tax laws during economic crises. An increase in tax offenses in such times is more socially acceptable.[22] However, such reluctance could encourage ongoing tax avoidance.[23] Moreover, in the context of the 2008-2010 global financial crisis, the International Monetary Fund indicated that despite the temporary relief offered to taxpayers, giving up tax enforcement in times of crisis is distortive, undermines equality, and harms the tax base

---

[16] Lesnik, T., Kracun, D., & Jagric, T. (2014). *Recession and tax compliance – The case of Slovenia.* INZINERINE EKONOMIKA-ENGINEERING ECONOMICS, 25(2), 130, 132.

[17] Wiseman, P. and Crustinger, M. (2020, April 15). *IMF: Global Economy will Suffer Worst Year Since Depression.* SEATTLE TIMES, https://www.seattletimes.com/business/imf-stung-by-virus-global-economy-will-shrink-3-in-2020/

[18] World Trade Organization [WTO]. (2020, April 8). *Trade set to plunge as COVID-19 pandemic upends global economy,* Press 855/Press release 8.4.2020, https://www.wto.org/english/news_e/pres20_e/pr855_e.htm This forecast was moderated later: WTO. (2020, June 22). Trade falls steeply in the first half of 2020. Press 858/Press release 22.6.2020, https://www.wto.org/english/news_e/pres20_e/pr855_e.htm.

[19] Fujita S., Moscarini, G. (2017). *Recall and unemployment.* AMERICAN ECONOMIC REVIEW, 107(12), 3875-3916, http://dx.doi.org/10.1257/aer.20131496

[20] Cai, H., & Liu, Q. (2009). *Competition and corporate tax avoidance: Evidence from Chinese industrial firms.* THE ECONOMIC JOURNAL, 119, pp. 764–795.

[21] Brondolo, J. (2009). *Collecting taxes during an economic crisis: Challenges and policy options.* IMF Fiscal Affairs Department, Staff Position Note, http://www.imf.org/external/pubs/ft/spn/2009/spn0917.pdf

[22] Posner, 2009, p. 6.

[23] Id, 7.

establishment in the medium term. The literature suggests that the tax authorities should change their approach in such times. They should improve communication with taxpayers and focus enforcement in areas where disobedience implies the greatest risk to tax collection.

The OECD[24] (Organization for Economic Cooperation and Development) distinguished emergency steps taken to stabilize economies in the short run, following the crisis burst, from measures that should be taken to rehabilitate national economies in the medium and long run. The latter should coordinate tax policies with health, trade, social, labor, financial, and monetary policies. The OECD listed short-term measures that countries took to handle the crisis. These measures included, among others, tax exemptions in certain circumstances; relief in depreciation calculations; and the extension of tax reporting deadlines, of tax payment deadlines, and of tax debts payment deadlines. In certain countries, these measures complemented subsidization and government payments, aiming to improve households' and businesses' cash flows and to encourage investments. In response to the COVID-19 economic crisis, the OECD recommended postponing tax payments as an alternative to low interest bank loans. Also, it recommended that countries consider giving temporary exemptions, or decreasing specific taxes such as property taxes and turnover taxes. In cases in which states gave direct financial assistance, the OECD suggested taxing them as income when given to richer households, but not to low-income households. It stressed that the scope of assistance through the tax system should depend on the level of state development[25] and its economic situation. The OECD warned that state assistance could trigger abuse. It urged tax authorities' awareness, recommending that they handle such cases by enforcement, combined with public explanation and communication with taxpayers.[26]

---

[24] OECD (2020). *Tax Administration Responses to COVID-19: Assisting Wider Government*. https://www.oecd.org/en/publications/tax-administration-responses-to-covid-19-assisting-wider-government_0dc51664-en.html

[25] OECD (2021). *Revenue statistics in Latin America and the Caribbean* 2021, 29-59, 24-25 https://tinyurl.com/26y6u6y3; Mankiw, G. (2020). *A proposal for social insurance during the pandemic*, https://tinyurl.com/4sxz8az4; Marron, D. (2020). *If we give everybody cash to boost the Coronavirus economy, let's tax it*. Tax Policy Center, https://tinyurl.com/2rwzm38m.

[26] OECD. (2021). *Revenue statistics in Latin America and the Caribbean* 2021, 29-59, 29-30, https://tinyurl.com/ye274p4m

THE ROLE-PLAY
TAX OBEDIENCE IN COVID-19 TIMES*

The Tax Authority has submitted three cases to the court in which it sued taxpayers who refused to pay income tax according to an assessment determined by the income tax assessor. Each taxpayer had their own explanation for their refusal to pay the tax:

Ronni: Ronni is the owner of a small jewelry design business located in the Zefat open mall. Ronni started her business without equity capital by convincing her bank manager to approve a 50,000 shekels business loan that she committed to pay back over the course of five years. She rented a small store in the open mall for two years and signed a two-year contract obligating her to pay the rent monthly. She also purchased raw materials and produced jewelry to present in the store for sale. Three months after the store's opening, the Coronavirus pandemic broke out and she was forced to close the store unexpectedly and immediately. Her landlord agreed to meet her halfway and collected only half of the rent amount agreed on in the contract for as long as the lockdown due to the Coronavirus continued, but he could not waive the whole amount as he was in need of the income as well. The store was closed during the entire period of the lockdown and even though Ronni opened her doors as soon as the government allowed her to do so, there were still very few customers. Ronni believes that this is a combined result of the governmental ban on overseas tourism, as she was aiming for tourists as her main clientele, and the harsh financial state that many have suffered due to the pandemic which leaves with them little disposable income to spend on things like jewelry (a luxury and not a necessity). Ronni claims that the Coronavirus pandemic has brought her to the verge of bankruptcy. She was not eligible for financial aid from the state because she started her business less than a year before the start of the pandemic. Since she had made no profit, she was not able to make payments towards her debts or pay her taxes.

Asher: For the past 30 years, Asher has owned a grocery store located not far from Ronni's store. Unlike Ronni, he had customers coming in during the pandemic, a lot more than usual and a lot more than he expected. Every time a lockdown was announced, his store would fill with hysterical shoppers buying anything they could get their hands on. In general, since the break of the pandemic, people have spent more time at home, so their consumption of groceries and household products has increased. Asher suddenly saw customers he hadn't seen coming in for years; they were scared to shop in the big supermarkets or shopping centers due to the fear of contracting COVID-19, so they preferred the local grocery store, which seemed safer to them. Like any savvy business owner, Asher took advantage of

---

* This role-play was developed by Nellie Munin and Yael Efron (2021) and used successfully in the tax law course at Zefat Academic College.

the situation and tastefully raised his prices a bit. After all, aren't supply and demand rules the basis of modern economics? Despite this, Asher is unwilling to pay his taxes. He is angry at his government that did not offer him any financial aid since he did not suffer a decrease in profits over the pandemic. Did he not pay taxes his whole life? Is he not scared to contract COVID-19 from his customers? Does he not provide an essential service while risking his life and his health? And, in any case, when he watched the news on TV, he was angered by all the poor business owners who had to close shop because the government deprived them of financial aid and decided that not paying his taxes was his way of protesting as a citizen in his country.

Sammy: Sammy owns a chain of well-known fashion stores that market clothing, accessories, and, in recent years, glasses. Sammy is known as one of the richest businessmen and as one of the largest employers in the country. After the outbreak of the pandemic, he did not hesitate to threaten the Israeli government. Along with a few other employers like him, he said that if the government does not allocate financial aid to them immediately, they will not allow their employees to return to work. The government gave in, and Sammy and a few others like him received government grants worth millions of shekels. Despite receiving the grant, Sammy fired 100 senior employees who received high salaries for their work, replacing them with new employees who earn less – while stating that he had done so due to difficulty stemming from the pandemic, when actually he had been planning this strategic move for a while, and was just waiting for the right moment. In addition, Sammy refuses to pay income tax. In his eyes, the government gave with one hand and is now trying to "take back" the grant with the other hand, masking it as income tax, and he will not have it. He read in the newspapers how many government grants have been given to businesses in Europe and in the United States. He has started seriously considering that maybe basing his business in Israel was not wise. He understands that the Israeli government has limited resources in comparison to these powerful countries. Still, he definitely thinks it is appropriate that Israel meets him and the other large-scale employers halfway, recognizing that if they would close their businesses in Israel then the unemployment rate would rise even higher than it has so far due to the COVID-19 pandemic.

The exercise's schedule and outline:

1) Set a date for submitting the written arguments to the instructors.
2) Set a date for classroom negotiations.
3) Classroom negotiations between the groups should last at least 45 minutes. Negotiators should attempt to reach an agreed-upon solution by that time.
4) Give the groups at least 30 minutes to present the agreements reached and/or points of disagreement between the participants.
5) Leave at least 20 minutes for exercise debrief and summary.
6) For further instructions and/or ideas regarding the exercise's setting, please consult part 2 of this book.

Instructions for performing this exercise

You belong to one of the following groups (see division into groups separately):

Group 1: the lawyers representing Ronni
Group 2: the lawyers representing Asher
Group 3: the lawyers representing Sammy
Group 4: the lawyers representing the tax authorities
Group 5: the court (the judges)

The tasks that are to be carried out by each of the groups:

1) You must establish a legal argument that supports your group's position, based on the basic bibliography for the exercise, listed below, and additional sources that you will locate yourselves.

2) You must devise a strategy for presenting your group's argument to the court.

3) Groups 1 through 3 must try to reach an agreement with the tax authorities (group 4) to avoid a court hearing and the risk of the court's unpredictable ruling. If you do reach an agreement, you will have to put it down on paper, signed by all group members (the lawyers for the individual and for the tax authorities). In addition to the written and signed agreement, you will have to submit a document that legally establishes the reasoning for the agreement you have reached. The court will either accept or reject your agreement, due to its possible impact on the overall tax policy and the message it conveys to the public.

The court's task (Group 5):

To receive a written legal argument from each group. To prepare questions for the oral arguments, and, after the court hearing, to present a ruling (with the legal reasoning for it, of course) for each of the three court cases.

Basic bibliography for the exercise:

Income Tax Ordinance Section 1 (Definition of the taxpayer) Section 2 (The obligation to pay tax) in the opening section 'it will be profitable, Definition of the source of income: business section 2(1), The relevant penal provisions.[2]

Nellie Munin & Karnit Malka-Tiv. *Tax Obedience in Corona Times* JOURNAL OF MULTIDISCIPLINARY RESEARCH, St. Thomas University, Florida, Vol. 13(2), Autumn 2021.

Nellie Munin & Karnit Malka-Tiv. *Tax Obedience in Corona Times*, IUP JOURNAL OF GOVERNANCE AND PUBLIC POLICY, vol. 16 (4), 46-68, 2022.

Bibliographic sources mentioned in the citations of these articles.

It is advisable and recommended to look for additional sources and use them to build a stronger legal foundation for your argument.

---

[2] Note that these sources refer to Israeli law, but the relevant definitions from any country's tax code can serve as basis of this role-play.

Sweet Surrender[*]

Introduction and background

This role-play focuses on the different and conflicting interests underlying consumption taxes on sugar sweetened beverages (SSBs). SSBs are known to cause severe health damage. They are recognized by international organizations such as the WHO as sources of global concern. Nevertheless, conflicting interests sometimes prevent the development of effective policies to regulate them. The exercise refers, among other things, to the following aspects:

- The effectiveness of the "polluter pays" policy, and Pigouvian taxes.[1]
- The effectiveness of consumption taxes to decrease consumption of SSBs, in comparison to other means.
- The conflicting interests involved in this dilemma.

The exercise's schedule and outline:

1) Set a date for submitting the written arguments to the instructors.
2) Set a date for classroom negotiations.
3) Classroom negotiations between the groups should last at least 45 minutes. Negotiators should attempt to reach an agreed-upon solution by that time.
4) Give the groups at least 30 minutes to present the agreements reached and/or points of disagreement between the participants.
5) Leave at least 20 minutes for exercise debrief and summary.
6) For further instructions and/or ideas regarding the exercise's setting, please consult part 2 of this book.

---

[*] This role-play was developed by Nellie Munin and Yael Efron (2023) and exercised successfully in the tax law course at Zefat Academic College.
[1] A Pigouvian tax, named after 1920 British economist Arthur C. Pigou, is a tax on a market transaction that creates an additional cost, borne by individuals not directly involved in the transaction. The tax aims to compensate the society for this cost.

The case background story

Like many countries around the world, the state of "Gluttonia" is currently experiencing a growing economic crisis. It is still burdened by a large debt that it has not been able to pay back due to the costs associated with managing the Coronavirus crisis. The global price increases caused by the Russia-Ukraine war are deepening the crisis and increasing government spending on products that the country needs to import for public use. The state is in a desperate search for sources of income that will help it overcome the crisis. The possibility of raising taxes on income has been ruled out. Such an increase would reduce work profitability and it could deepen the already-existing recession and increase unemployment, something that politicians are not interested in. They fear that the situation could lead to the fall of the government and to early elections in the near future.

The Minister of Finance proposed a brilliant idea, in his opinion: due to the fact that the people of Gluttonia have a sweet tooth, the minister offers to impose a consumption tax on SSBs. To stay on the frustrated residents' good side, he proposes that the government justify the tax imposition with unassailable reasoning - the tax on sweets will be justified because it aims to protect the health of the citizens from the dangers of obesity. Obesity is a global epidemic that causes diseases such as diabetes, heart problems, and cancer. Complications of these diseases are among the leading causes of death in Gluttonia.

The government of Gluttonia warmly welcomes the proposal; it presents a bill to amend tax laws to the parliament and notes in the law's memorandum that such taxes have already been successfully imposed in Israel and the United States. The World Health Organization (WHO) warmly supports its position, maintaining that the more countries that enact such laws, the more the world will move towards the goals promoted by the WHO.

Large segments of the public are unwilling to accept the new tax, and will fight in court to ensure that this law will not be enacted. Among other things, all those involved plan to participate in the discussion on the proposed law in the parliament's legislative committee to voice their position.

For the purposes of this exercise, assume that the legal system structure and tax laws in this country (Gluttonia) are identical to those in your country.

The chairman of the legislative committee in Gluttonia's parliament defined the questions that will be discussed in the committee, including the following:

> A. Is there an economic rationale for imposing a tax to collect revenues for the state, when its success will lead to a significant reduction in the use of the taxed goods, along with the subsequent reduction of the tax collected?
>
> B. Is it appropriate to apply the "polluter pays" principle through the tax system?
>
> C. Is the tax system the most effective tool for directing desirable behavior in this case?
>
> D. Is it a proportional tool compared to alternative tools?
>
> E. What are the implications of the use of tax for the various stakeholders?
>
> F. What are the relevant fundamental rights of the residents in this matter, and what is the proper balance between them and the right to collect taxes in this case?

G. To what extent should the state demonstrate paternalism towards its residents and which circumstances justify it?

Instructions for performing the exercise

The class is divided into 5 groups (the number of groups may depend on the size of the class).

You belong to one of the following groups:

Group 1: The lawyers representing the government of the state of Gluttonia.

Group 2: The lawyers for the non-profit organization "HelpUs," representing the weaker segments of the population in Gluttonia.

Group 3: The lawyers representing the association of SSB manufacturers/importers and marketers in Gluttonia.

Group 4: The lawyers representing the Ministry of Health of Gluttonia.

Group 5: Representatives of the World Health Organization.

The tasks to be performed for each of the interest groups:

You must establish a legal argument supporting the position of the group you represent, based on the basic bibliography for the exercise detailed below, as well as additional sources that you will identify yourselves.

You must develop a strategy for presenting your group's argument within a policy debate to be held in the Legislation Committee of Gluttonia's Parliament prior to the laws being put to a vote in Parliament.

When the discussions held in the committee end, you will be required to present the agreements reached between the groups regarding the proposed legislation, to the extent that you successfully achieved such agreements.

Basic bibliography for the exercise:
It is desirable and recommended to search for additional sources and rely on them to establish the argument.

Rifaat, Azam. "*The Interpretation of Tax Law: True Tax and Human Rights in the Supreme Court Ruling.*" MISHPAT VE'ASAKIM 18 (2014): 401-465. [Hebrew]. https://www.runi.ac.il/media/2ajbaqcl/azam.pdf

EUROPEAN JOURNAL OF POLITICAL ECONOMY – *References to a collection of articles on the topic "The Polluter Pays"* https://www.sciencedirect.com/science/article/abs/pii/017626809500007K

Taxation of Sugary Drinks

WHO (2022). *WHO calls on countries to tax sugar-sweetened beverages to save lives* https://tinyurl.com/bdefv6as

Israeli Government Decision No. 263 regarding the promotion of a healthy lifestyle [Hebrew]. https://www.gov.il/he/departments/policies/dec263_2021

Israeli Customs Tariff Order, Purchase Tax on Soft Drinks (Amendment No. 4), 2021 [Hebrew] - https://tinyurl.com/2fkbd6sn

Merav Peleg-Gabay (2021). *Taxation of Soft Drinks for Health Reasons*. KNESSET RESEARCH AND INFORMATION CENTER [Hebrew]. https://tinyurl.com/48pr3sj5f

Bank of Israel (2022). *Preliminary analysis of trends in the purchase of sugary drinks following the imposition of a tax on them.* [Hebrew] https://tinyurl.com/2x7sxua3.

Nellie Munin (2023). *Revocation of Israel's tax on sugar-sweetened beverages: A blessing or a curse?* THE IUP JOURNAL OF INTERNATIONAL RELATIONS, vol. 17(3), 19-42.

Research on Sugary Drink Taxation in the United States:

American Public Health Association (2016) *Impact of the Berkeley Excise Tax on Sugar-Sweetened Beverage Consumption* (abstract).

Berkeley Soda Tax Campaign website: https://ecologycenter.org/berkeley-soda-tax-campaign/

AMERICAN JOURNAL OF PREVENTIVE MEDICINE (2015). *Cost effectiveness of Sugar-Sweetened Beverages Excise Tax in the U.S.* https://tinyurl.com/mw5p8u9b

Private instructions - Group 1: The lawyers representing the government of the state of Gluttonia

You see great importance in the enactment of the laws, and you intend to stand firmly behind their enactment. Four main reasons motivate you:

The country's "budget hole" and the ease of collection of the consumption tax, which would fill the public coffers relatively quickly.

Gluttonia's positioning as a developed nation in the international community. The state of Gluttonia suffers repeatedly from criticism in international forums, such as the World Health Organization, for the way it handles issues of public health

If the World Health Organization's claim is correct – that taxation will reduce obesity, which leads to diabetes, heart problems and cancer – then, in the long run, the state will be able to save on the expenses associated with treating these problems.

Another reason, which you will not openly admit, is that the proposed law provides a golden opportunity to bring into the tax-paying circle populations that rely on the state and regularly avoid paying other taxes, some for ideological reasons and some due to financial hardship.

You are aware that the opposition will attack the government, claiming that it has chosen an easy and fast solution without seeking more justifiable alternatives and without thoroughly examining the proposed legislation's implications. You must prepare good responses to these claims.

You know that you should try to sway stakeholders who may have an interest in the legislation, such as the importers, manufacturers, and marketers of the regulated products, to see things the way you do because they have strong political power that can influence the legislature.

Private instructions - Group 2: The lawyers for the non-profit organization "HelpUs," representing the weaker segments of the population in Gluttonia

You are leaving no stone unturned in your opposition to the proposed laws and intend to fight to the bitter end against their enactment. You have several arguments to support your position:

Consumption taxes mainly hurt the weaker segments of society. You believe that sources of revenue should be sought to collect the missing funds from the stronger sectors, such as the high-tech industry, which has earned millions in recent years and was not even affected during the COVID-19 pandemic.

You suspect that the government is "leeching" off the weaker segments of society due to the assumption that they have no lobby and will struggle to become organized and united and fund lawyers to represent them and their interests. The government found it convenient to choose an alternative that harms them, rather than alternatives that harm well-organized sectors with political power.

You suspect that, due to political instability, the government is seeking easy solutions to fill the budget gap without fully examining the implications of its proposal. You are confident that there are better alternatives to solving the problem that will reflect more social and distributive justice.

You know that, among other things, you will be confronted with the claim that preventing obesity, which leads to diseases (such as diabetes, heart problems, and cancer) that are common in the population you represent, is in your client's interest. You are preparing to respond to this claim.

You acknowledge that "the weaker segments" is a generic term for various groups in the population, with different behavior patterns and different morals regarding tax payment. You recognize that part of this population avoids paying taxes at all costs and may not really be a part of the "weaker segments" of society. It is considered to be so only because it avoids reporting its full income to the tax authorities, causing it to be perceived as part of the population that has no or very low income. With that being said, you are aware of the fact that this segment of the population that you represent may have the political power to influence decision-makers behind the scenes. Therefore, you do not believe that your role is to distinguish between the different groups that have decided to join under this umbrella term of "weaker segments." However, you are aware that you may be attacked on this basis, and your preparation must include good answers for such an attack.

Private instructions - Group 3: The lawyers representing the association of SSB manufacturers/importers and marketers in Gluttonia

The entities you represent are ambivalent:

On the one hand, your clients are concerned that the law will increase the price of products in a way that will reduce their consumption (which is its stated goal). This will reduce their income, so they are not interested in this outcome.

On the other hand, you have wanted to raise the prices of your products for a long time, as their production and import costs have risen significantly because of the Coronavirus pandemic and the Russia-Ukraine war. However, you were afraid to do so because of the increasing public criticism of the rising costs of living, especially since you are aware that your products are a significant part of the basic products consumed by weaker segments of society. You estimate that the confusion that will occur with the implementation of the new laws will allow you to raise the prices of your products beyond the tax increase, without being recognized by the consumers and without having to face public protest. In this regard, you see the proposed laws as a business opportunity. You estimate that the profit you will make from this will cover the loss from the reduced consumption and may even be greater.

You know that the desire and tendency to tax these products according to the "polluter pays" principle is increasing around the world, and it is clear to you that, in the long run, the state of Gluttonia will not be able to avoid it anyway. Therefore, you understand that the significance of supporting the non-enactment of the law is, at best, only buying a window of time whose size is unknown, and that in the long run this move will be made in any case. So, it may be better for you to start preparing for it now.

With that being said, from a reputational perspective, you want to appear as supporters of your loyal customers: the weaker segments of society.

Finally, it's hard to ignore the global trend of "green-washing," in which corporations that produce or import harmful products strive to present a public image of health awareness to cover up the actual harm caused by their products.

Private instructions - Group 4: The lawyers representing the Ministry of Health of Gluttonia

You are less interested in the method - in this case, taxation - and more interested in the health goal. Deep down, you are not sure that taxation will achieve the desired result. For example, in Gluttonia, the experience with taxing cigarettes and alcohol showed that it did not succeed in reducing usage. However, the World Health Organization claims that such taxes have been proven effective at achieving their goals on a global level.

The very move raises awareness of the issues that are important to you, and therefore you are co-operating with Gluttonia's ministry of finance. You believe that if taxation does not solve the problem, you may be able to demand the use of more severe measures, in the future, such as administrative or criminal sanctions for behavior that does not align with the public interest.

It is also important for you to convey to the international community, especially to the relevant international organizations that constantly pressure you, that the state of Gluttonia is part of the community of nations and that it is not indifferent to global criticism but rather tries to take health promotion steps, as other countries have done.

Precisely because the state of Gluttonia is not a large or significantly influential country in the areas with which you entrusted, and because it is generally ignored in the global decision-making process, you believe that there is an opportunity here for pioneering action that will put Gluttonia at the forefront of international behavior designers. If it conveys power to countries that have already enacted laws on the subject, including important countries in world politics such as the United States and India, such countries will no longer be able to ignore Gluttonia in relevant international organizations.

Another incentive, which you do not want to disclose to the other groups, is that the Minister of Finance has promised to increase your office's budget from the "tax pie" that will be collected if these taxes are successfully imposed and collected.

Private instructions - Group 5: Representatives of the World Health Organization

You are less interested in method - in this case, taxation - and more interested in the health goal. World Health Organization data shows that taxing according to the "polluter pays" principle is effective and achieves its goal.

The very move raises awareness of the issues that matter to you, and therefore you are working in collaboration with the government of Gluttonia. You believe that if taxation does not solve the problem in practice, you can demand the use of more severe measures in the future, such as administrative or criminal sanctions for behavior that does not align with the public interest (as was done, for example, in Israel under the Container Deposit Law, 1999).

You represent international community organizations that are trying to find solutions to health problems (obesity leading to diabetes, heart problems, and cancer) caused by sugar-rich products. You see the big global picture, the growing rates of damage, and understand that it must come to an end. Economically, you are aware of the enormous costs involved in dealing with these problems and know that if they were solved the money could be directed towards more worthy goals.

Another motivation, which you do not want to reveal to other groups, is that your organization has not been very successful in the past few years in advancing its goals and the chances of achieving the goals set in international agreements are diminishing. There are significant disputes and conflicting interests among the member countries. Multinational corporations that harm public health through their products are using economic advantages to gain political power and pressure countries to turn a blind eye to low standards of corporate behavior.

At the forefront of your mind is the echo of U.S. President Trump's ominous threat that he will withdraw the U.S. from international organizations (and, of course, stop its huge contribution to their funding). Therefore, it is important for you to "turn over every stone" and take advantage of every opportunity to try to maintain relevance and to focus the public and media attention on your positive actions and your desired image.

You understand that an argument against the position of the weaker segments of the population could harm your image and play into the hands of those who represent opposing interests. So, you must frame your arguments in such a way that it is clear that you are actually protecting the weaker classes in the long run.

Tax on Disposables[*]

Introduction and background

This role-play focuses on the different and conflicting interests underlying consumption taxes on disposable utensils. Their intensive use is known to cause severe environmental damage. Consequently, they are recognized by international organizations as sources of global concern. Nevertheless, conflicting interests sometimes prevent the development of effective policies to regulate them. The exercise refers, among other things, to the following aspects:

- The effectiveness of the "polluter pays" policy and Pigouvian taxes.[1]
- The effectiveness of consumption taxes to decrease consumption of these products, compared to other means.
- The conflicting interests involved in this dilemma.

The exercise's schedule and outline:

1) Set a date for submitting the written arguments to the instructors.
2) Set a date for classroom negotiations.
3) Classroom negotiations between the groups should last at least 45 minutes. Negotiators should attempt to reach an agreed-upon solution in that time.
4) Give the groups at least 30 minutes to present the agreements reached and/or points of disagreement between the participants.
5) Leave at least 20 minutes for exercise debrief and summary.
6) For further instructions and/or ideas regarding the exercise's setting, please consult part 2 of this book.

---

[*] This role-play was developed by Nellie Munin and Yael Efron (2023) and exercised successfully in the tax law course at Zefat Academic College.

[1] A Pigouvian tax, named after 1920 British economist Arthur C. Pigou, is a tax on a market transaction that creates an additional cost, borne by individuals not directly involved in the transaction. The tax aims to compensate the society for this cost.

The case background story

Like many countries around the world, the state of Gluttonia is currently experiencing a growing economic crisis. It is still burdened by a large debt that it has not been able to pay back, due to the costs associated with managing the Coronavirus crisis. The global price increases caused by the Russia-Ukraine war are deepening the crisis and increasing government spending on products that the country needs to import for public use. The state is in a desperate search for sources of income that will help it overcome the crisis. The possibility of raising taxes on income has been ruled out. Such an increase would reduce work profitability and could deepen the already-existing recession and increase unemployment, something that politicians are not interested in. They fear that the situation could lead to the fall of the government and to early elections in the near future.

The Minister of Finance proposed a brilliant idea, in his opinion: due to the fact that the people of Gluttonia are very fond of large social gatherings, in which they serve food and refreshments using disposable plastic utensils, the minister offered to impose a consumption tax on disposable utensils. In order to stay on the frustrated residents' good side, he proposes that the government justify the tax imposition with unassailable reasoning: it aims to protect the planet from pollution that exacerbates the threat of global warming and damage to nature, including vital ecological systems.

The government of Gluttonia warmly welcomes the proposal; it presents a bill to amend tax laws to the parliament and even notes in the law's memorandum that such taxes have already been successfully imposed in Israel and in the United States. The OECD warmly supports its position, maintaining that the more countries that enact such laws, the more the world will move towards the OECD's goals.

Large segments of the public are unwilling to accept the new tax and they will fight in court to ensure that this law will not be enacted. Among other things, all those involved plan to participate in the discussion on the proposed law in the parliament's legislative committee to voice their position.

For the purposes of this exercise, assume that the legal system structure and tax laws in this country (Gluttonia) are identical to those in your country.

The chairman of the legislative committee in Gluttonia's parliament defined the questions that will be discussed in the committee, including the following:

A. Is there an economic rationale for imposing taxes to collect revenues for the state, when its success will lead to a significant reduction in the use of the taxed goods, along with the subsequent reduction of the tax collected?

B. Is it appropriate to apply the "polluter pays" principle through the tax system?

C. Is the tax system the most effective tool for directing desirable behavior in this case?

D. Is it a proportional tool compared to alternative tools?

E. What are the implications of the use of tax for the various stakeholders?

F. What are the relevant fundamental rights of the residents in this matter, and what is the proper balance between them and the right to collect taxes in this case?

G. To what extent should the state demonstrate paternalism towards its residents and which circumstances justify it?

Instructions for performing the exercise
The class is divided into 5 groups (the number of groups may depend on its size).

You belong to one of the following groups:

Group 1: The lawyers representing the government of the state of Gluttonia.

Group 2: The lawyers for the non-profit organization "HelpUs," representing the weaker segments of the population in Gluttonia.

Group 3: The lawyers representing the association of disposable product manufacturers/importers and marketers in Gluttonia.

Group 4: The lawyers representing the Ministry of Environment of Gluttonia.

Group 5: Representatives of the OECD.

The tasks to be performed for each of the interest groups:

1) You must establish a legal argument supporting your group's position, based on the basic bibliography for the exercise, detailed below, as well as additional sources that you will identify yourselves.

2) You must develop a strategy for presenting your group's argument within a policy debate to be held in the Legislation Committee of Gluttonia's Parliament before the laws are put to a vote in Parliament.

3) When the discussions held in the committee end, you will be required to present in class the agreements reached between the groups regarding the proposed legislation, to the extent that you successfully achieved such agreements.

Basic bibliography for the exercise:
It is desirable and recommended to search for additional sources and rely on them to establish the argument.

Rifaat, Azam. "*The Interpretation of Tax Law: True Tax and Human Rights in the Supreme Court Jurisprudence.*" Mishpat Ve'Asakim 18 (2014): 401-465. [Hebrew]. https://papers.ssrn.com/sol3/papers.cfm?abstract_id=2864397

European Journal of Political Economy – References to a collection of articles on the topic "The Polluter Pays" https://www.sciencedirect.com/science/article/abs/pii/017626809500007K

Disposable utensils

- Government Decision 261 on reducing the use of disposable plastic utensils. [Hebrew]. https://www.gov.il/he/departments/policies/dec261_2021

- Customs tariff order and exemptions and purchase tax on goods (Amendment No. 8), 2022 [Hebrew]. https://bit.ly/3FWDdTI

- Tel Aviv and Central Trade Chamber. A comprehensive and updated report on the new purchase tax on disposable plastic utensils. [Hebrew]. https://www.chamber.org.il/foreigntrade/1109/1111/125309/

- Shiri Specter-Ben Ari (2021). *Taxation of disposable plastic utensils*. Knesset Research and Information Center. [Hebrew]. https://tinyurl.com/mrxp6y2j

- *Ministry of Environmental Protection, Frequently Asked Questions about the taxation of disposable plastic utensils.* [Hebrew]. https://www.gov.il/he/departments/faq/why_pay_more

- OECD, *Environment Directorate, Environment Policy Committee, Working Party on Integrating Environmental and Economic Policies, Preventing single-use plastic waste: implications of different policy approaches*, July 2021 https://one.oecd.org/document/ENV/WKP(2021)14/en/pdf

- Israeli Consumers Council. Comparative information on the deposit law on beverage containers, 1999. https://www.consumers.org.il/category/deposit-law-general

Private instructions - Group 1: The lawyers representing the government of the state of Gluttonia

You see great importance in the enactment of the law, and you intend to stand firmly behind its enactment. Four main reasons motivate you:

1) The "budget hole" that the country has fallen into and the ease of collection of the consumption tax; the fact that it would fill the public coffers relatively quickly is also a factor.

2) Gluttonia's positioning as a developed nation in the international community. The state of Gluttonia suffers repeatedly from criticism in international forums, such as the OECD, for the way it handles environmental issues. In the environmental field, this has an impact that extends beyond Gluttonia's borders and it is not well-regarded by neighboring countries.

3) If the OECD's claim is correct - that taxation will reduce the harm to the environment - then in the long run, the state will be able to save on the expenses associated with treating these problems.

4) Another reason, which you will not openly admit, is that the proposed law provides a golden opportunity to bring into the tax-paying circle populations that rely on the state and regularly avoid paying other taxes, some for ideological reasons and some due to financial hardship.

You are aware that the opposition will attack the government, claiming that it has chosen an easy and fast solution without seeking more justifiable alternatives and without thoroughly examining the proposed legislation's implications. You must prepare good responses to these claims.

You know that you should try to sway stakeholders who may have an interest in the legislation, such as the importers, manufacturers, and marketers of the regulated products, to see things the way you do because they have strong political power that can influence the legislature.

Private instructions - Group 2: The lawyers for the non-profit organization "HelpUs," representing the weaker segments of the population in Gluttonia

You are leaving no stone unturned in your opposition to the proposed laws and intend to fight to the bitter end against their enactment. You have several arguments to support your position:

1) Consumption taxes mainly hurt the weaker segments of society. You believe that sources of revenue should be sought to collect the missing funds from the stronger sectors, such as the high-tech industry, which has earned millions in recent years and was not even affected during the COVID-19 pandemic.

2) You suspect that the government is "leeching" off the weaker segments of society due to the assumption that they have no lobby and that they will struggle to become organized and united and fund lawyers to represent them and their interests. The government found it convenient to choose an alternative that harms them, rather than alternatives that harm well-organized sectors with political power.

3) You suspect that, due to political instability, the government is seeking easy solutions to fill the budget gap without fully examining the implications of its proposals. You are confident that there are better alternatives to solving the problem that will reflect more social and distributive justice.

You acknowledge that "the weaker segments" is a generic term for various groups in the population, with different behavior patterns and different morals regarding tax payment. You recognize that part of this population avoids paying taxes at all costs and may not really be a part of the "weaker segments" of society. It is considered to be so only because it avoids reporting its full income to the tax authorities, causing it to be perceived as part of the population with no or very little income. With that being said, you are aware of the fact that this segment of the population you represent may have the political power to influence decision-makers behind the scenes. Therefore, you do not believe that your role is to distinguish between the different groups that have decided to join under this umbrella term of "weaker segments." However, you are aware that you may be attacked on this basis, and your preparation must include good answers prepared for such an attack.

Private instructions - Group 3: The lawyers representing the association of disposable product manufacturers/importers and marketers in Gluttonia

The entities you represent are ambivalent about the law:

1) On the one hand, your clients are concerned that the law will increase the price of disposables in a way that will reduce their consumption (which is its stated goal). This will reduce their income, so they are not interested in this outcome.

2) On the other hand, you have wanted to raise the prices of your products for a long time, as their production and import costs have risen significantly because of the Coronavirus pandemic and the Russia-Ukraine war. However, you were afraid to do so because of the increasing public criticism of the rising cost of living, especially since you know that your products are a significant part of the basic products consumed by weaker segments of society. You estimate that the confusion that will occur with the implementation of the new law will allow you to raise the prices of your products beyond the tax increase, without being recognized by the consumers and without having to face public protest. In this regard, you see the proposed law as a business opportunity. You estimate that the profit you will make from this will cover the loss from the reduced consumption and may even be greater.

3) You know that the desire and tendency to tax these products according to the "polluter pays" principle is increasing around the world, and it is clear to you that in the long run, the state of Gluttonia will not be able to avoid it anyway. Therefore, you understand that the significance of supporting the non-enactment of the law is, at best, only buying a window of time whose size is unknown, and that in the long run, this move will be made in any case. So, it may be better for you to start preparing for it now.

4) With that being said, from a reputational perspective, you want to appear as supporters of your loyal customers: the weaker segments of society.

5) Finally, it's hard to ignore the global trend of "green-washing," in which corporations that produce or import harmful products strive to present a public image of awareness of environmental issues to cover up the actual harm caused by their products.

Private instructions - Group 4: The lawyers representing the Ministry of Environment of Gluttonia

1) You are less interested in the method - in this case, taxation - and more interested in the health or environmental goal. Deep down, you are not sure that taxation will achieve the desired result. For example, in Gluttonia, the experience with taxing cigarettes and alcohol showed that it did not succeed in reducing usage, although the World Health Organization claims that such taxes have been proven effective at achieving their goal on a global level.

2) However, the very move raises awareness of the issues that are important to you and, therefore, you are cooperating with Gluttonia's ministry of finance. You believe that if taxation does not solve the problem, you may be able to demand the use of more severe measures, in the future, such as administrative or criminal sanctions for behavior that does not align with the public interest.

It is also important for you to convey to the international community, especially to the relevant international organizations that constantly pressure you, that the state of Gluttonia is part of the community of nations and that it is not indifferent to global criticism, but rather tries to take steps to promote the environment, as other countries have done.

Precisely because the state of Gluttonia is not a large and or significantly influential country in the areas with which you are entrusted, and because it is generally ignored in the global decision-making process, you believe that there is an opportunity here for pioneering action that will put Gluttonia at the forefront of international behavior designers. If it conveys power to countries that have already enacted laws on the subject- including important countries in world politics such as the United States and India- such countries will no longer be able to ignore Gluttonia in relevant international organizations.

Another incentive, which you do not want to disclose to the other groups, is that the Minister of Finance has promised to increase your office's budget from the "tax pie" that will be collected if these taxes are successfully imposed and collected.

Private instructions - Group 5: Representatives of the OECD

1) You are less interested in the method - in this case, taxation - and more interested in the environmental goal. OECD data shows that the tax on plastic bags has been proven effective while the effectiveness of taxes on drink containers, for example, is less clear.

2) However, the very move raises awareness of the issues that matter to you, and, therefore, you are working in collaboration with the government of Gluttonia. You believe that if taxation does not solve the problem in practice, you can demand the use of more severe measures in the future, such as administrative or criminal sanctions for behavior that does not align with the public interest (as was done, for example, in Israel under the Container Deposit Law, 1999).

3) You represent international community organizations that are trying to find solutions to the problem of environmental pollution caused by disposable utensils. You see the big global picture, the growing rate of damage, and understand that it must come to an end. Economically, you are aware of the enormous costs involved in dealing with these problems and know that if they were solved, the money could be directed towards other worthy goals.

4) Another motivation, which you do not want to reveal to other groups, is that your organization has not been very successful in the past few years in advancing its goals and the chances of achieving the goals set in international agreements are diminishing. There are significant disputes and conflicting interests among the member countries. Multinational corporations that harm public health and harm the environment through their production, which only sees the bottom line, are gaining political power and putting pressure on countries to turn a blind eye to low standards of corporate behavior.

5) At the forefront of your mind is the echo of the U.S. President Trump's ominous threat that he will withdraw the U.S. from international organizations (and, of course, stop its huge contribution to their funding). Therefore, it is important for you to "turn over every stone" and take advantage of every opportunity to try to maintain relevance and to focus the public and media attention on your blessed actions and your desired image.

You understand that an argument against the position of the weaker segments of the population could harm your image and play into the hands of those who represent opposing interests. So you must frame your arguments in such a way that makes it clear that you are actually protecting the weaker classes in the long run.

Harmful tax competition: to participate or not to participate?[1]

'Prisoner's Dilemma' games illustrate conflicts of interest between parties.[2] They are based on a familiar scenario: two prisoners are incarcerated and face interrogation. If neither prisoner divulges any information, they will both go free due to lack of evidence. However, the police aim to coax at least one of them into talking. The promise is that if one prisoner speaks up, they will be spared at the expense of the other, who will be incriminated. With no means of communication, participants cannot ensure that the other won't speak first and implicate them. Ultimately, there is no guarantee that both won't eventually talk, resulting in mutual incrimination.

In scenarios involving conflicting interests, a comparable risk arises. This conflict pertains to disputes between states. A coalition of states establishes specific rules with the goal of achieving a balanced equilibrium of interests. However, due to conflicting agendas, each state faces the temptation to deceive the other party—ostensibly adhering to the agreed-upon 'rules of the game' while subtly deviating from them to advance its own interests at the other party's expense. Such a strategy is effective only as long as the deviation from the rules is minor. However, as the scope of deviation augments, and the other party opts for a similar strategy ("tit-for-tat"), all parties may lose.

In this 'Prisoner's Dilemma' game, the conflict of interests illustrates the global phenomenon of harmful tax competition, whereby states use unfair practices to attract investors and potential taxpayers to them at the expense of other countries, e.g., by acting as tax havens. To prevent such practices, the participating countries set forth an agreed-upon body of fair rules, corresponding to the real OECD – BEPS (Organization for European Cooperation and Development – Base Erosion and Profit Shifting) rules,[3] set forth in 2015. However, the parties to the game must struggle with the temptation to deviate from these rules, to attract more tax revenues at the expense of their allies. The game illustrates that the

---

[1] The framework for the game is inspired by a well-known Prisoner's Dilemma game developed by Ebner and Winkler and was adapted to the Tax Law context by Nellie Munin. For the original game with detailed notes on preparing, conducting and debriefing the game, see: Noam Ebner & Yifat Winkler, *The Pasta Wars: A Prisoner's Dilemma Simulation-Game* Ebner, 40 SIMULATION & GAMING 134 (2008).

[2] The term was coined by ALLBERT W. TUCKER, A TWO-PERSON DILEMMA, presented at the Stanford University Psychology Seminar (1950) but was conceptualized by MERRILL M. FLOOD & MELVIN DRESHER, A STUDY OF RATIONAL BEHAVIOR IN THE CONTEXT OF CONFLICT (RAND Corp., unpublished manuscript, 1950). See WILLIAM POUNDSTONE, PRISONER'S DILEMMA (Anchor Books 1992).

[3] See more details in the OECD website: https://www.oecd.org/en/topics/base-erosion-and-profit-shifting-beps.html

more parties give in to this temptation to deviate, the greater the general damage to the entire group will be.

Instructions

Divide the class into four groups and read the instructions together. Give each group a sheet with the instructions, a slip sheet, and a balance sheet.

There should be no communication between the four groups. Messages from each group are passed to the instructor each round, using a slip from the slip sheet held by each group.

Each country must decide separately what its policy will be for the next month. They do not know what the other countries will do and will find out only after all slips are handed to the instructor.

The game is played for two consecutive rounds.

Towards the **third round**: The OECD Secretariat announces that since the global financial crisis severely hit the global economy, any effect of the Members' tax policy may be <u>doubled</u> in the next round. Consequently, the Members decide to send their representatives to a coordination meeting. It should be mentioned that the years of alliance did not wipe out the bad memories of the allies, and their relationships bear mutual suspicion.

Towards the **fourth round**: the financial crisis that hits the global economy makes market term shift, including the options for profit and loss, much more extreme. According to the OECD Secretariat, expected profit or loss may be <u>quadrupled</u>. Due to the obvious potential danger to the alliance's market, it is further announced that the sanctions for breaching the agreements will be extended proportionally to be $400,000 per each month of breach. The Members decide to meet again. This is the last meeting – no other meeting will be possible.

After the last round, ask each country:

How much did each of you gain/lose?

If there were a ninth round – what would you do?

Would you form a 'coalition' in the future? With whom?

Questions for discussion:

- What can be learned from this exercise regarding international taxation interests?

- What are some of the similarities and differences you can find when comparing this game to taxation practices you know?

- Considering your experience from this game and real-life, if you were to draft a new tax policy, what would you make sure to include in it?

Background

After hundreds of years of free (and sometimes wild) tax competition, the OECD rules, and particularly the 2015 BEPS, aim to establish global cooperation to ensure fair competition. Over 140 countries and jurisdictions globally are collaborating to implement the BEPS measures.

All four countries participating in this exercise are OECD Members. However, Alpha and Beta are large, economically strong developed countries. Gamma and Delta, the other partners, are smaller in size and economically weaker countries that joined the alliance to enjoy the economic benefits the OECD membership offers. Alpha and Beta are economic patrons of Gamma and Delta and they were struggling to obtain Gamma and Beta's OECD membership. In fact, Alpha and Beta were keen to get a political hold in Gamma and Delta, to prevent these countries from turning to other influential countries, which are Alpha and Beta's political rivals. In addition, Alpha and Beta hope that their businesses may have access to cheap labor and services in Gamma and Delta.

Alpha and Beta led the process of drafting the BEPS rules, planning them in the best way to suit their economies and interests. Gamma and Delta agreed to the rules because they wanted access to the prestigious OECD club, but in fact they know very well that their weak economies depend heavily on nurturing and encouraging what the OECD considers harmful tax competition.

If the four partners respect OECD rules against harmful tax competition (HTC), each of them will gain net $100,000 per year. If one of them engages in HTC, it would be fined by $100,000 per that year. This sum will be contributed to the OECD budget and will only be used to finance further enforcement, so the Members cannot enjoy it for other purposes.

The Conflict

Unfortunately, in recent years, due to the global financial and economic crisis, all four allies face economic temptation and political pressure by local industries to engage in HTC. As their financial and economic situation disintegrated, each of them (separately) concluded that if only one country will breach the rules, it may gain $300,000 per year. So, even having to pay a $100,000 fine it will still enjoy a net gain of $200,000. If two countries breach the rules, each will enjoy a $200,000 gain, diminished to $100,000 net gain after paying the fine. If three breach the rules, each will enjoy a $100,000 gain, but the fine will totally diminish it, so the net gain will be 0. However, if all four countries breach the rules, each will lose $300,000 per year.

Members breaching Rules	Gross Profit	Net profit (after fine payment)	Members obeying rules	Net profit
0	****	****	4	100,000
1	300,000	200,000	3	100,000
2	200,000	100,000	2	100,000
3	100,000	0	1	100,000
4	****	-300,000	****	****

To engage or not to engage in HTC?
Policy Decision Slip

Year # 1 Country _____ Decision: _____	Year # 2 Country _____ Decision: _____
Year # 3 Country _____ Decision: _____	Year # 4 Country _____ Decision: _____
Year # 5 Country _____ Decision: _____	Year # 6 Country _____ Decision: _____
Year # 7 Country _____ Decision: _____	Year # 8 Country _____ Decision: _____

Profit / Loss Balance Sheet

Year #	Our choice	Members breaching rules	Members obeying rules	This Year's Profit / Loss
Total Profit / Loss:				

Resident or Non-Resident?
A Tax Policy Dilemma[*]

The moral justification for a state's right to tax its residents stems from the understanding that residents benefit from public services provided by the state and should therefore contribute to their funding. However, globalization, with its increased mobility and new opportunities for generating income, continually challenges the traditional concept of residency. This shift often undermines a state's claim to tax or leads to conflicting tax demands from multiple states. This role-play activity explores and illustrates this complex dilemma.

Background

Rami is a citizen of Dinaria, a (fictional) country on an island near the coasts of Alaska. Rami is single and works as a world-renowned engineer and geologist, known for his expertise in oil and gas exploration. Since 2000, he has primarily resided on gas and oil rigs in the North Sea. He only returns to land to buy equipment, for medical appointments, and to visit close friends and relatives.

At the outset of their latest oil and gas exploration endeavor in Dinarian territorial waters, a group made up of three corporations (two American and one Dutch) hired Rami to consult for them, and in so doing, he traveled to Dinaria from time to time, each visit lasting several days. During the process of building the natural gas rig facing Dinaria's shores, he also spent time there to consult and oversee the building and set-up process. Rami was paid for this work as a freelancer by one of the American companies.

The Dinarian income tax authority issued Rami an assessment for the year 2018, calculated based on his income from across the world, which totaled almost 6 million DD (Dinarian Dollars), because, in 2018 and the two years preceding, he stayed in Dinaria (primarily on rigs located in Dinaria's territorial waters) a total of 425 days, and therefore he is a Dinarian resident for tax purposes. Furthermore, the Dinarian authority verified with its counterparts in other states that no other tax authority claimed residency status for Rami in the years in question.

Rami challenged this assessment, claiming that since 2000 he has not been a resident of Dinaria. However, he was not able to identify a different primary residence and insisted that he routinely travels from rig to rig, primarily in the North Sea but also in other areas.

---

[*] This role-play was developed by Nellie Munin and Yael Efron (2022) and used successfully in the Tax Law course at Zefat Academic College.

The Dinarian tax authority investigated the case and found that Rami maintains a savings account in Dinaria that he has not touched since he left; his only remaining living relative in Dinaria is an elderly aunt living in Hope, the capital of Dinaria; and that he holds a Dinarian credit card which he uses when buying food and pharmaceuticals when he leaves the rig and stays in Dinaria. Since 2005, Rami has not been insured by any national health program in Dinaria and has contributed from his salary to Dinarian public health taxes or social security. The tax authority did not find an apartment in Rami's name in any state. Rami manages bank accounts with modest amounts of money in several states, including Dinaria, and he uses several credit cards which he uses from time to time to fund his basic needs in the state he enters after leaving a rig.

Due to the complexity of the case and its wider implications, the finance minister of Dinaria appointed a public committee to examine the subject. Representatives of the relevant stakeholders are invited to the finance ministry for a hearing, after which the committee will submit its recommendations to the minister.

Instructions for conducting the Simulation:
You are responsible for one of the following groups (as assigned by your instructor):

Group 1: Rami and his legal team: arguing that he does not owe income tax in Dinaria for 2018 from his income from around the world, and, at most, is only required to pay income tax from the salary he received in Dinarian territory that year, which amounts to 50,000 DD.
Interests:

- To lessen Rami's taxable income.
- To establish a precedent for Rami's tax obligations, based on his particular lifestyle, that would apply in future tax years.

Group 2: Representatives of the Dinarian tax authority (income tax division): arguing that Rami is obligated to pay taxes in Dinaria on his worldwide income, amounting to 6 million DD in the 2018 tax year, because in that year Rami was a resident of Dinaria for tax purposes.
Interests:

- To enlarge Rami's taxable income.
- To establish a precedent for Rami's tax obligations, based on his particular lifestyle, that would apply in future tax years and to other taxpayers in similar situations.

Group 3: Representatives of the state revenue authority in the ministry of finance: considering if it is necessary to amend the national rules of tax residency, given the many cases dealing with the definition of tax residency being brought to the courts due to globalization's enhancement.
Interests:

- To ensure as much income tax as possible to fill Dinaria's coffers.
- To ensure that taxpayers won't be deterred from receiving income in Dinaria.
- To ensure that the law is as clear as possible so that collection and application will run smoothly.

Group 4: Representatives of the community of international businesspersons in Dinaria.
Interests:

- To ensure that the suggested tax policy will not discourage Dinarian international experts from sharing their expertise and assisting the development of Dinarian businesses, causing a "brain drain" in Dinaria.

- To the extent possible, to persuade the state to offer attractive taxation terms to such experts, to promote their interest in cooperating with local industries.

Group 5: Representatives of the community of local businesspersons in Dinaria: supporting the tax authority's stance and alerting the relevant groups that deviating from said policy could lead to frustration and feelings of discrimination amongst them, seeing as they find themselves bearing the burden of funding infrastructure and services that Dinarians running international businesses also enjoy.
Interests:

- To ensure that the Dinarian business community won't bear too heavy a tax burden while Dinarian businesspersons engaging in international dealings evade taxes, even though they enjoy the same business environment that facilitates their income.

- To the extent possible, to limit the competition from said parties and promote the livelihood of the local business community.

Group 6: The public committee mandated with making recommendations to the finance minister. The committee must consider the following questions:

- What is the proper balance between the interests of each side regarding the definition of residency for tax purposes?

- Is amending the law necessary for reaching a better balance or clarifying the rules?

- If the answer is no – on what basis?

- If the answer is yes – what is the suggested change in the tax residency rules and on what basis?

The assignments for each interest group:

1) You must establish a legal argument that supports the position of the group you represent, relying on sources that you find independently.

2) You must formulate a negotiation strategy with the other interest groups and a strategy for presenting your group's argument before the Public Finance Committee.

The assignments for the public committee (Group 6):

After receiving the written arguments from the members of each group, you must formulate questions for oral argument, and afterward formulate a well-based decision regarding the proposed legislation.

Public International Law

THE CHALLENGE OF TEACHING PUBLIC INTERNATIONAL LAW (PIL) AND HOW ROLE-PLAYS CAN ASSIST[1]

The United Nations General Assembly declared the 1990s to be the Decade of International Law in November 1989 when it ratified Resolution 44/23. In this resolution, the United Nations called for improving the teaching, learning, and disseminating of international law. In response to this UN Resolution, the Institut de Droit International suggested that international law be taught in all law schools so that no graduate may practice without at least a rudimentary understanding of the topic.[2] In Israel, as in other areas in the world, PIL rules are tightly linked to daily life and effect domestic law. Israel has been a party to PIL conflicts since its establishment but is also an active member of many PIL forums such as the UN, the WTO, and the OECD. To expose Israeli law students to the immense importance of this legal discipline, a course on PIL is taught in the first year of law school. This chapter is intended to increase to the awareness of educators teaching about the Middle East and those who seek to expose law students to PIL rules generally.

Many students find PIL challenging. First, in the beginning of the course, it is difficult to asses the relevance of PIL to their future legal career. They don't come across the numerous examples of the spread of international norms into domestic law until later in the course. It is common for graduates to grasp the full significance of the theoretical concepts that underpin international legal and commercial systems only after completing their studies.[3] Second, discomfort is fueled by the numerous inconsistencies between national legislation in Israel and international standards. International courts frequently criticize Israeli policy. In some instances, when comparing the rulings of these courts involving Israel with those made in comparable circumstances regarding other nations, there are times when it appears that the PIL criteria have been applied selectively and inconsistently. In addition, Israel's local courts'

---

[1] For more details and for a legal analysis for two of the role-plays in this chapter ("Little Golano" and "Flashpoint: Syria") see Nellie Munin & Yael Efron, *Role Plays Bring Theory to life in a Multicultural Learning Environment*, 66(2) JOURNAL OF LEGAL EDUCATION (2017).

[2] Institut de Droit International [The Inst. of Int'l Law], The Teaching of Public and Private International Law 1 (1997), https://www.idi-iil.org/app/uploads/2017/06/1997_str_01_en.pdf.

[3] In his guest lecture to the students of ZAC law school on May 13, 2013, Former Chief Justice Aharon Barak described Israel as a "living laboratory of international norms." For his description of the Israeli legal system, see Aharon Barak, *Some Reflections on the Israeli Legal System and Its Judiciary*, 6(1) Electronic J. Comp. L. (Apr. 2002). For the notion of Israel as a "laboratory" for legal norms, see also DAPHNE BARAK-EREZ, *The National Security Constitution and the Israeli Condition*, ISRAELI CONSTITUTION IN THE MAKING (Gideon Sapir, Daphne Barak-Erez & Aharon Barak eds., 2013) 429, 429.

interpretation of international law is upsetting and perplexing to those who disagree with Israel's policies as well as those who support them. The third factor contributing to the hardship of some of our learners is linguistic barriers. Most Israeli students do not speak English as their first language. To make matters worse, many of them speak Arabic at home and Hebrew as a second language, thus it is not even their second language. As a result, many of them find it challenging to understand the case law found in the course bibliography. This may be true in other countries where the teaching language isn't English. Furthermore, minority group members in Israel may also feel frustrated as they learn more about the differences between the ideals iterated in international conventions promoting equality and some domestic policies, which sustain inequalities. Finally, students frequently convey their dissatisfaction with PIL's incapacity to resolve current international conflicts.

Our PIL classes are made more difficult by the diverse student group, which acts as a miniature version of Israel. It is extremely risky to lead an informed conversation about the legitimacy of these occurrences in a nation where current events frequently reflect issues with international law. For instance, bringing up the annexation of the Golan Heights in class when its residents are present may cause strong feelings. Another current example relates to the war in Gaza in the context of humanitarian law, which incites conflict between those who grieve the harm done to innocent people across the border and those who actively took part in the combat or were struck by Hamas hostilities. To prevent "explosions" in the classroom, discussions about territorial disputes, self-determination, violating international waters, and the laws of war are always meticulously prepared. The course primarily focuses on introducing fundamental ideas and procedures, significant organizations and tribunals, and prominent case law that exemplifies these ideas and institutions to overcome some of these difficulties. Where applicable, specific references to Israeli cases are made. At the end of the course, role-play games are chosen as a way to summarize the topic covered and prepare students for the final exam. This is done to foster a positive attitude, increase student interest in the material, and guarantee retention of the information presented.

This section of the book shares three plots developed by the editors for role-plays in the context of the PIL course. In terms of factual details, they rely on the "pseudo-reality" method,[4] which uses a plausible yet unreal factual backdrop. The reality facade can be enhanced using props, such as maps, pictures, and other documents. Conflicting interests chosen for each scenario rely on the material covered in the PIL course. This way, as the participants chose an agreed-upon solution to the conflict, they must consider the comparative weight of each interest involved. In all exercises, the parties have to decide whether to opt for a legal or an economic/pragmatic approach to reach mutually agreed solutions. All three games involve real legal norms, presented on the backdrop of a factionary scenario. We discuss some of the similarities and differences between the fictional story and the real-life facts of the regional disputes in the Middle East in an article published in the Journal of Legal Education.[5] Instructors teaching these areas of interest are welcome to draw insights from this comparison and incorporate it into their preparation or debrief.

---

[4] Noam Ebner & Yael Efron, *Using Tomorrow's Headlines for Today's Training: Creating PseudoReality in Conflict Resolution Simulation-Games*, 21(3) HARV. NEGOT. J. 377 (2005).

[5] Yael Efron & Nellie Munin, *Role Plays Bring Theory to life in a Multicultural Learning Environment*, 66 JOURNAL OF LEGAL EDUCATION 309, 320-23 (2017).

The Authors' Experience

We have played theses role-plays at our law school in Zefat Academic College (ZAC) in Israel for six consecutive years, involving a total of over 300 students. Despite the differences amongst the role-plays, similar observations were recorded, and students' feedback was consistent across the many experiences we shared. The role-plays all demonstrated a clear contribution to the learning and skill acquisition of PIL students, which we are pleased to share here. A detailed analysis of how each game contributes to the students' learning could be found in the abovementioned article,[6] but since they directly address the challenges we described above, we wish to briefly share them here as well.

The first step in setting up these role-plays is always carefully thinking about the group make up. It is important for us that teams are culturally and academically diverse. Since the students are expected to work together as a group, the various points of view, skills, and capabilities directly contribute to the learning. As the students engage in the legal research for the legal brief required to assist their case, students who are less comfortable with oral expression can shine. At the same time, direct negotiations allow students who are less versed in research and writing but are confident speakers to express themselves as advocates. In scenarios involving third-party neutrals, students with dispute resolution skills and inclination can stand out.

The scenarios present students with the intricate challenges of negotiating with interest groups that ascribe conflicting interpretations to the same international regulations or advocate for alternative norms. For example, in "Flashpoint," the rule of domestic sovereignty contradicts the international policy regarding use of chemical weapons. To advocate for their case, students must be familiar with these rules, and the role-plays serve as an incentive to revisit and summarize the course materials. Furthermore, the exercises allow students to experience the benefit and effectiveness of international agreements, compared with other methods for resolving international conflicts. In "Little Golano," for example, we found that all the groups diverted from the strict terms of the international treaty which concluded the war between the parties ninety-nine years ago. Instead, they drafted a pragmatic compromise that better served both parties' current economic and political interests.

The exercises allow students to experience the political pressures prescribed by the client they represent, while trying to reconcile their client's interests with the interests of their counterparts. They must be versed in the legal standards governing the case as well as with the alternatives to negotiated agreements, while employing sophisticated communication skills.[7] The exercises also offer students an opportunity to compare the effectiveness of a rule-oriented approach to that of an interest-based approach.[8]

When debriefing the games, we make a point of drawing the students' attention to the resemblance of dilemmas introduced by the imaginary plot of the role-play to real-life conflicts. We also stress in the debrief the crucial role of empathy. This is exceptionally important in groups where participants are parties to similar conflicts themselves. We do this by asking participants specifically what surprised them about their assigned role and whether anything that their counterparty presented affected their

---

[6] Ibid, at 326-29.

[7] Essentially, they are required to conduct principled negotiations. ROGER FISHER & WILLIAM URY, GETTING TO YES: NEGOTIATING AGREEMENT WITHOUT GIVING IN (3rd ed., 2011); LEIGH L. THOMPSON, THE MIND AND HEART OF THE NEGOTIATOR 77-79 (5th ed. 2011).

[8] Fisher & Ury, *ibid*, at 42-57.

understanding of the conflict. Most students acknowledged their ability to empathize with the other side, while several admitted difficulties in doing so. While emotions and logic often compete in real-life conflicts,[9] it seems that the constructive analysis throughout the exercise was facilitated by the positive atmosphere enabled by detaching dilemmas from real-life contexts during the role-plays. In all our years of experience playing these games, we never encountered incidents of emotional outbursts, despite the infusion of emotional components into the scenario. In this sense, the role-plays prove that emotions and logic are not mutually exclusive and that, by composed and thoughtful analysis, emotions can be addressed in a civilized manner, and even contribute to constructive solutions.[10]

We use the debrief to highlight the game's contribution to the development of skills required in legal practice. Participants appreciate the need to thoroughly prepare, just like with a real legal case. By allowing the negotiating groups to present their agreements to the whole class, we highlight the notion that there is no single solution to the problem at hand. Diverse solutions can be found to a similar dilemma. The exercises force the students to implement the theories and case law taught in the PIL course, so they can effectively advocate their positions. They make them carefully build a case strategy and think of negotiation tactics. The experience encourages collaboration and teamwork. It also allows students to practice public speaking. In our experience, while some preferred to avoid this, others admitted that the enthusiastic discussion in the group made them forget their fears.

We discovered that role-plays are a highly efficient and effective educational tool for addressing the challenges in teaching PIL outlined earlier. This is particularly true for classes where students are directly involved in real conflicts. The reputation of role-plays has become well-known among students, and they eagerly look forward to them each year. In fact, they have even requested that we extend this teaching method to other courses, a request we gladly fulfilled, and we gladly share with colleagues.

---

[9] See BERNARD S. MAYER, THE CONFLICT PARADOX: SEVEN DILEMMAS AT THE CORE OF DISPUTES 167-200 (2015).
[10] Id. at 176-80.

CONVERGING![1]

Simulation Overview

In *Converging!* participants are set in a scenario that blends real and fictional events, forming a 'pseudo-reality': a situation familiar enough to spark interest, motivation, and identification yet controlled and delineated to allow for maximum learning and skill-building.

At its core, the simulation's framework is familiar: two disputing parties and a third-party neutral, all possessing both shared and private information. Parties must choose whether to fall into familiar patterns of competition and coercion, or endeavor to construct a collaborative process and achieve co-operative outcomes with their perceived enemies.

Certain elements in the simulation's setup dictate that careful attention be paid to the early stages of the simulation's initiation (for example, each party is composed of several members, each having personal information and interests that may be divergent from those of other team members, necessitating careful thought to role assignment). The introduction of trainer-initiated changes and interventions in the scenario necessitates special attention to the simulation's management. Additionally, the Teachers' Manual in Part 2 of this book provides an extensive Debriefing Guide, to address the various training goals this simulation can achieve.

---

[1] This simulation is an adaptation made by Nellie Munin and Yael Efron to the original simulation created by Noam Ebner & Yael Efron. The original *Converging!* Simulation game won the 2007 E-PARCC's Honorable Mention Award at the Maxwell School Collaborative Governance Initiative competition, Syracuse University (2007). Its e-version is available at: https://www.maxwell.syr.edu/parcc/eparcc/simulations/2007_5_Simulation/.
The original version paralleled the Israeli-Palestinian conflict. However, this 'pseudo reality' simulation resembles other international disputes, e.g., between Russia and Ukraine, China and Tiwan, Morocco and Spain, Cyprus and Turkey, and others. Despite the fact the original scenario was written some twenty years ago, it is, unfortunately, still extremely timely and relevant. We find great benefit in teaching about the intricacies of such a dispute using role-plays, and the reasons for this are detailed in a separate chapter in this book. However, we always encourage instructors who wish to use this simulation game to do so with grave sensitivity and caution (not only in these dire times), and to leave plenty of room for expressions of distress and for facilitation of emotions.

Designed for dedicated and committed participants, *Converging!* engrosses participants in the simulated environment for a long period of time, ranging from one to three days, or from about six to twenty hours. This investment supports two major learning outcomes:

- In-depth understanding of the complexities of intractable conflicts.[2]
- Advanced skill-building in conflict resolution, negotiation, and mediation.

While it can be employed with participants at an introductory level, the simulation is particularly suited for participants with some background (at least) in either international territorial conflicts or conflict resolution, e.g., students of conflict resolution or public international law, or professionals working in conflicted regions around the world.

The background scenario depicts the political and social conflict in a fictional territory, weaving in the planned evacuation of a Roritanian city – Dan - located in the disputed territory in East Autopia. Such an evacuation is anticipated in many negotiations aiming to resolve territorial disputes. The interrelatedness between the Autopian city of Jen and the Roritanian city Dan complicates matters, lending complexity to the exercise.

Additional themes woven against this backdrop include the internal struggle on the Autopian side between the Freedom Fighters (FF) and the National Patriots (NP), the building of a disputed wall between Roritania and Autopia, and a Roritanian military operation in the area. Political and social motives depicted in the scenario have led both parties to send unofficial delegates to talks held in Cyprus, under the unofficial auspices of a team of UN mediators, in an attempt to reach a local, negotiated settlement.

Rather than replicate the oft-tried (and well-exhausted) method of throwing participants into the calamitous pond of the entire Roritanian-Autopian conflict and instructing them to solve it, this simulation offers an alternative method to learn these issues by dealing with them on a smaller scale. Participants are given the opportunity to focus on the immediate realities in the disputed territory, on the big-picture realities of the conflict as a whole, or on both. Through trainer intervention, participants are constantly moved between these two foci, mirroring the real-life complexity of trying to negotiate any isolated or localized issue in the conflict, in the shadow of the larger conflict.

The simulation is designed for maximum versatility. The storyline can be updated easily and regularly to accommodate any changes in any regional political reality. The roles of the UN mediators can be stressed in mediation skill-building training or dropped altogether to allow participants to flex their unassisted negotiation skills. New roles can easily be developed (or the provided roles adapted) to allow for participants' real-life preferences and experiences.

---

[2] Intractability refers to conflicts that seem to be stuck for a long time in an increasingly destructive spiral, yet the parties seem unable to extricate themselves, either alone or with outside help. When the issues of the conflict stem from identities and values, the adversary is perceived so dangerous that the costs of the battle feel justified. Barbara Gray, Peter T. Coleman & Linda L. Putnam, *Introduction: Intractable Conflict: New Perspectives on the Causes and Conditions for Change*, 50 AM. BEHAV. SCIENTIST 1415, 1416 (2007).

Logistics, Setup and Game Management Instructions

Number of Roles: 10-20 (up to 8 Roritanian roles, 8 Autopian roles and 4 UN mediator roles)
[Optimal group size is 12-13 participants, with 5 players each on the Autopian and Roritanian teams and 2-3 UN mediators. This allows for maximum individual participation and group management. However, roles are provided for up to 20 players. In still larger groups, several simulation-groups can work concurrently, with the trainer either rotating between them or employing training assistants.]

- **Setup and Preparation Time**: 1-2 hours
- **Running Time**: 6-20 hours
- **Level**: Intermediate to Advanced

Debriefing Time

1 hour debrief recommended for every 4 hours of simulation running time. In addition to a post-game debriefing session, trainers might choose to conduct impromptu or pre-planned debriefing sessions during the game's running time. See further instructions below and the Teacher's Manual (Part 2 of this book).

Background Preparation

If the simulation is used to teach about a specific (current or historic) territorial conflict, trainers might choose to assign reading material before handing out the simulation information packs, or to provide participants with time to conduct independent background research in the library or on the Internet.

Role Assignment

A. Divide participants Roritanian, Autopian, and UN teams.

While the trainer can consider personality, experience, or participant-preference in role assignment, or opt for random selection, it is vital that one member of the Roritanian Team be assigned the settler role (role #2) and that one member of the Autopian Team be assigned the role of Freedom Fighters (FF) representative (role #5). These roles are key for ensuring the formation of internal and external opposition (and, occasionally, surprising coalitions).

B. Hand out the following material:
To each member of the Roritanian team:
Public Information
Private Instructions for the Roritanian Team
A map of the conflicted territory
One 'Personal Role Information' from the Roritanian characters.

To each member of the UN team:
Public Information
Private Instructions for the UN Team
A map of the conflicted territory

One 'Personal Role Information' from the UN characters.

To each member of the Autopian team:
Public Information
Private Instructions for the Autopian Team
A map of the conflicted territory
One 'Personal Role Information' from the Autopian characters.

Participant Instructions

Instruct participants to read their information carefully, and to try to flesh out their instructions with their own knowledge, emotions, and experience. Explain that by "owning" the role in this manner, the simulation will not only become more lifelike, but it will also enable them to understand what parties to conflict truly experience; resulting insights will, therefore, be highly transferable to real-life situations.

Role Preparation

Once roles have been assigned, allow students at least one hour for reading and individual preparation. You might even consider giving the material out the evening before the simulation begins.

Ask all members of each team to stay in the same room during the individual preparation period. This will prevent participants from getting 'lost' during this extended period and will encourage a natural transition to the group discussion period.

According to the scenario information, participants meet with their own team before meeting the other. Announce that once the individual preparation period is up, each team will meet as a group for 45 minutes or an hour before meeting the other group. This time is to be used for the team to get to know each other 'in-role,' discuss issues, interests, and priorities, divide labor etc. The UN team will use this to discuss their intervention strategy, and perhaps to arrange the meeting room. This time will serve as a transition period during which participants will try on and try out their new roles and get used to addressing each other in-role as colleagues.

Room Setup

Allow participants to set up the meeting room as they wish, or specifically assign this task to the UN team. Preferably, the room should have a whiteboard and/or a flipchart and comfortable seating (remember the duration of the simulation!).

The group may periodically opt to break out of the meeting for consultations. Try to have a couple of spaces available adjacent to the primary meeting room for this purpose.

3rd Party Intervention

According to the instructions given to the parties, the UN mediators are expected to be relatively passive observers at the beginning, taking a more active role when this is requested by the parties or dictated by circumstances. The participants in the UN roles might be a bit uncertain regarding their authority and timing at first. This is part of the process: they are expected to identify situations and process-points suitable for their intervention and earn the parties' trust and acceptance through their words and behavior rather than these being dictated by instructions. You might choose to stress this to them during the team preparation time. The UN team's intervention will usually begin to be increasingly necessary after the first 'situation' temporarily halts the talks (see below). Of course, the UN role can be written to be more involved or directive (to make the 3rd party role clearer) or written out altogether (to stress unassisted negotiation skills).

Gametime

Once the time for team preparation is up, 'Gametime' begins. If a party takes more time to discuss things among its members, they need to be aware that the other party is already waiting for them in the meeting room, and there may be a 'process-price' to pay. Parties arrive, are seated, and spend some time on formalities (introductions, etc.) although some groups might quickly jump to conflict on procedural issues ('how come they have one representative more than we do?') or make early demands ('If the attack on Jen is not halted immediately, we will not sit at the same table with the Roritanians!'). After some time has passed, parties will usually (but not always) reach a point where they intuitively try and set a general agenda for the talks, or perhaps even plunge into an in-depth negotiation on one of the issues.

Interruption: Targeted Assassination Situation

At Gametime +1 (1 hour after the joint session has begun), break in on the group's discussion, regardless of what they are doing or discussing. Hand the teams envelopes containing their instructions for *Situation: Targeted Assassination*. This causes an instant disruption of the talks and an Autopian walkout. The negotiations are put on hold, parties will caucus to discuss their next move, and the UN team will probably try to persuade the parties to return to the table. This incident not only shakes the process up, it also introduces participants to the complexity of negotiating in an environment subject to the impact of real-time external events. Participants will now be aware of the possibility of trainer-initiated scenario changes, causing a sharp dynamic change: enhanced awareness and reduced complacency.

Continued Game Management

The Autopian Team's instructions dictate that they return to the table after no more than half an hour (although sometimes they might stretch this, or the Roritanian Team might stage a counter walkout). The negotiations usually resume after some rocky minutes (usually involving the formation of some declaration by the Roritanian Team or by both Teams jointly).

From this moment on, game management, from the trainer's point of view, is entirely a balance between the amount of time available and the parties' progress. On the one hand, one wants to avoid an artificial rush to settlement (such as 'Let's hurry up and reach agreement on everything before lunch so we can have the day free'). Conversely, a trainer might want to avoid a situation in which parties approach the final deadline without any headway at all. For while this might indeed go a long way towards introducing participants to the reality of protracted peace talks, it results in disheartened and de-motivated participants. To allow the trainer to change the game's dynamics and pace, two different types of interruptions or interventions are provided:

Incentives & Setbacks are meant to have minor effect, throw in a bit of optimism or pessimism, trust or distrust, acceleration or deceleration.

Situations are mini-scenarios, which, in their own right, demand that the participants drop whatever was previously engrossing them and focus on an emergency situation demanding their immediate attention. The outcome of a *Situation* can have great effect on the continuing negotiation dynamic: parties who worked together to solve the *Situation*'s crisis might bring that sense of collaboration with them back to the 'main' negotiation table, while a *Situation* crisis handled badly will lead to continuing attitudes of distrust and blame.

It should be stressed that the trainer need not use all the *Situations*, all the *Incentives & Setbacks* – or any of them (beyond the 'Assassination' *Situation*). Trainers can pick and choose, judging which might be best utilized to fine-tune the game dynamic in any desired direction. Trainers can improvise their own interruptions, whether on the spot or based on recent (or predicted) events in the news.

This fine-tuning aside, the amount of time available for the simulation will usually dictate the flow of the game and the frequency of trainer interventions. As a rule of thumb, it is suggested that the trainer intervene again at least at the following two points:

One hour before the end of the first half of the time allocated for the simulation, the trainer should announce that the coordinators for all parties have requested that by 'halftime' the parties will have reached an agreed-upon agenda for the remainder of the negotiations (if they have not already done so). This will serve to focus participants on what they came here to do, nudging them gently (albeit a bit artificially) away from the play-acting the first few game hours allow for and encouraging them towards the application of conflict resolution skills in a decidedly non-conducive atmosphere.

One hour before the end of the time allocated for the simulation, the trainer should announce that the coordinators for all parties have requested that the participants write up any agreements they have reached. Participants might ignore this at first, especially if no or little agreement has been achieved. The trainer should repeat this instruction 15 minutes later, stressing that 'agreements' can relate not only to settled issues but also to an agreed upon agenda for future talks, a joint declaration, or any other joint statements or agreed principles.

When the allotted time is up, help parties break out of character, take a deep breath, and move on to debrief (See the Teacher's Manual in Part 2 of this book). Beyond debrief sessions, consider using forms for participant self-assessment (before, during, and after the simulation) and for receiving participant feedback on the simulation or the workshop, such as the sample forms for these purposes provided below (See the Teacher's Manual in Part 2 of this book).

Use of Props

Imaginative trainers will find many ways to develop and employ props during this simulation. Here are a few possibilities:

Provide nametags for participants, each with a Roritanian, Autopian, or UN flag on it.

Provide place cards for each participant (these can also be in the national colors). Players will often color or decorate them, or perhaps create a game name for themselves suitable to their personal role.

When initiating a trainer-intervention such as a *Situation* or a *Setback*, do so in a way that startles and shakes people up. Inflate a balloon and pop it behind everybody's backs or set off a small confetti bomb to stress the explosive nature of the news.

Consider providing a transparency of the map included in the scenario, for participants to project on a whiteboard and draw on.

Consider providing additional maps, pictures, relevant clippings from current newspaper headlines, etc.

Public Information

In June 1970, Roritania launched a swift two-week war, surprising its long-standing adversary, Autopia (both situated in the Eleusian Region), and capturing significant portions of its territory, in the East and in the West. Since then, many Roritanians have moved into the occupied Autopian lands. Some did so for ideological reasons, believing the land rightfully belongs to them, while others were drawn by the affordable housing prices.

Life under Roritanian occupation has caused considerable hardship for the Autopian population, fueling the rise of violent groups who argue that political solutions alone will not reclaim their land. Instead, they advocate for a determined, armed struggle. Over the years, these violent acts have resulted in numerous casualties for Roritania. The past decade has been the bloodiest of all.

The past year has seen noticeable change in the political arena of the Eleusian geographic area, with numerous rigorous international peace initiatives. As the freedom battle initiated by Autopian militia groups against Roritania enters its seventh year, it is unclear if the situation should be defined as "The Eleusian Peace Process" or whether the term "The Roritaian-Autopian Conflict" is more apt.

Recently, Roritania decided to evacuate the city of Dan, situated in North-Eastern Autopia, which has suffered significant losses. The military explained that the city's proximity to the nearby Autopian city of Jen makes it impossible to ensure the safety of Dan's residents. Furthermore, they emphasized that the resources required to secure the city could be more effectively deployed elsewhere.

John the Great, the Autopian president and the head of the National Patriots (NP) political party, is not the charismatic father figure that his late predecessor was. As a result, the NP – and the Autopian people – are suffering from internal rifts. The Freedom Fighters (FF), an extremist religious organization with radical views towards Roritania and the West, surprised the world last year not only by participating in the political process for the first time, but by winning – decisively – in the general elections. The National Patriot's monopoly on the Autopian internal political scene is a thing of the past. Arguments over control of the NP's security forces sparked exchanges of gunfire between the two political groups, as well as kidnappings and assassination attempts. Recently, the FF has ousted the NP from West Autopia by force, completely dominating this area while the NP continues to cling to its old power bases in East Autopia (where Jen and Dan are located). Most of the nations of the world have not recognized the FF-led West Autopia as a separate state and refuse to deal with the FF. The ensuing diplomatic confusion complicates the transferring of international aid to Autopia and to aid agencies the two parts of it.

Roritania's unilateral disengagement from West Autopia was carried out in two years ago. Ten thousand settlers were evacuated from their homes in these areas, and their houses - along with army bases evacuated by the Roritanian Defense Forces (RDF) - were bulldozed into rubble. Roritanian society and politics were thrown into turmoil as a result of these events. Shortly after Roritania's evacuation from West Autopia, the Roritanian centrist Forward party was voted into power, and its leader assumed the post of Prime Minister. He has announced his plan to continue to take unilateral steps, in the absence of a negotiated agreement. Meeting last month with the U.S. President, the Roritanian Prime Minister announced his "Convergence Plan," according to which isolated Roritanian settlements in East Autopia would be evacuated and some settlement blocs closer to Roritania's border would be connected to Roritania by means of including them within the envelope of the security barrier Roritania has been constructing over the past few years.

The realization of this plan has been delayed, due to the upheavals on the Autopian side. At present, there is no contact between Roritanian figures and any representatives of the Autopian government, with the exclusion of its president. Roritania has halted its withdrawal from East Autopian cities kept under Roritanian control for the past few years, claiming to have apprehended suicide bombers originating in these cities. Autopian militants have resumed firing rockets from West Autopia at Roritanian cities.

The Roritanian Prime Minister recently announced that Dan, a small city in the northern East Autopia, would be evacuated at the end of this month; Roritanian military presence in the area would also cease. He stressed that this step would be performed unilaterally due to the absence of a Autopian negotiating partner and that Roritania would continue to take unilateral measures to set its borders according to its security needs.

Roritania, seeing its last opportunity to act against the militant groups and arms factories in the northern East Autopian city of Jen before pulling out of the area, is preparing for a large-scale incursion. RDF troops have already entered the city and the refugee camp, searching houses for armaments and militants. The last RDF incursion into Jen, five years ago, took a heavy toll on both sides, and caused a local humanitarian crisis. Jen has been kept under close RDF scrutiny ever since; the damage caused has yet to be repaired and, due to the situation, elections have not been held in the city.

Heading a shaky coalition, the Roritanian Prime Minister relies heavily on his coalition partner, the left-of-center Labor Party, for political support. While supporting the convergence plan, Labor sees the plan's unilateral nature as its key long-term weakness. Labor officials open a backdoor channel to the Autopians, hoping to achieve a mutually agreed upon handover of power and territory, and perhaps a first step towards resuming regular negotiations. Labor leaders are confident that the Roritanian Prime Minister will adopt any reasonable agreement reached by them with the Autopians rather than risking the collapse of his government.

Through contacts from the previous rounds of negotiations in the area of Eleusia, Labor leaders contact the Governor of Jen and the local NP commander. Faced with the reality of the RDF incursion and realizing that to a great degree the fate of the Autopian nation could turn on what occurs in Jen, they agree to negotiate. They promise that if a just and reasonable agreement is reached, they would pressure their NP president of East Autopia and the FF Prime Minister of West Autopia to endorse it; if they would not, they would be blamed and castigated for all damages resulting from the RDF incursion in Jen.

The coordinators of the upcoming talks have reached these procedural agreements:

1) They would select non-professional and non-partisan negotiators, a trusted and representative group, and charge them with reaching the best deal possible.

2) The talks would be held in Nicosia, Cyprus, a city with its own ongoing drama of conflict and peacemaking. The talks' time-frame will be limited to the two weeks remaining until the planned evacuation of Dan, and a secluded hotel will be booked for that period of time.

3) Third party neutrals would be involved in the process, both to mediate difficult situations and as a means of giving the talks credibility in the future. The coordinators requested assistance from the chief of the UN's permanent mission to Cyprus, situated there to help monitor and facilitate the local peace process. Due to the temporary hiatus in activity on the Cyprus front, the chief of mission agreed to assist the talks by assigning several of his staff to help. It was agreed that they would be assigned observer status for the first part of the talks, taking a more active role only if expressly requested to by the parties. During the second part of the talks, as time becomes shorter, they will intervene more actively.

4) Secrecy of the talks is paramount; any leakage would end them. Therefore, the groups will not convene ahead of time, and each member will arrive separately, leaving his cell phone at home. The talks will be quarantined – no messages will go in or out except periodic updates sent by each team's coordinator. The only outgoing messages will be actual agreements, passed on through the UN neutrals.

5) Arriving in Nicosia, each delegate finds a note in his room asking him to come meet the other members of his team. A private meeting room will be used, and the meeting's purpose is to get to know each other and to prepare for the first upcoming meeting with the other side.

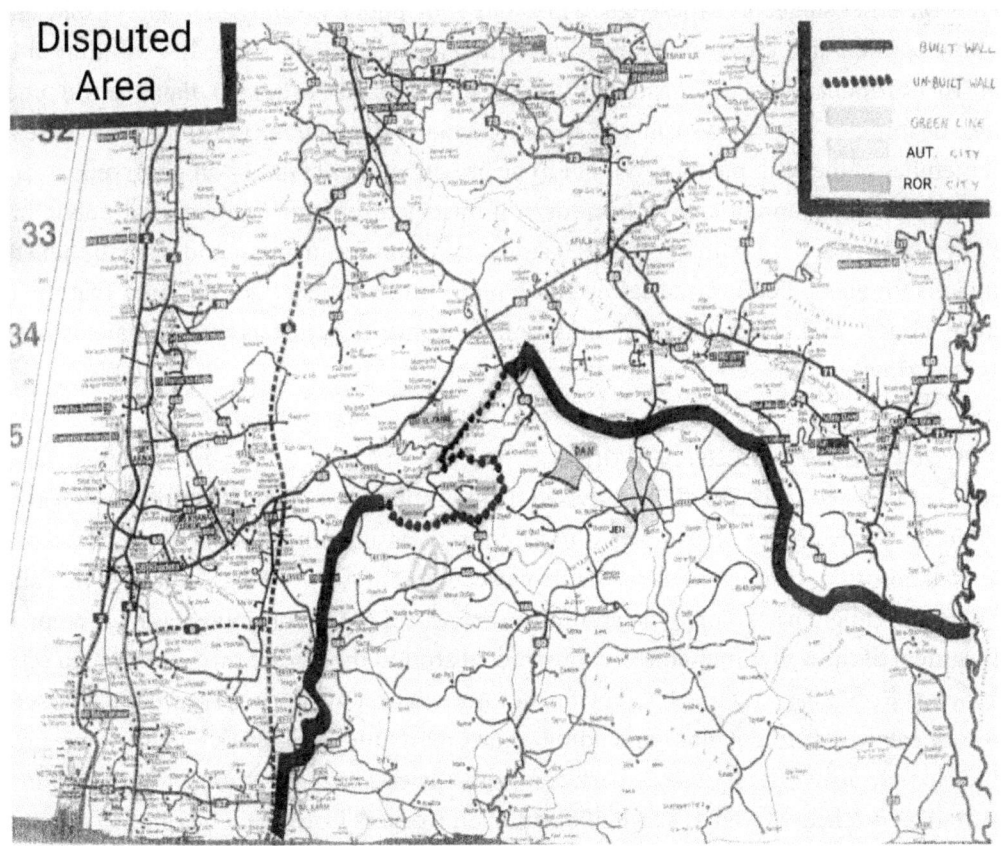

Private Information for the Roritanian Delegation

This is the first time you are meeting as a group, and the one thing most of you have in common is that you never expected to be Roritania's representative in negotiations with the Autopians. Of course, you are familiar with most of the issues; whether you live near Jen, walk the streets of Roritania, or do military reserve duty in the Autopian territories, the conflict is a fact of life. You are excited at the talks' potential, but apprehensive about ensuring Roritania's main interests are satisfied. Bad agreements mean more terror and more deaths. In such a small country, everything hits close to home; whatever happens here will affect you, your families, your friends and your country. Before meeting the other side, read this background summary.

Convergence

The East Autopia's convergence plan is a done deal. The Roritanian Prime Minister *must* implement it in terms of internal politics – it's what he was elected to do – and he has made a firm commitment to the U.S. President.

The city of Dan will definitely be evacuated, on schedule. Established by pioneer Roritanians 30 years ago, Dan is isolated in the heart of Autopian-populated areas, and its very existence causes friction with the Autopians. The Roritanian government is working to put together a compensation package for the 20,000 inhabitants of Dan, who will all be evacuated. Not all these inhabitants have agreed to evacuate; the ideological settlers amongst them view the uprooting of a Roritanian city as a cataclysmic tragedy. The huge political price for forcibly evacuating them might limit your ability to make too many concessions on other subjects at these talks, to avoid your public's feeling that you've sold out. Being able to show considerable concessions from the Autopian side might make this withdrawal easier to carry out. The Roritanian Prime Minister has stressed that internal Roritanian dialogue will precede any withdrawal he initiates, to avoid a social rift. In this spirit, the Roritanian coordinator for these talks has invited a member of the settlement movement to be present at these talks as an observer.

Dan is a carefully planned city with modern infrastructure, street system, and public buildings, etc. The city houses a college with about 2,000 students, commercial areas, and a small industrial area providing jobs for about 2,000 workers. The Roritanian Prime Minister has declared that the city's infrastructure, houses, and community buildings will be dismantled, just as the settlements in the West Autopia were. However, this subject is deemed negotiable.

Withdrawal Line and Security Wall

The Roritanian Defence Force (RDF) has advised that the still uncompleted Security Wall between East Autopia and Roritania proper be completed in its entirety, as a continuous barrier. RDF troops would cross the Wall only in hot pursuit of terrorists. In closed sessions, the RDF has conceded that alternative security measures might be explored in certain sectors instead of the continuous wall concept, but only if a vital segment of the wall is immediately constructed around the bloc of three Roritanian settlements and Fountain, a Roritanian city inhabited by former Autopians. One purpose served by this segment of wall is to connect the settlement bloc – including its Prosperity Industrial Park – to Roritania proper and ensure the bloc's security. The industrial park comprises several dozen factories, which employ close to 3,000 Roritanian workers as well as about 500 Autopian workers from the Jen region. The second purpose is to deny suicide bombers' access to Northern Roritania by infiltration via the Roritanian city of Fountain, where a majority of former Autopians live.

Security Considerations

Occupying less territory makes the RDF's job easier. Defending along a fixed line is simpler than policing Autopian cities. After convergence, fewer casualties among soldiers and settlers alike (to say nothing of Autopians) are expected. The fewer the cities, settlements, and roads to be defended, the less manpower needed to be dedicated to the region. Less day-to-day friction with the Autopians might reduce motivation for terrorism. On the other hand, the pullout will reduce Roritania's on-the-ground intelligence-gathering capability. In addition, Roritania has always depended on the deterrent effect of its military might to keep its neighbors at bay. If the evacuation of Dan is viewed as a capitulation to terror, terror organizations will be hailed as the liberators who banished the RDF and their stock will rise amongst terror-enablers within the Autopian population.

No Linkage

A major concern is that any change in the status quo potentially sets a precedent to be cited in future negotiations. While reaching agreement here can create a positive background for future talks, do not agree to *any* linkage between these and future negotiations. Roritania has never before evacuated a city located east of the ceasefire borders of the 1970 war. Several others exist further south, and Roritania intends to hold on to at least some of them.

Political Considerations

The recent turnaround in Autopian internal politics has left Roritania in a bind: after treating the Autopian National Patriots (NP) as the other side's legitimate representing authority, Roritania is faced with the fact that a terrorist organization (the FF) has taken over West Autopia. Roritania and most Western countries refuse to recognize the FF regime in West Autopia unless it meets three conditions: renouncing violence, recognizing Roritania, and respecting past agreements between Roritania and the NP. The FF has yet to meet any of these conditions. The NP, although certainly not Roritania's friend, is considered more moderate: at least it would stand accountable with regard to previous peace agreements and cease-fires. Roritania has much to gain by strengthening the NP at the FF's expense – and much to lose if East Autopia would be overrun by the FF (like West Autopia was). Additionally, faced with a possible agreement, internal Autopian politics may force the FF into adopting a more moderate line.

The Jen Incursion

Jen has been a hornet's nest of terrorist activity for the past few years, and suicide bombers originating in Jen have struck at buses, restaurants, and bus stations across Roritania, killing hundreds of civilians. While you certainly feel empathy for Jen's inhabitants living in cramped living conditions and enduring searches and curfews, you also know that terror organizations promote these problems by hiding their operations and operators amongst the civilian population.

The RDF estimates there are 10,000 firearms in Jen, besides the weapons held by the semi-functioning, NP-controlled, Autopian police forces. The RDF is particularly worried that militants have smuggled rocket launchers into Jen, capable of striking at the nearby Roritanian city of Afulu. Their primary mission is to capture these arms stockpiles. The RDF also plans to demolish the homes of three suicide bombers and to arrest local terrorist leaders, leaving the terrorist infrastructure in Jen in shambles in the hope that more moderate elements might gain control. During the RDF's last incursion into Jen, the Autopians claimed that Roritanian civilians were committing war crimes. A UN commission later found none of the accusations were even close to the truth.

Before you sit down with the Autopian team, review the boundaries of your negotiating mandate:

The evacuation of Dan *will* be executed.

Allow no formal linkage between these talks and this evacuation to any other talks or withdrawal plans.

Full security must be achieved along the border line.

The strategic threat posed by the weapons caches in Jen *must* be neutralized.

Beyond these points, anything and everything is negotiable at your discretion. You can affect not only the big picture, but you can also reach immediate, local, or interim agreements regarding the Jen incursion, the security wall, or any other issue. These agreements can be put into immediate effect by notifying your coordinator. Your job is to achieve an agreement that best serves Roritania's interests.

Use your preparation time well; you will soon be meeting with the Autopian team.

Private Information for the Autopian Delegation

This is the first time you're meeting as a group. None of you ever expected to represent Autopia in negotiations with the Roritanians on such existential issues. Of course, you are all familiar with most of the issues. Whether you live in a refugee camp, walk the streets of Jen, or get held up for hours at the Roritanian occupiers' checkpoints, the conflict is a fact of life. Bad agreements, from Autopia's standpoint, mean more Roritanian aggression and more deaths. In such a small state, everything hits close to home; whatever happens here will have immediate effects on you, your families, and your country. You don't trust Roritania, and you're not sure whether to trust the Roritanian delegation. Before you sit down with them, here is a background summary necessary for the talks.

Jen

Little has changed in Jen since the death of the former Autopian leader and the transfer of power to John the Great. The Roritanian army continues to maintain checkpoints around the city, strangling commerce and cutting the city off from its outlying areas and other Autopian cities. As a result of the occupation, Jen's inhabitants did not participate in the general election held in January, and the FF's victory has not had much effect here. The area is still under the control of the pro-NP Governor, and most of the local security forces are NP loyalists. However, the FF has been increasingly flexing its muscles in the region and will certainly attempt to use any Roritanian withdrawal as a pretext for attempting to take over local power bases. Since the FF's takeover in West Autopia, the sporadic violence between NP and FF throughout East Autopia has not passed over Jen. In acknowledgement of the shift in the Autopian political scene, the talk's coordinator has invited a representative from FF in Jen to participate in the talks as an observer.

You feel uncomfortable. Back home, Roritarian soldiers are entering the city and arrests have begun. This may be the only way to stop the killing. Last time the Roritanian Army entered Jen five years ago, hundreds were killed. The world stood silently by as the Roritarians destroyed an Autopian city. Only the Autopian resistance, killing hundreds of the invaders, left the city some pride. The FF and religious martyrs have promised to resist. Foreseeing the violent Roritanian reaction to this, you feel responsible to prevent a massacre and a humanitarian crisis. **You must do whatever you can to stop, slow down, or limit the attack.**

Roritanian Withdrawal

You have no objection to Roritania's withdrawal. The Roritanian Prime Minister's coordination of the convergence plan with the Americans and not the Autopians, though, is insulting. These talks are a chance for the Autopian voice to be heard, but the looming ultimatum angers you. Make it clear that you *will* demand your right to be heard on the issue of Roritanian withdrawal. This disengagement should be the first step, linked to future withdrawals in East Autopia.

The Roritanian city of Dan, built on Autopian land, has always been a bone of contention. The open sewage running through the streets of the Jen refugee camp, contrasts with the Roritanian villas across the valley in Dan. It might be enjoyable to watch Roritanian bulldozers tear down the city just as they tore down hundreds of houses in Jen. However, the handover of these homes, undamaged, could have benefits. Refugees, left homeless by Roritania's last invasion, could move into Dan. Evacuating Jen's refugee camp, housing some 50,000 people, could allow Jen to get a fresh start. Dan's modern infrastructure, commercial areas, and public buildings are far beyond anything you could hope to establish on your own. The city also currently houses a college with about 2,000 students, commercial areas, and a small industrial area providing jobs for about 2,000 workers (including about 500 workers from Jen, when the RDF allows them to enter Dan).

Withdrawal Line and Security Wall

You strongly object to the so-called Security Wall. Although primarily built along the Ceasefire border line, in some regions it cuts deeply into Autopian lands. The Wall serves as a physical barrier, denying thousands of Autopians access to employment in Roritania, after almost 40 years of occupation had made you dependent on the Roritanians for employment. The Wall also ends any territorial hopes Autopians may have *west* of the Border Line, in Roritanina proper. Many people in Jen once lived in now Roritanian cities, before the Roritanians expelled them in the 1950 war; some have never come to terms with Roritania's existence. Parts of the Wall are still unbuilt, and *you want to prevent their completion*. At the very least, arrangements should be made to allow free passage into Roritania. In particular, you hope to stop the Wall from being built around the three Roritanian settlements built on Autopian lands west of Jen. In this area, the Wall diverges from the Border Line, tears off a big chunk of Autopian land, and will block thousands of laborers from Jen from employment in the Prosperity Industrial Park. In addition, the planned Wall will cut off family and business ties between residents of Jen and Fountain, the Roritanian city where many former Autopians live. The Governor has stressed that you must keep the larger picture of Autopian national interests in mind at all times. These demand that Roritania withdraw to the Ceasefire Border Line, dismantle parts of the wall, and cease to build the unfinished segments. Settling for less might set a dangerous precedent.

Control of Jen and Dan

While the Autopian internal situation has not yet degenerated into civil war, gunfire is being exchanged daily between NP and FF militants, as the FF attempts to consolidate its power and the NP struggles to attain its former supremacy. After the Roritanians withdraw from Jen, a major power struggle will take place in that city between the FF and the remnants of the NP security forces loyal to John the Great. The city of Dan could play an important role in this struggle. If the FF gains control of the evacuated city, it could use the opportunity to set up an FF-governed city, threatening the supremacy of the NP in East Autopia, including Jen proper. An agreed handover of power directly to the Governor might just allow him to retain control.

Economic Considerations

A unilateral Roritanian pullback might seem to be a considerable concession, but would in reality strangle Jen economically by denying its inhabitants employment in Roritanian industrial parks and business opportunities in Fountain. New peace initiatives are often supported by international resources. Such funding could enable Jen's renovation. If an agreement is reached and implemented, there could be positive local and national effects. Jen might become the focus of East Autopian political activity, having positive effects on local commerce. Security in the area might encourage the establishment of a

Roritanian-Autopian joint industrial park, solving Jen's 60% unemployment rate while Roritanian companies enjoy access to East Autopia markets.

At the very least, you **must**:

Achieve at least some rapid concessions on the ground in Jen.

Attain at least some concession on the issue of the Security Wall, the most symbolic to the Autopian public. Under no circumstances can the entire Wall be built.

Achieve an organized handover of power, preserving Autopian dignity.

Although local interim agreements like these can be made, do *not* agree to a *final, overall* solution to the conflict with the Roritanians achieving anything less than a pullback to the Ceasefire Border Line.

Beyond these, anything and everything is negotiable at your discretion. Any agreements reached can be put into immediate effect by notifying your coordinator. Your job is to achieve an agreement that best serves Autopia's interests. Use your preparation time well; you will soon be meeting with the Roritanian team.

Private Instructions for the UN Team

The UN team has been assigned the mission of facilitating informal Track II talks between Autopians and Roritanian ahead of Roritania carrying out the recently announced withdrawal in north-east Autopia. Your chief of mission is not participating in these talks himself; as the talks are not between official representatives of the parties, the UN involvement must remain low-profile. He has selected you all for your experience in third-party roles gained working on the Cyprus issue. You have been assigned observer status during the first part of these unofficial, top-secret, behind-the-scenes talks. However, the chief of mission has allowed you to take a more active role in mediating or facilitating the negotiations, provided the parties agree to this. At any rate, during the later phases of the talks you will definitely intervene to speed things up; time is running out for everyone. Successful UN intervention would be an important feather in the team's cap.

This is the first time you've met as a group. Of course, you are all familiar with most of the issues – you follow them on the news and read briefings; some of you have dealt with them professionally. You are careful to keep abreast of developments in the region. In addition, your chief of mission has provided you with the following briefing paper, covering what seem to be the parties' interests and viewpoints, what the UN's view, is and what your job is.

Convergence

The convergence plan itself is a done deal – the Roritanian Prime Minister will be able to implement it in terms of internal politics and has made a firm promise to the U.S. President on this issue. He has too much riding on this to let it slip.

The Roritanian Prime Minister is planning to evacuate the city of Dan. Established 30 years ago by a small group of settlers, the city now numbers some 20,000 inhabitants. Dan is a carefully planned city with a very modern infrastructure, street system, and public buildings, etc. The city houses a college with about 2,000 students, commercial areas and a small industrial area providing jobs for about 2,000 workers. Dan is isolated in the heart of Autopian areas, and its existence causes much friction with the Autopians. This is the first time the Roritanians have considered the possibility of evacuating an entire city; in the West Autopia evacuation last summer 25 small settlements, totaling about 10,000 inhabitants altogether, were evacuated.

Withdrawal Line and Security Wall

The exact pullback line has not yet been declared. The Roritanian Prime Minister's security advisors have aired their opinion that the security wall being built between East Autopia and Roritania should be completed in a continuous manner over the entire withdrawal line so as to prevent suicide bombers' free access to Northern Roritania. You think the Roritanians might agree to leave parts of the wall unbuilt if the Autopians agree to alternative security measures.

Security Issues

On one hand, less territory actually held by Roritania makes the RDF's job easier. Defending along a fixed line is much simpler than continued presence in Autopian cities. Less day-to-day friction between the parties might reduce motivation for terrorism, particularly for suicide bombers. On the other hand,

Roritania has always depended on military deterrence to keep its neighbors at bay. If the disengagement is viewed as capitulation to terror or as a retreat under fire, terrorist organizations would be seen as liberators who banished the RDF and this would encourage their further activity. This would be compounded by Roritania having reduced its on-the-ground intelligence-gathering capability.

Linkage and Future Negotiations
Roritania will try to avoid setting precedents that could be cited in future negotiations; such linkage may be important to the Autopians. Overcoming this may take creativity on your part. Positive results from these talks just might result in full-blown peace talks for the entire Eluesian region.

The Jen Incursion
Jen is one of the Eleusian Region's most cramped, underdeveloped towns. One of its neighborhoods is actually a refugee camp, with scarce electricity and sewage running in the streets. You can't understand how the Roritanians can live with this happening in their backyard. Jen has been a hornet's nest of militant activity for the past few years; a breeding ground for suicide bombers and terrorists who take refuge amongst the civilian population. There are thousands of firearms in the camp, illegal under international agreements. The CIA has reported attempts by the FF to smuggle in artillery and ground-to-air missiles – with possible success. In the RDF's last large-scale operation in Jen, five years ago, troops met fierce local resistance and took heavy casualties. Autopian claims of massacred civilians and war crimes committed by soldiers were investigated by a UN commission, which found that 54 Autopians had been killed and that the accusations of massacres were inaccurate and inflated, to say the least.

Political Considerations
Ever since the attempts to initiate a peace process between the parties began over 15 years ago, the NP party has always been Roritania's negotiating partner. The recent turnaround in Autopian internal politics has Roritania and the world in a bind: after enabling and encouraging the Autopians to set up their own institutions and treating the NP as the other side's legitimate representing authority, this body has been taken over by a group viewed by Roritania and most Western countries as a terrorist organization. These countries refuse to recognize the FF-led regime in West Autopia unless it meets three conditions: renouncing violence, recognizing Roritania, and respecting past agreements between Roritania and the NP; The FF has yet to meet any of these conditions. While the UN has not yet reached any resolution on the subject, you have received reports from administrators of UN-backed aid organizations on their dealings with the new Autopian reality. On the one hand, they are finding it difficult to get aid money transferred into the Autopian areas due to Western concerns that the money will be used to fund militant and terrorist activity. On the other hand, they report a lack of transparency and accountability, and admit that they themselves cannot be certain where the money is ending up and whether it is being used for peaceful goals.

Although elements of the NP have been involved in attacks against Roritania, they are considered more moderate and are at least accountable to Roritania and the world with regard to previous peace agreements and cease-fires. While NP leaders have addressed the UN's General Assembly FF is viewed as a radical group with extreme religious orientation, with little (if any) international support.

UN Interests:

Restoring dialogue to promote quiet in this volatile region.

Achieving tangible results, which can create a more favorable atmosphere of dialogue in the Elusian region, with an eye towards other current hotspots.

Regaining favor with both parties, who have not had a favorable view of UN assistance in recent years.

Possible UN Incentives:

In addition to its willingness to facilitate the talks, the UN can offer its own involvement and other incentives to get a peace process off the ground.

If the situation warrants it, you can consider the following proposals:

The UN can provide on-the-ground monitoring for implementation of any agreement reached.

The UN can provide up to $10,000,000 for humanitarian efforts and urban development in Jen; an effort can be made to seek similar investments from the EU and the World Bank.

The UN can provide consultants on civil engineering and urban development.

Use your preparation time to work out your game plan - you will soon be meeting with the delegations.

Personal Role Information - Roritanian Team # 1

A professor of International Relations at Roritania University, you specialize in the Roritanian-Autopian conflict from a historical perspective. You've never felt the urge to actively promote change, but having been asked by a childhood friend, now a cabinet member from the Labor party, to take part in these talks, you've reconsidered. Success here could springboard your friend into a position from which he could make you a serious offer, leading to an interesting career change into politics. Labor's program is to steer things back to the negotiating table, despite anything the Roritanian Prime Minister or the Autopean leadership might say or do. While making promises of linking this pullback to any other concessions is categorically forbidden, he's told you there is no reason it can't be informally used as an incentive. After all, if we're talking to them now, we'll be talking to them again before future pullbacks. Labor lags far behind the Roritanian Prime Minister's party in the polls and needs you to achieve an agreement that it can take credit for during a future election.

Personal Role Information - Roritanian Team # 2

You know that other members of the delegation may not be happy with your presence, but you won't let this keep you a passive observer. A resident of the Imar settlement in Autopia, you have been active in the settlement movement for the past decade. You can't believe that the Roritanian Prime Minister, after all his right-wing posturing in the past, is capitulating. The entire East Autopia should be part of Roritania proper. The previous concept of cooperation with the Autopians was all a big mistake, one that cost Roritania dearly. The disengagement from West Autopia two years ago has proved to be a costly mistake: West Autopia has been taken over by the FF and is serving as a launching-pad for rockets into Roritanian cities and towns. You know that the settlers of Dan are willing to be relocated, but fear that this precedent could form the basis for uprooting other settlements, including your own. You understand you cannot prevent the withdrawal, but perhaps you can affect its scope and the nature of the precedent set. You want the government to adopt a scorched-earth policy, leaving no Roritanian-built structures or infrastructure in the settlements evacuated for the Autopians to enjoy.

Personal Role Information - Roritanian Team # 3

You are a civil engineer, living in soon-to-be evacuated Dan. Three years ago, you ended a career of 15 years as a lieutenant colonel in the Army Engineering Corps. You were asked to provide expert input on engineering issues at these talks; you also have strong views on other topics. You believe a continuous Security Wall is vital for Roritania; any gap would require extraordinary alternative measures to prevent infiltrations. Having heard rumors regarding the talks, your neighbors pressed you to make sure they receive adequate compensation for their homes. Of course, these talks seem to have nothing to do with this issue, but you are keeping it in mind. You have mixed feelings on the question of demolishing the city. You spent two years building your own home and know that demolishing it would painful. On the other hand, seeing an Autopian family simply move into it might hurt just as badly. You know that with a concerted effort, all traces of the city could be simply erased from the earth in a few days.

Personal Role Information - Roritanian Team # 4

A former diplomat, you were asked to join the talks as someone who could lend a wider perspective. You think the city of Dan, once evacuated, should be turned over to the Autopians undamaged, as needless destruction would do little to promote reconciliation. While the Security Wall concept is one good idea, other alternatives could be implemented at no security risk in certain areas. Gain your delegation's trust in you by sharing the experience you have gained at previous dialogue attempts, but don't divulge your other purpose at those talks. Your diplomatic position serves as a cover for your position in Roritania's internal intelligence agency. Working undercover, you are on the lookout for secrecy infringements – disclosure of military or government secrets to Autopians by Roritanian delegates to the peace negotiations. When disclosure is done inadvertently, delicately prevent it by steering the subject away. If this doesn't work, you might warn the speaker privately, or report him. Here as negotiator and undercover agent, stress the first, acting naturally and according to your own views – but keep the other in mind. Of course, your identity mustn't be revealed to your team or the Autopians.

Personal Role Information - Roritanian Team # 5

When your son was killed during military service in Autopia, your whole life changed. Working through the pain by sharing with other parents who have undergone similar experiences, you eventually became director of Roritania's Veteran Memorial Organization. In such a small country, personal grief is shared by the whole community; your position gives you a certain degree of influence over politicians and policymakers. You believe that Roritania has made a big mistake by remaining in East Autopia as occupiers. The settlements have locked Roritania into an indefensible position, strategically as well as morally. The sooner they are dismantled, the sooner the RDF can pull out of East Roritania. Saving precious lives, this would also prevent the deterioration of morale and morality among Roritanian soldiers and civilians and return the army to performing its original mission of protecting Roritania's borders. Roritania should simply get up and leave, without any demonstrative demolition or humiliating physical barriers preserving the dispute. Immediate bilateral talks can then lead to security agreements and cooperation far more valuable than walls.

Personal Role Information - Roritanian Team # 6

It seems coincidental that you were requested to join the talks just as you were considering a career-change to public affairs. During your successful business career, you've formed a wide worldview which you think can be implemented on the community and international levels as well. In your experience, commerce goes a long way towards allowing co-existence. People making money together might argue over the size of their piece of the pie, but they rarely kill the goose that lays their golden eggs. The freer access Roritanians and Autopians have to each other's markets - the more joint ventures and partnerships, and the more interdependence created between the two economies - the better. You realize that initially the Roritanian side might seemingly have to give more, as the Autopian economy is currently in shambles, but eventually it would pay off financially as well as by reducing terrorism and violent friction.

Personal Role Information - Roritanian Team # 7

Four years ago, you were offered the position of Project Director for the founding of a Labor Party youth wing. Labor had just lost the elections and the party was in shambles, but someone must have been thinking ahead. You agreed, not so much from any political belief, but rather to pay the rent. Today, with Labor wielding immense parliamentary power as the Roritarian Prime Minister's primary coalition partner, you find yourself, at age 25, running an organization consisting of over 5000 members, young activists who will form the backbone of the next election campaign. Your generation will soon be asked to make historic decisions, and your position may set you at the forefront; you feel you need to know more. You are here mainly to meet the other side, to hear their side of the story, and to discover whether they can be trusted, or at least worked with. You sense that the way these talks go will profoundly affect your political outlook, and due to your influence on the party activists, your impressions may affect how Labor will lean in the future. One thing you know for certain: if Labor can't claim credit for reaching agreement with the Autopians, they don't stand a chance of upsetting the Roritanian Prime Minister in the upcoming elections.

Personal Role Information - Roritanian Team # 8

A respected journalist for Roritania's second largest newspaper, you had to promise you would never write this story unless both parties agreed. Not only could shining a spotlight on the talks end them instantly, but it might also put the participants, particularly those on the Autopian side, in severe danger. You appreciate their willingness to come to the table, risking condemnation by their peers as collaborators. You've covered many rounds of talks in the past, criticizing what each side was doing wrong, and prophesizing the talks' end right on time. But last week, you received a phone call from a Labor source, offering you a chance to *join* these talks and put your money where your mouth is. Although used to observing, your bluff was called, and you hope you can translate this experience into negotiating skills. You can also provide input on use of the media to promote any initiative that may result from these talks. Perhaps there will be a media representative on the Autopian team, and at least you could propose doing some joint work.

Personal Role Information - Autopian Team # 1

You are a retired history teacher in Jen, but your family originally comes from Osher, today a major city in Roritania. Your childhood is filled with your parents' stories about their expulsion from Osher in 1950 and moving between various refugee camps before settling permanently in Jen. You see part of your identity as being a living history of the Autopian experience. You feel that you are responsible not only to the inhabitants of Jen, but to the whole Autopian nation, in Autopia and abroad. Eventually, you hope to see both Autopia and Roritania open to the return of hundreds of thousands of Autopian refugees. You would also like to see your students studying in the modern, air-conditioned classrooms of Dan, and dream of the day when Jen will house a university, the only Autopian university in the area.

Personal Role Information - Autopian Team # 2

You are the childhood friend and trusted confidante of the NP military commander in Jen, as well as his second-in-command, and you were sent to be his eyes and ears at the talks. He has asked you to prevent the FF representative from dominating the talks, and to work towards an orderly handover of power in Jen by the Roritanians to the Governor, whose administration is reliant on the NP movement. You also need control of Dan – whether standing or razed – to prevent the FF from gaining control of the area and moving in thousands of FF supporters and their families. You know that one of the Roritanians' main interests in the latest incursion is the seizing of the FF's arms caches. You are also worried about the FF's weapons and would be happy for them to be extracted from the city to weaken FF. When the FF took over West Autopia, many NP authority figures either escaped to East Autopia or were executed. Careful, though - you don't want to appear to be a collaborator with Roritania.

Personal Role Information -Autopian Team # 3

An attorney by training, you have been the right-hand person to the Governor of Jen's for years. You know that, to keep the Governor in power, you must do whatever you can to bring the current invasion by the RDF to a halt, or at least enable immediate humanitarian relief. The Governor is a long-time NP supporter, and the FF will certainly seek to use its new-found power to remove him as soon as they are able. When the FF took over West Autopia, many NP authority figures either escaped to East Autopia or were executed. The Governor needs the Roritanians to pass control of Jen over to him in an orderly fashion once they withdraw their troops. Similarly, he needs them to hand Dan over to his authority to prevent it from becoming an FF-dominated city. Any way the FF can be weakened along the way is fine by you, so long as it doesn't lead to civil war. Your own family owns several shops in the Roritanian city Fountain, northeast of Jen, selling farm produce from around Jen. If the planned wall cuts off delivery routes to these stores, your family business will crash.

Personal Role Information - Autopian Team #4

You represent one of Jen's wealthiest and most influential families. Your family has formed secret partnerships with several Roritanian factories operating in the Prosperity Industrial Park. Due to your connections, many of your relatives in Jen have been given jobs in these plants. You know that if security arrangements reduce the Industrial Park's profitability, or if access to it is denied to Autopian workers from Jen, you stand to lose a lot of money. You have used a lot of your family's influence in the past to keep the Governor in power, and you won't hesitate to seek a return on the favor by leaning on the personal representative you are sure he has included in the group. If the Governor doesn't choose to structure his priorities correctly, maybe the FF representative will offer you a better deal.

Personal Role Information - Autopian Team #5

Realizing that agreements will eventually be reached in these talks or in others, the FF has decided to take part. Its recent victory in the general elections showed that only the FF truly represent the *real* interests of the Autopian people. After the FF takeover in West Autopia, you feel it is just a matter of time before the FF consolidates its power in East Autopia as well. As a high-ranking FF leader in Jen, you have no intention of staying in a passive observer role at these talks. When the Roritanians leave the region, the FF will be putting pressure on the Governor and the remnants of the NP in the Jen region to accept the new reality, and the better you help this process along, the more your own standing is likely to skyrocket.

Any attacks on Roritanian troops or civilians are not only justified, they serve a holy purpose. The proof of this is that God is forcing the Roritanians to turn tail and leave the Autopian lands in West Autopia and now Dan. You have no mandate - or desire - to offer the Roritanians a cease fire; they only understand violence. On the other hand, you may reach agreement with the NP on how life in Jen will go on once the Roritanians are gone. At the very least, you want the NP's assurance that elections for local government will be held as soon as possible, with external observers; you feel that violence aside, the FF may have a chance of politically ousting the whole corrupt NP administration and bureaucracy.

Personal Role Information - Autopian Team # 6

Despite the fact that you raised your children on moderate religious values of charity, brotherhood, and community, and set a good example for them by being a well-respected leader of the Jen community, impoverished life in the refugee camp made your teenaged son easy prey for the FF recruiters. Promised paradise and financial aid for his family, he died a martyr's death as a suicide bomber at a bus stop in the capital of Roritania, killing 5 soldiers. Although your son's comrades from the FF told you that you should be proud of his martyrdom, and a small aid package was received, your grief overcomes your hatred towards the Roritanians as well as any religious consolation. You also have the rest of your family to consider, and have a bad feeling the Roritanians will demolish your home in retribution for your son's actions unless the invasion into Jen is halted.

Personal Role Information - Autopian Team # 7

A doctor in the Jen Medical Center, a 20-bed clinic in the center of the city, you feel guilty being here while you picture the Roritarian tanks and bulldozers moving into Jen. You were in the thick of it last time and you still can't erase the nightmarish memories of dozens of wounded patients in your clinic. Even after the Roritanians withdrew, the destroyed sewer system, the lack of water, food, and medicine, and the denial of access to Roritanian hospitals just 20 minutes away kept you busy for months. As the city's infrastructure has not properly been repaired since then, this time might be even worse. The clinic's director told you before you left: "Forget the fighting, the land, the history. Your job is to keep people alive." You can't help but fantasize about directing a medical center in the modern Dan medical clinic.

Personal Role Information - Autopian Team # 8

Director of the local Jen radio station, you are sure the Roritanians have already taken over your broadcasting offices. You've never let Roritanian sensitivities concern you when speaking your mind and spreading the truth. Acting in concert with local radio initiatives all over East Autopia, your station gives ordinary citizens a chance to tell their own personal stories. Most focus on their treatment by the Roritanian Army, while some discuss issues of national pride. As a public service, you also provide reports on movements of Roritanian Army units, traffic conditions at army checkpoints, and warnings of helicopter gunship sightings. You feel you are contributing to the Autopians' national identity. Your station stresses the common factors and the shared characteristics among stories from different locales. Your main concern at these talks is to stress the need to always keep the common Autopian issues at the forefront, as opposed to focusing on Jen alone. It has taken a long time for solidarity to form, and infighting would be the worst thing that could happen to the Autopian cause now.

Personal Role Information - UN Team # 1

You have been working on the Cyprus issue for the past couple of years, observing and reporting on the different aspects of the peace efforts. Although you were in contact with all the higher-ups on both sides, it was always in a junior role. This assignment seems to be an opportunity to have a real effect on important decisions. You never expected to be in the role of international mediator, but you sure are glad you took Conflict Resolution 101 in college. You'll be watching the parties closely during the opening phases of negotiation, trying to figure out a process that would help them discuss things productively.

Personal Role Information - UN Team #2

After completing your graduate degree in International Relations, you've been working with the United Nations for the past seven years, mainly as a junior staffer on low-level negotiation groups on international trade issues. One thing you've witnessed is the power of joint economic gains to pave the road to agreement even between the bitterest of enemies.

This assignment might be your chance to break out of the pack and stand out, perhaps earning yourself a permanent post on the UN's Eleusian team. You are optimistic about the positive role the UN can play in ongoing conflicts in the Eleusian region, and the Roritanian-Autopian conflict is probably the best place to start. It's time those conflict resolution courses you took in college start paying off for you. You'll be watching the parties closely during the opening phases of negotiation, trying to figure out what their real interests are.

Personal Role Information - UN Team # 3

As an experienced CIA field agent, you worked your way into the UN administration long ago and have been working undercover at different posts around the Eleusian Region since you finished your training at Langley 8 years ago. None of your colleagues to the UN mission in Cyprus know of your CIA role; they consider you one of them. You've accompanied several peacemaking rounds in the Eleusian Region and have seen how fragile diplomacy is. You've spent the past 3 years here on Cyprus, assisting the Secretary-General's peace initiative while at the same time reporting home to Washington and keeping an eye out for U.S. interests.

You feel there isn't much about the Roritanian-Autopian conflict you don't know, and if asked to mediate, you could actually put your knowledge of the situation to good use; both to help the parties out and to keep an eye out for issues in which the U.S. might have an interest.

Personal Role Information - UN Team # 4

A career aid administrator, for nearly ten years, you have served in various capacities at UN missions across the Eleusian Region, and now Cyprus. You had hoped your next position would take you back to UN Headquarters, preparing you to assume a senior mission role. You were surprised by the orders attaching you to the Roritanian-Autopian project staff. Your boss impressed upon you the importance of your team's mission – if these negotiations are fruitful, they could jump-start the whole peace process. The fact that success here could save thousands of lives excites you, and you feel a heavy burden of responsibility. His promise to help you get posted back to New York if these talks are fruitful is also a powerful incentive. You will put every ounce of energy you've got into this and feel that, if need be, you can help the parties reach agreement by sheer persistence and will. You decide not to be put off by any amount of stonewalling or walkouts – you're going to keep coming up with fresh, inventive ideas to solve the issues the parties raise.

Situations

Following are several messages to the teams, describing unexpected situations that could affect the negotiations. Instructors should introduce a situation to disrupt the talks, using discretion as to if and when would be an appropriate moment in the negotiations to do so.

Situation: Targeted Assassination
(Hand this announcement to members of the Roritanian team)

Message from the Roritanian Coordinator
A targeted killing of a Autopian terrorist leader took place this morning in Jen. Helicopters were able to target an extremist religious leader, whose speeches called on terrorist groups to kill every living Roritanians, and whose religious center – the largest and most influential in Jen – served to shield terrorist cells.

Situation: Targeted Assassination
(Hand this announcement to members of the Autopian team)

Message from the Autopian Coordinator
A religious leader and orator in Jen's largest religious center, has been killed in a rocket attack launched on his car by Roritanian helicopters while he was on his way to prayers. His wife and two sons, accompanying him in the vehicle, were seriously injured.

You cannot continue, under these circumstances, to negotiate with the Roritanians. Get up, make a scene, let them know how you feel and leave the negotiation room for at least 15 minutes.

Since holding these talks is critical, you may return to the room no later than 30 minutes from now, but only after the UN neutrals intervene and request you to reconsider your walkout.

Situation: Targeted Assassination
(Hand this announcement to members of the UN team)

Message from the UN Chief of Mission:
Roritania has targeted and killed a prominent religious figure in Jen known for encouraging and shielding militant activities. His family was also injured.

This may be your chance to intervene; perhaps you should be leading this dialogue from now on. Prepare to do so.

Situation: Ambulances
(Hand this announcement to members of the Roritanian team)

Message from the Roritanian Coordinator
Autopian and Red Cross sources report at least 20 critically wounded in Jen, far beyond the treatment capacity of the local medical center. In order to avoid unnecessary fatalities, and avoid adverse media attention, you are authorized to suggest they be treated at an Roritanian hospital in Afulu, 15 minutes away. Keep the following interests in mind:

In the past, such gestures have been used to smuggle terrorists and bombs into Roritania. Attaining the names of the Autopian wounded can help intelligence efforts – as the army would be able to determine if it has neutralized people on its list.

Treatment of these wounds is a very expensive matter.

Situation: Ambulances
(Hand this announcement to members of the Autopian team)

Message from the Autopian Coordinator
Autopian and Red Cross sources report at least 20 critically wounded in Jen, far beyond the treatment capacity of the local medical center. You must arrange for their evacuation to a Roritanian hospital in Afulu, 15 minutes away.

This treatment is a minimal duty of the offensive army. There should be no unnecessary delays, ambulance searches etc., as every minute could mean life and death.

Situation: Hostage Soldier
(Hand this announcement to members of all teams)

An RDF soldier has been kidnapped while patrolling on the outskirts of Jen and is being held somewhere in the city by a splinter cell affiliated with the FF. The group is demanding release of all the Autopian prisoners held in Roritanian jails in return for his safe release.

A spokesman for the Roritanian government has rejected the demand, warning that if the soldier is not immediately released, the Jen incursion will continue with unprecedented intensity. 'We will ensure the welfare of our kidnapped soldier,' he said, 'even if we have to dismantle every house in Jen to find him.'

Situation: Trapped Child
(Hand this announcement to members of the Roritanian team)

Message from Roritanian Coordinator
Autopian and Red Cross sources report a 3-year-old girl trapped under the ruins of a home destroyed by the RDF. These reports have also been picked up by the world media. The RDF chief of staff ordered a cessation of military operations in that sector of the city and has sent engineers and heavy equipment in rescue the child.

As the rescue team moved in, they came under heavy fire from terrorists in the buildings on either side, suffering several casualties. Broadcasting the team's mission in the Autopian language on megaphones has not helped. Trapped in a courtyard halfway to the target, the team didn't try to break out as this would involve extremely heavy damage to the residential neighborhood. For similar reasons, and out of concern that the engineering equipment might be damaged and decrease the possibility of a successful rescue, the RDF has not yet sent in a relief force, instead broadcasting an ultimatum insisting that the terrorists cease fire within an hour. Nobody is sure the girl has that much time.

You have half an hour, at most, to find an agreed solution.

Situation: Trapped Child
(Hand this announcement to members of the Autopian team)

Message from Autopian Coordinator

The Roritaians have mowed down an apartment building with their huge bulldozers, burying a 3 years old girl under the rubble. Her mother insists she's still alive, and her pleas for help are being broadcast all over the world.

The Roritanians moved another bulldozing unit into the city, which was immediately attacked by FF fighters. Trapped in a courtyard and surrounded, the Roritanians suddenly claimed they had come to save the child. Not trusting a word the Roritanians say, the FF believed this was a ploy, and that once permitted to pass the equipment would be used to further destroy the city. Caught up in the heat of a successful battle, the fighters have surrounded the Roritanian group and are now wiring explosives round the entire courtyard, scoffing at a Roritanian ultimatum to disperse within one hour. The Governor of Jen has put his foot down, forbidding an attack on the Roritanians so as not to have the child's blood on his hands. The FF has agreed to wait for an hour for the Roritanian ultimatum to pass and let the Governor figure this one out. Afterwards, they've let it be known, they would attack the Roritanian force and wipe it out. Nobody is sure the girl has that much time.

If you can work out an agreement that saves the girl, protects the city, and doesn't cause the FF to lose face, the Governor will be able to persuade them to let him implement it.

You have half an hour, at most, to find an agreed solution.

Situation: Trapped Child
(Hand this announcement to members of the UN team)

Message from the UN Chief of Mission
A critical situation has erupted in Jen. A little girl is buried alive under a bulldozed building. Roritania claims it sent a rescue team of engineers, but it was attacked by militants and is unable to advance. The FF, whose militants have surrounded the Roritanian team, claims it is just another force sent to destroy buildings and they intend to destroy it.

You feel this may be a make-or-break event for these talks; they might not survive the death of the child and a potential hostage situation. Each team has given the other a one-hour ultimatum.

Nobody is sure the girl has that much time.

You have half an hour, at most, to help the teams reach an agreed solution.

Setbacks & Incentives

(Either pass these announcements out as updates from the teams' coordinators, or announce them as if they were radio broadcasts)

Setbacks:
A 15-year-old suicide bomber from a village near Jen blew himself up inside a crowded Roritanian mall. 13 Roritanian civilians were killed. Security forces think the bomber infiltrated into Roritania in the area of Fountain.

Delayed at an RDF checkpoint on her way to a hospital in Roritania, a pregnant Autopian woman went into premature labor, and the baby was stillborn.

In the northeast of Jen, a stray rocket fired by a Roritanian helicopter set hundreds of acres of farmland on fire, destroying this year's crops as well as hundreds of olive trees.

A former East Autopian NP leader sentenced by Roritania to life imprisonment, has been killed in prison. Roritanian sources say he was killed by a prisoner identified with the FF.

Incentives:
An EU consortium is willing to invest $10,000,000 to develop a joint Autopian-Roritanian industrial park, providing the park itself is located on the Autopian side of the Ceasefire Border Line.

The UN has announced its willingness to deploy troops as observers or peacekeepers in the implementation stage of any Roritanian-Autopian agreement.

Ford Company has announced its intentions to open a production line in the Eleusian Region. Although Ford is also considering building the factory in neighbouring countries, the company announced that, in keeping with Ford's policy of promoting peace and prosperity worldwide, it would build the factory in a stable area in East Autopia – if one were to be found.

Little Golano[*]

General Information

99 years ago, the bloody War of 1910 between the U.S. and Mexico ended with the two countries signing a treaty including a cessation of hostilities and delineating the border between the two countries in the San Golano River area. According to the treaty, Mexico kept all areas south of the San Golano River, and the U.S. retained all lands north of the river (control of the river itself was not discussed in the treaty). The exception to this rule was an area south of the river, of about 100 square kilometers, known as "Little Golano." Both sides had laid claim to Little Golano before the war, and recurrent clashes between Mexican villagers and American ranch owners and prospectors had served as one of the war's major triggers. This disputed territory, it was decided, would remain under U.S. control for 100 years, after which time it would revert to Mexico.

Since then, the U.S. has developed Little Golano in various ways. A huge biotechnological industrial park was constructed, and the town of Golan Falls was built along both riverbanks. Further down the river, the natural mating grounds of the Tuli Turtle at Yifi Point were declared a nature preserve, and many ecotourism projects including lodges and expedition operators have developed between Yifi Point and Golan Falls.

Six months from now, the handover date set down in the treaty will arrive. Despite requests through diplomatic channels from the Mexican government over the past decade, several U.S. administrations have refrained from taking a clear stance on the issue of the Little Golano region. So far, no federal agency has been set up to deal with the issue. State Department spokespeople have been vague on the issue and have recently replied to journalists' questions with phrases such as "if this should come about" or "the proposed handover."

Increasingly, news channels are airing in-depth features on Little Golano. Schoolchildren in Mexican villages near Little Golano are shown preparing banners and decorations for the handover celebrations, and their parents speak longingly about returning to their ancestral homes. Reruns are shown of the Mexican President's recent election campaign speeches, in which he focused on the handover as an issue of national pride and promised to make sure the U.S. respected its commitment.

On the U.S. side, protests are shown taking place in front of the White House calling for the U.S. to remain in Little Golano. Many of the protestors belong to environmental groups, concerned that the ex-

---

[*] Noam Ebner & Yael Efron, *Little Golano: An International Conflict Management Simulation* (2011). This role-play was awarded first prize at the 2009 E-PARCC Competition for Collaborative Governance at Syracuse University. Available at: https://www.maxwell.syr.edu/research/article/little-golano
Its adaptation to the public international law classes at ZAC was created by Munin and Efron.

tensive conservation efforts conducted in Little Golano will be swept aside by a wave of Mexican farmers pouring into the area and cultivating it. Also protesting the pullout is an umbrella organization called "U.S. First," which was set up to oppose the pullout by coordinating the activities of many right-wing, conservative, and patriotism-oriented organizations. Both movements enjoy public support in the U.S.

Tension is steadily rising between the two nations, and the cooperation that characterized U.S-Mexican relations throughout the 1980s and 1990s is deteriorating. Tourists from the U.S. are encountering harassment and a general "go home" sentiment in Mexican cities. In the U.S., anti-Hispanic hate crime is on the rise. Heated exchanges between Mexico and the U.S. in the United Nations have become a day-to-day event, and both countries anxiously upped their military training, fearing an outburst of hatred as the date for the handing over of Little Golano, stated in treaty, approaches.

Under pressure from the UN Secretary-General, both countries have agreed to send senior-level negotiators to bilateral talks in Geneva, Switzerland.

Instructions for the U.S. Negotiating Team

You are the United States Undersecretary for International Affairs. Along with your two colleagues, your job is to engage the Mexican negotiating team in such a way as to serve the U.S.'s best interests. The following is a summary of a briefing session held in Washington, D.C.

General

Little Golano was never, until recently, an important issue on the political agenda. The war on terror, U.S. troops on Middle Eastern grounds, and the economy have tended to sideline everything else. While official U.S policymakers never rejected the treaty, facts on the ground have made it increasingly difficult to even imagine literal compliance with it. An estimated 30,000 American citizens live in the disputed region, have set down roots, and established livelihoods. The town of Golan Falls, built along both sides of the San Golano River, is a strongly unified community. The townspeople are working the media, appealing to the President and the rest of the nation not to abandon them. The President, well aware of his ratings in the polls, shudders at the thought of evacuating U.S citizens from the area and of victorious Mexican peasants burning U.S flags in the town hall.

Political and Diplomatic Considerations

If these negotiations do not seem to lead in a direction that serves U.S. interests, you would be willing to refuse to comply voluntarily with the treaty and submit the issue to the International Court of Justice. While not sure if you'd win, you estimate it would take the ICJ at least five years to decide the issue. This would have the effect creating the perception that you are not giving up without a fight. You know the Mexicans might not be able to afford that delay – much as they would like to get a chance to rake the U.S over the coals at the ICJ.

On the other hand, working out a negotiated solution serving American interests and not seen as capitulation to Mexican pressure would be a diplomatic achievement that could strengthen the President's position, promote the U.S.'s public image, and contribute to keeping your party in power in the upcoming election.

Security Issues

While choosing the makeup of the negotiating team, the President decided not to include a representative from the Department of Defense, not wanting the Mexicans to perceive that he was looking towards an escalation. However, the team includes a representative from the Department of Homeland Security, and security issues were detailed in the briefing you all received.

The administration views the ever-rising wave of illegal immigration from Mexico as a first-class security concern. In all U.S-Mexico border states, unemployment and crime are on the rise, and more and more resources need to be expended just to keep the streets safe and local government functioning. In addition, the immigrant-smuggling channels are being used to smuggle drugs and weapons into the U.S. It is only a matter of time before terrorists use these channels to enter the country.

Little Golano serves as a buffer zone in a very vulnerable region. The San Golano River is at its lowest here and is easily fordable. Without U.S presence on both sides of the river, you fear the area might become an open backdoor into the U.S. You fear Mexico might try to divert part of the river's water southwards for agricultural use, lowering the water level even more and making it easier to cross.

Ordinarily, the U.S would not be concerned at all by the threat of military action by Mexico to seize the region by force. However, the U.S military is nearly over-tasked as it is, and it would certainly be spread thin if it became necessary to dedicate considerable resources to a new front with Mexico. Additionally, open hostilities might lead Mexico to turn a blind eye to terrorists taking advantage of the opportunity to enter the U.S. Keep the Mexican delegation away from considering this option.

Economic Aspects

The Little Golano Biotechnological Industrial Park (BIP) is situated on the south bank of the river. The park is powered by electricity produced from the river itself at the adjacent power plant, which also provides power for the entire town. The river also supplies many of the elements necessary for the different experiments and production processes carried out in the BIP. If the U.S government were to compensate the BIP's owners for the loss of the park, or for the cost of resituating it elsewhere, it would cost between one and two billion dollars. The BIP employs over 4,000 workers and shutting down would have huge repercussions.

The BIP's main purpose, however, remains a secret known only to the park's owners and the top levels of the U.S government. The San Golano River is home to a unique underwater weed, not found anywhere else on the planet. While much research remains to be done, and at least several years remain before drugs derived from the weed can be approved and marketed, scientists believe that a serum derived from this weed enables the human body to successfully defend itself against viruses from Influenza to HIV, and ultimately ensure the survival of mankind. The prestige and financial reward for developing this serum are incalculable. The Pentagon views this serum as the ultimate answer to the threat posed by bioterrorists equipped with vials of smallpox or SARS; enabling its production is seen as a major security concern.

Environmental groups, worried about the Mexicans polluting the San Golano River, are exerting heavy political pressure on the President. The BIP's owners and the Pentagon, concerned that river pollution harms the weed or alters its properties, are also exerting similar pressure.

About 100,000 tourists from the U.S and abroad visit the region's natural parks and ecotourism projects, generating an estimated 50 million dollars in annual revenue and supporting over a thousand jobs.

While nobody thinks that this situation can be defused simply by buying the Mexicans off, the President has authorized you to use up to 3 billion dollars, for whatever purposes you deem necessary, in order to achieve a good outcome.

Take time to prepare yourselves, individually and as a team. When you feel ready, go to the conference room to meet with your Mexican counterparts.

Good luck!!!

Instructions for the Mexican Negotiating Team

You are the Mexican Assistant Minister for International Affairs. Along with your two colleagues, your job is to engage the U.S. negotiating team in such a way as to serve Mexico's best interests. The following is a summary of a briefing session held in Mexico City before your departure for Geneva.

General:

This is a crucial moment in Mexican history. One hundred years ago, Mexico forced the U.S. to admit that the Little Golano region was truly Mexican, but in order to spare bloodshed on both sides, Mexico had agreed to wait a century before regaining control of the area. You now fear that this moment of historic justice might be denied due to U.S. greed; you fear your government may have been too naïve in simply believing the U.S. would respect its treaty agreements.

Political and Diplomatic Issues

The Mexican President has promised the nation, time and again, that their patience would pay off, and that the Mexican flag would soon wave in Little Golano once more. In fact, this appeal to national pride enabled his rise to power in the last election.

If the Americans refuse to withdraw, Mexico could always appeal to the International Court of Justice. However, such a procedure could take years to reach a conclusion. The Mexican people expect to see results, and soon. Developers are already planning villages for construction in the area, and Mexican courts have been swamped with litigation concerning rights to plots of land in the area filed by descendants of the villagers and farmers forced off their land a hundred years ago.

Any agreement reached with the U.S. negotiating team must take into account the honor and the needs of the Mexican people, and under no circumstances can it seem as if Mexico is backing down. If any concessions need to be made, it must be done in return for valuable concessions from the Americans.

Mexico had been demanding that the U.S. formally hand over the Little Golano region to Mexico, evacuate all its citizens from the area, and desist from any military operations on the south side of the river. The U.S. has so far avoided stating a clear position on the issue, giving rise to a sense of distrust on your side. Mexico has been enjoying much support in the United Nations over this issue and feels that should it stand strong against the U.S., the world would support it.

Economic Issues

The U.S. has invested billions of dollars in infrastructure in the region. The value of the homes, the roads, the community buildings, and the industrial park is immense. If the U.S. could be persuaded to pack up and leave everything as it is, this would be a perfect outcome from your point of view. Although you could suggest compensating it for the infrastructure or the added value of the development, Mexico's economy is on the brink of collapse; this U.S. pullout is supposed to help it, not push it over the edge.

If possible, you should try and achieve a handover of the Biotechnological Industrial Park (BIP). You can consider offering some degree of joint operation of the park, cashing in on the Americans' experience and expertise; however, you could always bring in outside experts to manage the Park; Japanese conglomerates have already approached you on this issue. One major benefit of the BIP's continued operation is that it can create over 3,000 jobs. Unemployment in that area of northern Mexico is estimated at about 20%; this could be an enormous help in that regard. You estimate that about one third of the jobs are positions for scientists and other highly trained specialists, but that the rest might be handled by less qualified employees.

Recently, Mexican scientists have discovered a special nutrient, derived from the shell of the Tuli Turtle's eggs, which has the potential to make agricultural crops flourish despite a shortage of water. The Tuli has been declared an endangered species by U.S. conservation groups, and its nesting grounds in the Little Golano region were declared a nature preserve. The nutrient's discovery has been kept secret so far, to prevent the greedy Americans from capitalizing on it and withholding it from Mexico. If some of the waters from the San Golano River would be diverted south into the agricultural areas, the combined effect of the nutrient and the new water system might just pull the entire population of the country above the poverty line.

Two years of drought in a row have cost Mexico nearly four billion dollars, and two outbreaks of avian flu took another two billion dollars. The country is on the verge of economic recession; the Little Golano handover might not only help Mexicans hold their heads up high but might also put money in their pockets.

Security Issues

Stepping up your military training in the areas close to the U.S. border was mainly a show for internal consumption. Not only could Mexico never hope to win even a limited war against the U.S., it could also not afford the total breaking off of relations this would entail with its main trading partner. However, in today's reality where the U.S. Army is spread across the globe, having to hold troops in reserve for a U.S.-Mexico flare up would put a strain on the U.S. military and economy. This might be a good pressure point to lean on.

You know that one of the U.S.'s major concerns is illegal immigration from Mexico. You have mixed interests on this issue. On the one hand, Mexican laborers who find work in the U.S. send money back home to their families, bringing more dollars into the country. On the other hand, it encourages corruption and lawlessness on the Mexican side of the border and does not enhance the country's image. If the Americans cooperate, you can offer them increased cooperation in preventing illegal immigration; if they don't, you can always threaten to stop patrolling your side of the border altogether.

You share one common enemy in the border region: drug smugglers. Mexico is trying to dispel its reputation as an easy conduit for drugs from South America to the U.S. The government's fight against the drug trade is a battle for survival between Mexican democracy and the drug syndicates constantly trying to set up powerbases in Mexico. This common interest might be a good one to raise when looking for ways to cooperate with the U.S.

Take time to prepare yourselves, individually and as a team. When you feel ready, go to the conference room to meet with your U.S. counterparts.

Good Luck!!!

Flashpoint Syria[*]

Simulation Overview

FlashPoint is a simulation game constructed as a teaching tool for the topics of conflict analysis and resolution, collaboration, negotiation, mediation, and public international law. It is set in a scenario that is primarily fictitious – but still blends in and incorporates real events, history, and detail, forming a 'pseudo-reality': a situation familiar enough to spark interest, motivation, and identification, yet controlled and delineated to allow for maximum learning and skill-building.[1] Set, as it is, in a scenario right out of today's headlines, it offers students the sense of applying their analysis and skills to real-world problems.

At its core, the simulation's framework is familiar: two disputing parties and a neutral third-party intervener, all possessing both shared and private information. Parties must choose whether to fall into familiar patterns of competition and coercion or endeavor to construct a collaborative process and achieve cooperative outcomes with their perceived adversaries.

Certain elements in the simulation's setup dictate that careful attention be paid to the early stages of the simulation's initiation (e.g., role-division and participant preparation). The introduction of trainer-initiated changes and interventions in the scenario necessitates special attention to the simulation's management. To this end, detailed simulation setup and management instructions have been provided. Additionally, the Teachers' Manual in Part 2 of this book provides an extensive Debriefing Guide, to address the wide variety of training-goals this simulation can achieve.

Designed for dedicated and committed participants, FlashPoint engrosses participants in the simulated environment for a long period of time, ranging from one to three days, or from about six to sixteen hours. These can be conducted in a continuous, intensive manner or in multiple sessions over several lessons. This investment engenders two major learning outcomes:

- In-depth understanding of the complexities of managing international conflict
- Advanced skill-building in conflict resolution, negotiation, and mediation skills

---

[*] Noam Ebner, Yael Efron & Nellie Munin, *Flashpoint: Syria, 2014—An International Conflict Management Simulation* (2014). Available at: http://dx.doi.org/10.2139/ssrn.2476968.
This role-play was developed originally by Munin and Efron, and after further adaptation by Ebner the role-play was submitted to the 2014 E-Parcc Competition for Collaborative Governance at Syracuse University, where it was awarded first prize.

[1] For more on this method, see Noam Ebner & Yael Efron, *Using Tomorrow's Headlines for Today's Training: Creating Pseudo-Reality in Conflict Resolution Simulation-Games*, 21(3) Negotiation Journal 377 (2005). Available at: http://ssrn.com/abstract=1292594

While it can be employed with participants at an introductory level, the simulation is particularly suited for participants with some background in conflict resolution, international relations, or public international law. It can incorporate students from more than one course (i.e., law students negotiating and mediation students serving as mediators). It has been used successfully with participants at both the graduate and undergraduate levels, as well as with groups whose participants hail from very diverse backgrounds.

The background scenario depicts a fictional dispute between Turkey and Syria, over a developing humanitarian crisis occurring in a piece of land claimed by both countries. Underlying this presenting issue is a broad range of international, national, and local interests, which must be resolved for a peaceful solution to be reached. However, power imbalances, as well as time pressure, present major obstacles to resolution. A team of UN mediators convenes negotiating teams from each country in an attempt to reach a negotiated settlement.

The simulation is designed for maximum versatility. The storyline can be updated easily and regularly to allow for any changes in regional or global political reality. 'Hot' issues – such as escalation in different areas in the Middle East or in the real-world internal politics of Turkey or Syria – can be spotlighted in order to allow the reality of the relations between the two countries, and the sentiments of their populations, to permeate the simulation. The roles of the UN mediators can be stressed in mediation skill-building training or dropped altogether in order to allow participants to flex their unassisted negotiation skills. New roles can easily be developed (or the provided roles adapted) to allow for participants' real-life preferences and experiences.

Logistics, Setup and Game Management Instructions

Number of Roles: 8-20 (up to 8 Turkish roles, 8 Syrian roles, and 4 UN mediator roles)

Optimal group size is 8-9 participants, with 3 players each on the Turkish and Syrian teams and 2-3 UN mediators. This allows for maximum individual participation and group management. However, suggestions are provided for incorporating up to 20 players in the simulation (see Game Variations). In still larger groups, several simulation groups can work concurrently, with the trainer either rotating between them or employing training assistants.

> **Setup and Preparation Time**: 1-2 hours (see section on Game Variations).
> **Running Time**: 6-16 hours (see section on Game Variations).
> **Level**: Intermediate to advanced.

Debriefing Time

At least one hour of debrief is recommended for every four hours of simulation running time. In addition to a post-game debriefing session, trainers might choose to conduct impromptu or pre-planned debriefing sessions during the game's running time (see further instructions below and in the Teacher's Manual (Part 2 of this book).

Background Preparation

When this simulation is used with groups with little knowledge of Syrian-Turkish relations, conflict in the Middle East, or international law, trainers might choose to assign reading material before handing out the simulation information packs, or to provide participants with time to conduct independent background research in the library or on the Internet. However, the simulation can be conducted on the basis of the material provided alone.

Role Assignment
a) Divide participants into three teams: Turkey, Syria, and the UN.

b) Hand out the following material:

To each member of the Turkish team:
Public Information
Private Information for the Representatives of the Turkish Government
A copy of the map (optional).

To each member of the UN team:
Public Information
Private Instructions for the UN Team
A copy of the map (optional).

To each member of the Syrian team:
Public Information
Private Information for the Representatives of the Syrian Government
A copy of the map (optional).

c) Assign each team member on the Turkish and Syrian teams a specific title, indicating their area of responsibility. To clarify: Each member of the team gets the same information. However, each is designated an undersecretary/assistant minister representing a particular department/ministry, which leads participants to prepare themselves, individually, to represent the interests pertinent to their office. This leads to better preparation and sets the stage for interesting intra-team dynamics, as team members see themselves as representing or safeguarding particular interests.

On the Turkish side, designate participants as assistant ministers of Health, Defense, and Justice. On the Syrian side, designate participants as assistant ministers of Foreign Affairs, Justice, and Defense. Have them note their title at the top of their private team instructions.

Participant Instructions
Instruct participants to read their information carefully, and to try and flesh out their instructions with their own knowledge, emotions, and experience. Explain that by "owning" the role in this manner, the simulation will not only become more lifelike but will also enable them to understand what parties to conflict truly experience, resulting insights will, therefore, be highly transferable to real-life situations.

Role Preparation
Once roles have been assigned, allow students at least one hour for reading and individual preparation. You might even consider giving the material out the evening before the simulation begins.

If students prepare their roles immediately before gametime, ask all members of each team to stay in the same room during the individual preparation period. This will avoid participants getting 'lost' during this extended period and will also encourage a natural transition to the group discussion period. If you have given the material out earlier, you might consider suggesting they add some individual research to flesh out their assigned role.

According to the scenario information, participants meet with their own team before meeting the other. Announce that once the individual preparation period is up, each team will meet as a group for 45 minutes or an hour before meeting the other group. This time is to be used for the team to get to know each other 'in-role,' discuss issues, interests, and priorities, divide labor, etc. The UN team will use this time to discuss their intervention strategy, to decide on their opening welcome to the parties, and to arrange the meeting room. This time will serve as a transition period during which participants will try on and try out their new roles and get used to addressing each other in-role as colleagues. If the simulation is being conducted in the framework of a study program involving negotiation and/or mediation, this might be a good opportunity to prime participants to keep the models learned in class in mind as they prepare for the upcoming process.

Room Setup

Assign the task of setting up the room and organizing seating arrangements to the UN team. Preferably, the room should have a whiteboard and/or a flipchart and comfortable seating (remember the duration of the simulation!).

The group may periodically opt to break out of the meeting for consultations. Try to have a couple of rooms available adjacent to the primary meeting room for this purpose.

3rd Party Intervention

You might choose to give the UN team particular instructions on how they should act, process-wise. You might ask them to be relatively passive observers at the beginning, taking a more active role when this is requested by the parties or dictated by circumstances. Alternatively, you might instruct them to conduct a controlled, semi-formal process – depending on your class framework and training goals. The participants in the UN roles might be a bit uncertain regarding their authority and timing at first (although your initial guidance should help them with this). This is part of the process: they are expected to identify situations and process-points suitable for their intervention and earn the parties' trust and acceptance through their words and behavior, rather than these being dictated by instructions. You might choose to stress this to them during the team preparation time. Of course, the UN role can be written to be more intervening or directive (in order to make the 3rd party role clearer), can be written out altogether (in order to stress unassisted negotiation skills in a two-party process), or can be limited to providing good offices. In general, the degree to which you choose to prime the UN team should depend on their experience and skill level in third-party intervention.

Gametime

Once the time for team preparation is up, the simulation opens with a joint session. If one party takes more time to discuss things among its members, they need to be aware that the other party is already waiting for them in the meeting room, and that there will be a 'process-price' to pay. Parties arrive and are seated, and spend some time on formalities (introductions etc.), although some groups might quickly jump to conflict on procedural issues (e.g., 'How come they have one representative more than we do?' or 'Are these talks going to be confidential?') or make early demands (e.g., 'If Syria does not immediately welcome our inspectors, we will not sit at the same table with their team!'). After some time has passed, parties will usually (but not always) reach a point where they intuitively try and set a general agenda for the talks, or perhaps even plunge into an in-depth negotiation on one of the issues.

FlashPoint is designed to be conducted entirely by participants, requiring no trainer intervention. This frees teachers up to take notes and prepare for debrief. Teachers wishing to consider a more active role in affecting the ebb and flow of the game can see suggestions for doing so in the Game Variations section, below. However, even teachers choosing to stay on the sidelines, for the most part, would do well to consider intervening at the following two points, to make sure that primary learning objectives are achieved:

One hour before the end of the first half of the time allocated for the simulation, if parties have not yet set an agenda for the substantive discussions (e.g., they have been bogged down for an hour over the question of who should speak first, suffered a walkout by one party, etc.) the trainer should announce that the Syrian and the Turkish Ministers of Foreign Affairs, who are following the talks closely, have requested that by 'halftime' the parties will have reached an agreed-upon agenda for the remainder of the negotiations. This will focus participants on what they came here to do, nudging them gently (albeit a bit artificially) away from the play-acting the first few game hours allow for and encouraging them towards applying of conflict resolution skills in what may have become a decidedly non-conducive atmosphere. You might even set a time by which they must submit a written agenda.

One hour before the end of the time allocated for the simulation, the trainer might announce that the coordinators for all parties have requested that the participants write up any agreements they have reached. Participants might ignore this at first, especially if no or little agreement has been achieved. The trainer should repeat this instruction 15 minutes later, stressing that 'agreements' can relate not only to sealed issues but also to an agreed-upon agenda for future talks, a joint declaration, or any other joint statements or agreed principles, including procedural agreements regarding these or future negotiations. The purpose of this intervention is to try to allow for students to have some sense of achievement, albeit minor, when the simulation is brought to a close. This has a positive effect on debrief, encouraging participants to engage without losing the valuable effect of the in-process frustration of slow or no progress. If any significant agreements have been reached (even if only a partial agreement) highlight this milestone by conducting a brief signing ceremony.

When the allotted time is up, help parties break out of character, take a deep breath, and move on to debrief (See further instructions below and the Teacher's Manual (Part 2 of this book). Beyond debrief sessions, consider using forms for participant self-reflection (before, during, and after the simulation) as well as for receiving participant feedback on the simulation or the workshop. Sample forms for these purposes are provided in the Teacher's Manual (Part 2).

Use of Props

Imaginative trainers will find many ways to develop and employ props during this simulation. Here are a few possibilities:

Provide nametags for participants, each with a Syrian, Turkish, or UN flag on it.

Provide place cards for each participant (these can also be in the national colors). Players will often color or decorate them, or perhaps create a game name for themselves suitable to their personal role.

Consider providing a transparency of the map included in the scenario for participants to project on a whiteboard and draw on.

Consider providing, pictures, relevant clippings from current newspapers, etc.

General Information
February, 2014.
With the entire world focusing on the internal conflict in Syria, a much larger conflagration is currently building up between Syria and its neighbor to the north – Turkey.

For the past three years, Syria has been engulfed in internal strife. Fierce battles have been fought all across the country between forces loyal to the Syrian government and various opposition groups. The struggle has taken a heavy toll in human life. According to the UN, over 100,000 people have been killed in Syria thus far – half of them estimated to be civilians caught in the shifting lines of fire.

The international community has expressed its dissatisfaction with the situation in Syria, focusing particularly on censuring the government's acts. The United Nations condemned the Syrian government's acts in using force against opposition protestors in the initial stages of the conflict, but as armed conflict broke out, Security Council resolutions calling for sanctions against Syria were vetoed by China and Russia. The UN and other international bodies have called for a ceasefire and for democratic elections to be held, but the Syrian government has ignored these calls. The government has repeatedly stated its position that the international community had no right to meddle in Syria's internal affairs and has protested the West's undermining of its legitimacy and infringement on Syria's sovereignty.

In 2013, tension between Syria and the international community peaked as fears that the Syrian government was using chemical weapons rose. The United States called off an offensive against the Syrian government at the very last minute when Syria declared it would turn its stockpile of chemical weapons over to international observers for extrication from the country and neutralizing. This disarmament has been successfully completed; the UN has announced that, to the best of its knowledge, there are no more chemical weapons in Syria, and the team of chemical disarmament experts has finished its work and departed the country. With the chemical weapons issue out of the way, the international community has focused less on intervening in the day-to-day fighting, focusing its efforts instead on bringing the parties together for peace talks.

Since the beginning of the conflict, Syria has closed its borders completely. However, opposition forces have taken over several border crossings, allowing weapons to funnel in – and refugees, fleeing the combat zones, to funnel out. Most of these refugees found their way to camps in Turkey. Turkey has given refuge to hundreds of thousands of Syrian citizens and has expressed its dissatisfaction with the Syrian government. The Syrian government, on the other hand, has accused Turkey of supplying weapons to opposition forces, and of repeated violation of Syrian airspace. There have been numerous clashes between Turkish and Syrian airplanes on the border between the two countries. Artillery fire from Syria has often impacted on Turkish soil, although whether fired by government or opposition forces and whether these were intentionally aimed or stray rounds is constantly a matter of mutual accusation. Tensions between Turkey and Syria are currently very high.

A month ago, an artillery round (reported in the news to have been fired by opposition forces) hit a Syrian fertilizer manufacturing plant near the Syrian-Turkish border. Given the fighting in the region, the plant had not been active for nearly two years. However, its storage areas remained full of fertilizer and other materials, and the explosion caused the entire factory to be engulfed in flames. The noxious smoke caused by highly flammable fertilizer materials has spread a dense cloud on both sides of the border. Given the fighting going on in the area, Syrian firefighters have been unable to fully extinguish the blaze, and a cloud of fumes continues to spread from the factory. The fumes on the Turkish side of the border have now spread to engulf the Turkish border town of Akcakale. This town had often been hit by artillery fire coming from the Syrian side of the border, but the damage now caused is at an unprecedented scale. Dozens of people are dying daily from reactions to the smoke, with hundreds more being hospitalized. Amongst the casualties are many Syrian refugees living in a temporary camp just outside the town. The Turkish government has proclaimed a national emergency in the area, and teams of medical and other experts and emergency forces are converging on Akcakale.

Turkey has demanded to send its own experts into the factory and its surroundings to control the blaze and determine the type of fumes being released. This is the only way, it says, to decide on proper treatment for the Turkish citizens and Syrian refugees who have been injured, as well as on the proper preventative measures needed to protect the inhabitants of the region.

Syria has refused Turkey's demand, stating unequivocally that nobody would be allowed to cross into Syria. It has flown fighter sorties over the border crossing and threatened to attack anyone who set foot on Syrian soil.

Syria suspects that Turkey is not only using this situation as a pretext to smuggle arms and supplies into Syria for delivery to opposition forces, but also that Turkey is seizing an opportune moment of Syrian weakness to introduce Turkish forces into the area surrounding the factory in order to lay claim to it. The factory, and about eight square miles of its surroundings, had originally been Turkish territory, which had been wrested away from a much-weakened Turkish Republic by the French Mandate which ruled the Syria region in the early 1920s, right after the First World War. There is now a small Syrian village in the area, Tell Abiad, populated by a few dozen Syrian families – some of them farmers and others employed in the fertilizer factory. Syria has often made it clear that this is Syrian territory, while Turkey has claimed that the territory (which they call Lower Akcakale) is Turkish. Turkey has recently re-raised this claim to support its demand to enter the area.

The Syrian government has offered to work cooperatively with Turkey in the sense of updating Turkey on the firefighting and fumes-control efforts, as well as providing data from tests conducted to identify the composition and concentration of the fumes. In addition, Syria has promised that if the fumes continue to pose harm to Turkish civilians, Syria will be willing to assist in humanitarian efforts on the Turkish side of the border, providing medical assistance and other supplies to injured or displaced Turkish civilians.

Turkey has claimed that by its behavior, Syria is in breach of the United Nations Chemical Weapons Convention (CWC), which makes it forbidden "[t]o develop, produce, otherwise acquire, stockpile or retain chemical weapons." Turkey claims that the treaty also governs factories producing large quantities of chemical products - seemingly for civilian use, but with potential use for chemical warfare. Turkey has also stated that it will see protracted Syrian refusal to allow Turkish experts into the site an act of chemical warfare on Turkey.

Several Syrian civilians – some living in the affected area in Syria, others residing in the Akcakale refugee camp in Turkey – have filed claims against both countries in the European Court of Human Rights owing to their failure to protect the right to life. They claim that this is both countries' duty, under the European Convention on Human Rights.

The Secretary-General of the United Nations has assigned a team from the UN's Mediation Unit to convene a meeting between representatives of Turkey and the Syrian government in Lucerne, Switzerland. In his message to both parties, he stated: "The purpose of this meeting is, at the least, to reach agreement regarding the humanitarian crisis currently developing in the Akcakale region. However, if either party would raise additional issues for bilateral discussion, the UN team is at your disposal for assistance."

Private Information for the Representatives of the Turkish Government

You are official representatives of the Turkish government; each of you is an assistant minister in each of your respective offices: the Ministry of Health, the Ministry of Defense, and the Ministry of Justice. The Turkish Prime Minister agreed to send such a high-level team to Lucerne because he knows how crucial this meeting is to Turkey's national interests.

The first priority, of course, is to protect Turkish lives. Syria must allow you to enter the Lower Akcakale territory, extinguish the blaze if it cannot do so itself, and figure out how to stop the fumes from spreading and killing yet more Turkish people.

Another reason to prioritize this is that as the fumes have spread, the stream of refugees from Syria to Turkey has greatly increased. Even though the fumes also threaten the Turkish area, the refugees' reason that they will at least receive better treatment from Turkish and international medical teams in Turkey than they would in Syria. Turkey's ability to provide for the hundreds of thousands of Syrian refugees already in Turkey has stretched the country's capacity to its limits; a continued flow of refugees could overwhelm it – endangering lives, the Turkish economy, and Turkey's reputation in the international community. In addition, Turkey cannot rule out the possibility that at least some of the 'refugees' may be undercover Syrian intelligence agents.

Turkish intelligence suspects that the source of the fumes is not really fertilizer and associated chemicals lying dormant in an inactive manufacturing plant. The plant was, they believe, a military installation for the stockpiling, and perhaps the manufacturing, of chemical weapons. There is no way to prove this without access to the factory surroundings. However, the nature of the injuries suffered by people in Akcakale is not of the type usually associated with fertilizer-related fumes. Turkish intelligence has not ruled out the possibility that the fire and fumes were caused intentionally by Syria to camouflage a deliberate attack on Turkey, which would tie up Turkish attention and forces and limit Turkish ability to supply the Syrian opposition forces.

Turkey's long-term interests include restoring its national honor by regaining and reclaiming the Lower Akcakale region. Advancing the international border into Syria, even by four or five miles, would also greatly lessen the chance of stray artillery and gunfire causing casualties in Akcakale and other Turkish villages in the region.

Turkish intelligence has covertly laid hand on some very valuable information. About five years ago, a survey conducted secretly by the Syrian government showed that the region, although relatively small, was likely to be rich in natural gas reserves. Unable to develop the gas field due to its financial situation, and later due to the state of internal conflict, Syria has kept the information in reserve for a more opportune time. Turkey's developing economy is a huge consumer of energy and has been moving towards natural gas. Currently, Turkey is dependent on Russia for gas and is considering a large-scale treaty with Israel to supply Turkey with gas from Israel's recent offshore discoveries in the Mediterranean. Having access to a local supply would allow Turkey to consider disengaging from both those partnerships and gaining, in the process, much more political freedom to maneuver in its quest to become a regional power. This freedom would be particularly welcome given that so many other countries competing for clout in the region are still struggling to recover from the upheavals caused by the Arab Spring that started in 2010. This quest for regional influence also dictates that Turkey must refuse any offers to resolve issues between it and Syria by more active UN intervention – that would be a clear sign of weakness. Participating in UN-sponsored dialogue initiatives, however, is not only a wise diplomatic move, but also necessary in terms of Turkey's bid for EU membership, recently renewed. Turkey must protect its image as a peace-loving country and a good partner. It also must gain recognition as a protector of human rights – and, therefore, it is of great importance that Syria pressure its citizens to withdraw their petitions to the European Court of Human Rights.

Finally, you know that while your Prime Minister is committed to seeing the Syrian President ultimately ousted from office, that might take some time. Meanwhile, the absence of low-level coordination with Syria – on issues of security, refugees, environment, and more is costing Turkey heavily. There are two issues on which you would like the Syrians to cooperate. The first is that drug smugglers are using the same routes into Turkey from Syria, and the flow of drugs into Turkey has tripled over the past year. The second would involve Syria stepping up to take some responsibility for the refugees currently being supported and cared for by Turkey. Even with the rift between your countries and the current developing crisis, some pragmatic discussion might enable cooperation on those issues.

Private Information for the Representatives of the Syrian Government

You are official representatives of the Syrian government; each of you is an assistant minister in each of your respective offices: the Ministry of Health, the Ministry of Defense, and the Ministry of Justice. The Syrian President has agreed to send such a high-level team to Lucerne, because he knows how crucial this meeting is to Syria's national interests.

Syria's immediate interest is to prevent foreign personnel, forces, or experts from entering into the region, which would threaten to completely topple the last vestiges of government-controlled stability in the region. Unstable regions are easy pickings for "opposition" – really, *rebel* – forces. In particular, Turkish personnel, even disguised as chemical or medical experts, are sure to be used in some manner to support the rebels with aid or arms. Finally, allowing a foreign power to take care of this situation would be a huge admission of weakness – and an image of weakness is the last thing the Syrian government can allow itself at this point in its struggle against the rebel forces.

Indeed, the Syrian administration is much more concerned about the situation vis-à-vis the rebels than it is with any danger or damage caused by the fumes spreading from the burning factory. Those are local issues; the threat posed by the rebels attempting to overrun the country is of far greater importance.

The truth of the matter is that foreign intervention in the factory would probably uncover the truth: the factory was indeed used for manufacturing and stockpiling chemical weapons. While Syria cooperated with the international team dismantling its chemical warfare program, it concealed the existence of three stockpiles – and this factory is one of them. The administration's intention was to maintain the weapons as a last-ditch resort against foreign enemies or the rebels. If the stockpile's existence is verified, Syria would certainly face international sanctions and perhaps military action; you yourself could wind up in front of a war tribunal.

Syria has no doubts about Turkish intentions to create facts on the ground enabling it to rekindle the dispute over the area surrounding the factory – Syrian territory! The Turkish government can orate all it wants about "national honor" being restored; you know that this is really about weakening Syria. Unless Turkey's intelligence forces are better than usually suspected, Turkey likely is not aware that Syria has secretly conducted surveys showing large reserves of natural gas in the area. If Turkey's intelligence forces discovered this, you certainly refuse to be plundered in this manner! You know that once the rebellion is quashed in Syria, you will need all your resources to restore the country to what it once was.

Syria is suspicious not only of the Turkish claim to the territory, but of other foreign intervention in the area as well. You know that once international forces enter a region they can remain there endlessly, and on their heels come a wave of multinational development contractors looking for fat reconstruction contracts. They would certainly be attracted to developing the gas fields; there is more than one way to plunder Syria's treasures! You've seen this happen in Iraq; you won't allow it to happen to your country.

Syrian-Turkish relations have been good over the past ten years – until the Turkish Prime Minister abruptly betrayed the Syrian President and began to openly support the rebels trying to oust him from politics. Your President has a long memory, and this may be payback time. Turkey is currently engaged in its bid for EU membership, and its actions in this conflict are sure to be closely monitored. You might have the opportunity to embarrass Turkey in terms of its handling of human rights situations, or of its unwillingness to participate in peaceful settlement of disputes. A weakened Turkey, at this moment, is good for Syria.

On the other hand, engaging in diplomacy – any diplomacy – on the international level provides the government with some much-needed legitimacy in this arena. Therefore, cooperating with Turkey on some issues might be in Syria's interest. As one example of this, perhaps you can use this as an opportunity to start winning back the hearts and minds of your country's people. These talks might offer an opportunity for Syria to cooperate with Turkey by becoming involved in caring for its refugees across the border in Turkey. Using this as a highly publicized (yet limited) demonstration of care for its citizens might score the government some points.

Private Information for the Representatives of the Secretary-General of the United Nations

The UN Mediation Unit has been assigned the mission of facilitating talks between the governments of Syria and Turkey. A new team set up for rapid deployment into real-time conflict areas and for dealing with immediate crises, you and all its other members have earned your spot in the unit through years of playing third-party roles in other parts of the world - working on endless rounds of talks on the Cyprus issue and addressing the Israel/Palestine conflict. As Turkish-Syrian bilateral relations have always been smooth, however, there is no one in the unit with specific experience pertaining to the situation. The internal Syrian conflict has held everybody's focus for so long that your team hadn't even noticed this new situation escalating until you were tapped for the job! Still, you are confident that you can help the parties work out their issues with your conflict resolution toolbox and all the patience in the world.

Well-versed on the internal Syrian conflict, it didn't take long to bring you up to speed on recent developments on the Turkish-Syrian border. In addition to the general information readily available in the public media (see the General Information sheet), your director has provided you with the following guidance regarding the UN's position and how it can help.

The Secretary-General is concerned about three issues:

First, that this issue might undermine the UN's efforts to address the much bigger problem of the civil war raging inside Syria by convening the Syrian government and the opposition leaders.

Second, that there is a very real danger that one side or the other would act unilaterally, and the current issue would trigger a full war between Turkey and Syria. Turkey's recent suggestion that Syria's intransigence was tantamount to waging chemical warfare against Turkey might be laying the foundation for justifying an upcoming Turkish invasion.

Third, the crisis is currently local. However, if the winds shifted and carried the fumes to neighboring countries such as Iran or Israel, there is no telling what will follow, and the stability of the entire region will be at risk.

In addition to these, the UN has the following interests:

1) Modeling a successful dialog process, to encourage the Syrian government to engage in dialog with the opposition with which it is currently at war. At the very least, you need to avoid a mediation fiasco which Syria can later point to as a reason for turning down future UN-backed initiatives focusing on the internal conflict. The UN has been ineffective and gridlocked so far regarding the internal Syrian conflict - you must avoid making that worse!

2) As it is now, the reason for gridlock in the UN is the Chinese and Russian vetoes cast on any resolution leveling sanctions against the Syrian government. You know that one reason for these vetoes lies in these countries' hopes to be awarded large contracts in reconstructing Syria once the government quashes the opposition. In particular, one area both these countries are casting their eyes towards is the very zone in which the current disaster is unfolding - both countries think there are oil or gas reserves in the area.

3) You have no definitive information - but you know that there is a chance that this is no innocent fertilizer factory. As the UN was responsible for carrying out the program for destroying all of Syria's chemical weapons, finding out that the Syrian government had withheld stockpiles of

weapons would be valuable information. It would also be *embarrassing* information, given that the UN has already declared that all chemical stockpiles had been dismantled and that its teams had dispersed. One way or another, this is certainly information the Secretary General would want to know should the opportunity to find out present itself.

4) This problem is snowballing: From an internal conflict to a potential conflict between states; from an environmental problem to a health nightmare and a refugee crisis. The sooner all this can be neutralized, the better. Time is not on your side.

You know that even though the countries' governments have accepted the Secretary-General's invitation to these talks, neither government will be particularly inclined towards further UN intervention. Therefore, while you can offer them some practical aid or incentives, it is more a question of whether they want to deal with each other than whether they want to deal with the UN.

Here are some resources the UN could provide, should parties be interested:

- The UN can provide on-the-ground monitoring for the implementation of any agreement reached. Given the volatile state of the region, this would require a peacekeeping force of several thousand troops ensure any monitoring personnel are adequately protected.

- The UN can provide up to $10,000,000 for humanitarian aid in Akcakale and the nearby refugee camps.

- The UN can provide experts on firefighting as well as medical personnel. It can also provide experts on working with refugees.

This doesn't seem to be a case where you can just throw money or resources at the issue and expect it to resolve itself. However, it never hurts to come to the table with something in your pocket. In the end, though, you know that getting anywhere at all with this conflict depends on your ability to encourage parties to cooperate with you and with each other.

Use your preparation time to work out your game plan - you will soon be meeting with the delegations.

Game Variations

FlashPoint can be tailored by teachers to achieve teaching goals optimally across a wide spectrum of programs of study and educational settings. This section includes guidance for four categories of variations:

Role additions, variations, and expansions.
Active game management.
Simulation updating and contextualizing.
Public international law-focused version.

Role variations

Changes can be made to the role structure of the game, to accommodate teaching goals, by incorporating more players in the game or adjusting participants' level of identification with the characters they are playing.

Incorporating more players in the game:

The game's basic structure accommodates 8 players: 3 members on each delegation, and 2 UN mediators. This number can be expanded to allow more players to participate in the same game, to allow for a shared learning experience. With large groups, though, breaking the group down into several separate simulations is recommended. Here are some ways to add players to a group, in an order recommended to have the best impact on the simulation's conduct:

Add another Assistant Minister to each group. These might be chosen according to current issues in Syrian/Turkish relations at the time of play. If nothing seems particularly suitable, add on roles of the Syrian Assistant Minister of Justice and the Turkish Assistant Minister of Foreign Affairs

Add an additional mediator (or two) to the UN team.

Assign each team another member – a legal counsel or a negotiation consultant. They might take a seat at the table or take a back-seat role – participants can work this issue out for themselves.

Add a local role to each team (e.g., the Turkish Mayor of Akcakale) as an observer or full team member.

Assign each team member an aide – a legal counsel or negotiation consultant. These should be back-seat roles.

In addition to adding roles, you might consider adding slight twists in the plot or in negotiator information to shift dynamics. For example, hand a note containing secret personal information to one or more individual members of negotiation teams regarding commercial/financial interests they have in the region, or personal political ambition that somehow affects to the story.

Adjusting Participants' Degree of Role Identification:

You might consider creating more in-depth briefings, handed out as personal information, for each individual player in the game. These might include professional, contextual information (e.g., providing the Turkish Assistant Minister of Defense with information regarding specific concerns or threats) or personal information (e.g., providing the Syrian Assistant Minister of Defense with personal ambitions to form close ties with the Turkish government or to portray himself as a reasonable statesman whom the international community might look to as a responsible alternative in the event the current Syrian government collapses).

If students have been given their roles ahead of the game (such as the night before game time), you might ask them to write themselves a brief personal "bio" for the character they are about to play (upbringing, education, experience, etc.).

Active Game Management

As noted, *FlashPoint* is designed to carry its own weight, process-wise. Participants with reasonable degrees of motivation will engage in the process for hours, making their own decisions on procedure, joint and separate meetings, in-role breaks, etc. Therefore, teachers can take on the role of observers, focusing on collecting issues to stress during debrief.

However, teachers may prefer to intervene in the process to achieve specific training goals. Common examples are interventions aimed at helping students stay on track with a particular process model or to demonstrate use of a particular technique. Beyond these contextual preferences, the desire for active game management, from the trainer's point of view, is often a balance between the amount of time available and the parties' progress. On the one hand, one wants to avoid an artificial rush to settlement (e.g., 'let's hurry up and reach agreement on everything before lunch so we can have the day free'). On the other, a trainer might want to avoid a situation in which parties approach the final deadline without any headway at all; while this might indeed go a long way towards introducing participants to the reality of protracted peace talks, it might also result in disheartened and demotivated participants. In that sense, it is often helpful for a trainer to be able to fine-tune the game's progress, pace-wise, allowing for optimal use of the time allotted for the simulation. It is important for teachers to keep in mind that while they would do well to "trust the process" provided by the game's structure and not come pre-equipped with a plan for dozens of interventions, interrupting the simulation's flow – they can, and should, consider interventions, breaks, in-process check-ins, or mini-debriefs as suitable to the context, the framework the simulation is conducted in, the students' learning habits, etc.

One common simulation management method is to incorporate teacher interventions, providing short breaks in the game routine. These could be in-role interventions (such as the teacher joining the UN team and serving as a mediator for a few minutes) or mini-breaks in which the teacher breaks the players out of their role for a short discussion, exercise, or debrief (note that the personal reflection sheets provided at the end of this book allow for such a mid-game self-debrief exercise).

Other interventions allow the trainer to change the game's dynamics and pace, by means of two different types of real-time game adjustments: *Incentives* and *Setbacks*. *Incentives* are occurrences or elements that offer positive opportunities or support for reaching agreement or for improving relations. *Setbacks* are occurrences that threaten to deteriorate progress already made or threaten the chances of reaching agreement. *Incentives* and *Setbacks* are meant to affect the dynamics at the table injecting a shot of optimism or pessimism, trust or distrust, acceleration or deceleration.

Trainers can decide on the best way to introduce *Incentives* or *Setbacks* into the room. They can make an announcement in the room, describing what took place as if they were making a radio broadcast; they might pass a note to the mediators describing the occurrence and charging them with introducing it into the room as they see fit; they might call for a break, saying each of the teams has received messages from home and handing them written information or instructions.

Here are some *Incentives* and *Setbacks* that work well in *FlashPoint*:

Incentives:

The UN has publicly announced its willingness to deploy troops as observers or peacekeepers in the implementation stage of any agreement between Syria and Turkey. If agreed to by both parties, these UN troops will also partake in protecting refugees and conducting anti-drug operations, as the UN recognizes these issues have a destabilizing effect in the region.

British Petroleum has announced its interest in drilling for gas in the Akcakale region, and is willing to add a reconstruction, rehabilitation, and development component to the project by employing refugees to build roads and facilities in the area. It would fund the building of pipelines to Turkey and other countries in the region. Of course, BP has cautioned, this project could be carried out only if the region was peaceful and environmentally safe.

Setbacks

A mortar shell has landed in a downtown market in Akcakale, killing 13 townspeople and 3 Syrian refugees. The shell was fired from somewhere in the region of the burning factory, probably using the smoke from the blaze as cover. In a press release from Ankara, the Turkish government has accused Syrian government troops of firing the shell. Syrian officials blame the Syrian opposition for the attack.

The President of Iran has invited the Syrian President to Tehran for discussions focusing on what he calls Turkey's ongoing aggression in the region. Iran has already backed Syria heavily in its internal conflict, and Turkey knows that Iran is looking for any excuse to become more involved in its internal affairs and to form a strong bloc limiting Turkey's regional aspirations.

It should be stressed that trainers need not use all of the *Incentives and Setbacks* listed– or any of them. Trainers can pick and choose, judging which might be best utilized to fine-tune the game dynamic in any desired direction. Trainers can improvise their own interruptions, whether on the spot or based on recent (or predicted) events in the news.

Simulation adaptation, contextualizing and updating

Many aspects of the *FlashPoint* scenario are left a bit ambiguous on purpose to allow the teacher a high degree of latitude to tailor the simulation to any particular course. Far from tampering with the simulation's basic structure, such adaptation is welcome and will likely to improve students' learning experience.

The same principle relates to the question of assigning students reading material. The simulation, as written, can be assigned as-is, with no further reading or preparation required on the students' part. However, that is not to say that reading external material interferes with the simulation in any way; on the contrary, teachers can choose any background material they consider beneficial to students in their field and assign it (e.g, relevant international treaties, general literature on conflict management, or specific reports on the disputed region). Similarly, they can assign students to conduct their own research, pointing them at particular topics or resources.

The use of maps and other visual materials is a helpful way to adapt the simulation to a particular type of use. While one teacher might want to use this to emphasize broad regional trends and circumstances, another might prefer to keep the focus as local as possible, and perhaps zoom in even further to allow students to deal with the nitty-gritty details of sketching out real-world treaties. Google Maps (www.google.com/maps) is one example of a useful tool which allows teachers to create maps showing different areas in different scales. To give students a sense of scale, teachers might create maps comparing the size of the region they choose to a region with which students are familiar, to give students a sense of proportion (for example, a map of Turkey and Syria overlying a map of the southern U.S., to demonstrate that, combined, they are roughly the size of Texas can be seen at http://mapfrappe.com/outlines?show=18423). Helpful sites for this purpose are http://overlapmaps.com/and http://mapfrappe.com/outlines.

This simulation was written at a particular point in time – early-to-mid -2014. As time goes by, facts on the ground might change; political realities and even territorial boundaries may change. There are two ways to approach this. One way is to leave the simulation as it is, and to ask students to play it out according to the material and not according to current historical fact. A second is to update the simulation, tweaking facts in the information here and there to align it with contemporary events; telling students that this is what you've done will allow them to overcome any gaps you may have missed or dealt with too generally. Keeping an eye on, or conducting a search through general news sites (such as www.cnn.com or www.bbc.co.uk) should provide the necessary material; teachers can also check out local news sites such as www.hurrietdailynews.com. [3]

One way to address the issues of adaptation, contextualizing and updating is to create a team of students charged with design issues. Teachers can assign this group to review the simulation before it is given out to the other students, and to make changes, create supplementary material, choose reading material, develop maps, etc. This group may also be tasked with creating in-simulation interruptions, interventions, incentives and setbacks (see "Active Game Management" above) either before the simulation begins or as it goes along. Students in the designer role will benefit from a unique experience and their learning experience will not be less than that of students in the role-play; they will certainly serve as a valuable resource to the class in the debrief session following the simulation.[4]

International Law

In this section, we show one interesting purpose for which *FlashPoint* can be used, and we also demonstrate how teachers might contextualize the simulation to teach a particular topic. *FlashPoint* can be used to demonstrate the relationship between international negotiation process and public international law, showing how each takes place in the shadow of the other. This variation works successfully in educational settings focused on international law or on international relations with an international law element included.

FlashPoint raises core international law issues including signing, upholding, and construction of treaties; the use of force, self-defense, or chemical weapons; cross-border natural resource management, cross-border environmental issues, territorial sovereignty, borders, human rights issues, and many others. As a result, international law will always find its way, to one extent or another, onto the negotiation table. The General Information includes links to two international conventions, to ensure this. Teachers

---

[3] For more on the benefits and challenges of using ongoing, real-life situations as the backdrop to simulations, and on ways of maximizing learning and student comfort, see Noam Ebner & Yael Efron, *Using Tomorrow's Headlines for Today's Training: Creating PseudoReality in Conflict Resolution Simulation-Games*, 21(3) Harv. Negot. J. 377 (2005).

[4] For discussion of such a designer role and its benefits, see Daniel Druckman & Noam Ebner, *Onstage, or behind the scenes? Relative learning benefits of simulation role-play and design*, 39(4) Simulation & Gaming 465 (2008).

wishing to stress the interplay between law and negotiation might add further material (real or fictitious). Beyond that, they might adjust the structure of the parties and the game to allow the legal aspects to be given more attention, by addressing directly, or orienting students towards, for example, the 4th Geneva Convention (1949), the Hague Conventions (1899, 1907), the Charter of the United Nations (1945), the agreements concluded between the EU and Turkey regarding the latter's EU candidacy, the Treaty on Functioning of the European Union (TFEU), the Treaty on European Union (TEU) , the EU Convention of Fundamental Rights (EUCFR) or the European Charter on Human Rights (ECHR).

One way to do this, already mentioned above, is to add a role of legal counsel onto each team. This role could be given to participants with a particularly strong background in international law. When possible, participants tapped for this role might receive the role information a week or more ahead of time, allowing them to research the legal aspects and implications.

An even stronger spotlight can be cast on the interplay of law and negotiation can be done by holding separate sessions in which each of these is highlighted. Here is one way to do this:

Hand out the role material a week or more before game time. Assign one to three students on either side as their delegation's legal counsel/team. Task them with treating the role information they have received as a legal case précis, and to prepare for a hearing of the case before an international court, which will take place before the negotiation sessions. You might play the role of the arbitrator/neutral/judge in the hearing or assign a participant to this role. Depending on learning goals, the hearing can be conducted briefly and informally, or as a full-blown mock court session, similar to a Jessup competition round, complete with written and oral pleadings and rebuttal. At the end of the hearing, announce that now that the case has been heard, the court/neutral recommends that parties take the UN up on its offer to provide mediation services.

The next session (which might follow immediately afterwards or begin the next day) is dedicated to the mediation process, which will continue until parties reach agreement or impasse, or until the activity's time runs out. In these sessions, the negotiation is to be conducted by the participants assigned the negotiator roles. However, it is interesting to note whether they allow their legal team to sit at the table, lead the way or participate in other ways. As the negotiations commence, note for later discussion how the legal mindset and frames affect the parties' negotiating behavior and the nature of the conversation. Also, note efforts made by the mediators or the negotiators to slip loose of the legal framing, and their success or failure. Other issues of interest may be the relationships between principles and counsel, counsel as agreement facilitator/inhibitor, the way parties relate to and use their BATNA[5] (success in court, as it has been framed by their legal counsel) and the type of language used in the negotiation.

---

[5] The best alternative to a negotiated agreement (BATNA) is a course of action a party will take if talks fail and no agreement can be reached during negotiations. ROGER FISHER & WILLIAM URY, GETTING TO YES: NEGOTIATING AGREEMENT WITHOUT GIVING IN (2011).

PART 2
Teacher's Manual

Conducting and Debriefing Educational Simulation Games/Noam Ebner[*]

Introduction

Conducting an educational role-play simulation with students is a deceptively complex task. Deceptive in that it may sometimes seem to teachers as if all they need to do is hand students a page of instructions and, *voila*, a learning experience unfolds. Similarly, it might seem to students as if all they need to do is play a game and, *voila*, they will have learned something. In reality, educational simulations require teachers to be mindful of a host of planning, timing, selecting, setting up, conducting, troubleshooting, and meaning-making activities along the way.

In this part, we will discuss these activities, providing teachers with a road map to follow through the life cycle of implementing an educational simulation.

Note that this part focuses on the actual set-up and conduct of simulations – preparing for the activity and playing it out. Some of the tasks included in the road map lie beyond this focus. For example, simulation choice and simulation design are described briefly in the lead-up to actual simulation preparation and conduct in order to prepare teachers to take them into account in their planning, as decisions made about these tasks will affect the simulation's actual conduct (for example, by determining the actual amount of time in a two-hour class that will be dedicated to student role-play activity as opposed to debriefing the activity).

---

[*] Noam Ebner is an expert in legal education and conflict resolution pedagogy. A former professor at Creighton University and chair of its online graduate program in negotiation and conflict resolution, Ebner has over twenty years of experience in online teaching, curricular design, and program development. Ebner has consulted for many academic programs in these areas, and has supported many teachers in the negotiation, conflict resolution, and ADR fields in their transition to teaching online. Ebner's writing on negotiation pedagogy and online negotiation and dispute resolution processes can be found at: https://papers.ssrn.com/sol3/cf_dev/AbsByAuth.cfm?per_id=425153

Phase I: Preliminary Considerations
(Some of the considerations listed here are described in greater detail in Phase II: Simulation Set-Up, below).

1) *Learning goals and pedagogical methods*

Before selecting a simulation, consider your educational goals. What are the learning outcomes you wish students to achieve? Why do you think they will be best achieved by engaging in a simulation? By sharpening your educational vision around the topic at hand in terms of substance and pedagogy, you will be better able to identify the suitable path to simulation.

2) *Simulation choice / design / tailoring*

Depending on your subject matter, there may already be simulations that were authored, tested, and improved by experts in the topical area, such as those offered in this book. Of course, not every simulation that addresses your topic will necessarily serve you well. Some of the other considerations in this section (e.g., your group size, the physical space available to you, the time at your disposal) might make an otherwise perfectly matched simulation unsuitable for your use. Similarly, other aspects of the simulation might render it less suitable upon consideration (e.g., the simulation requires students to apply some understanding of a second subject area that is not covered in your course or is covered later on). Before moving on to search for an alternate simulation, consider whether the simulation can be tailored to suit your purposes. Would writing in another role, or eliminating an existing role, serve this purpose? Would augmenting the role information with additional detail, or instructing students to disregard certain information in the role information, bring the simulation in line with your educational goals and the resources you wish to dedicate to the simulation? Often, small tweaks to existing simulations can accommodate specific teachers' requirements. Of course, you might choose to forgo using pre-designed simulations and instead design one yourself. While design considerations and process guidance are beyond the scope of this book, a helpful first step would be to read through all the simulations provided in this book, with an eye to their structure and the different types of balance and conflict created between parties' roles.

3) *Participant group size*

In deciding to run a simulation, consider the number of students in the class. Some simulations are designed to be conducted in dyads, with each student paired with/against another. Others have students performing in a small group or in a small group acting as a team in an interaction with several other teams of students. Some simulations allow users to expand the 'natural' number of participants (e.g., by having students play their role as a team rather than as an individual). Some are unlikely to work well if there are too many participants; others, if there are too few. Read the simulations' instructions regarding group size before adopting it for use in your classroom. Also, consider whether your educational purpose requires all students to be involved in the same simulation (in which case, a single large-group simulation is required) or whether it may be beneficial to run multiple small-group simulations, such as for the purposes of comparing different processes and outcomes (in which case pairing 40 students into 20 dyads is preferred).

4) *Participant preparation requirements*

Most simulations require students to prepare for their role ahead of time. However, the extent of preparation differs impacting its suitability to your purposes. Some simulations provide students with all the information they need, and their preparatory task is limited to analyzing the situation and/or data based on a concept or a model they've studied in the classroom (as an example, the "The United Currency Wars" in this book). Other simulations provide students with a framework for the upcoming interaction and some general information, but requires students to prepare beyond studying this material by conducting independent research (for example, any moot court simulation, or the "Disposables Tax" simulation in this book).

5) *Simulation time decisions*

Simulations require time for three sets of tasks; participant preparation, simulation conduct, and debrief. These can be combined to one consecutive timeframe, or they can be pieced out over separate time slots. For example, you might assign students their roles to read, instructing them to begin the simulation after 20 minutes of preparation, and to complete it within an hour, dedicating the rest of the lesson to debrief. Alternatively, you might assign them their roles to read ahead of class, conduct the simulation throughout an entire class period, and conduct the debrief in the next lesson. Consider the natural length of your class lessons and the time requirements of each of the three tasks, and plan accordingly.

6) *Simulation space requirements*

Different simulations require different spatial arrangements. While the specifics of this will be discussed below (regarding the simulation set-up), space decisions must be considered at the preliminary stage as well, as they can affect your decisions as to which simulation to use, or even whether to use simulation in the first place. Some simulations (such as "Let There Be Gas!" in this book) require a large open space in which large groups can interact. Others (such as "The Currency Wars" in this book) require a reasonable amount of privacy and quiet surroundings as they can be conducted in many pairs or small groups working on separate simulations with each other. Others do not require any spatial arrangements, as they can be conducted solely online (such as "Colonel Chicken Goes Abroad" in this book).

Phase II: Simulation Set-Up

1) *Role Assignment*

In most simulations, each participant is assigned a specific role, or placed on a specific team. Assigning students to their roles can be done in a number of ways:

Random assignment: Hand out roles to students in a random order, or according to a list compiled at random.

Self-grouping: Ask students to divide into pairs, trios, two groups, or whatever configuration serves the simulations purpose. Depending on the configuration, students in each group will work as counterparts or teammates with another group as its counterpart (as in the "The Currency Wars" simulation, in this book, for example).

Self-assignment: If students are familiar with the various roles in the simulation, you might invite them to choose the roles they prefer to play.

Assign key roles: In some simulations, certain roles have special importance for the simulation's success. For example, in a model European Union simulating a meeting of the European Council, dozens of participants might play the roles of participating member state representatives, but two roles - the European Council President and the President of the European Commission – are charged with running the meeting and facilitating negotiations. Teachers might consider assigning such key roles, as well as team/group leaders roles, to particularly engaged, proactive, dependable, and/or skilled students.

Role-identification: Some simulations relate to issues pertaining to participants' real-life activities, opinions, values, or beliefs. Playing a role one identifies with might contribute to one's motivation; playing a role counter to one's belief might encourage perspective-taking and seeing things from another point of view. However, at some point over- or under-identification with a role can interfere with a participant's learning experience. Keep this in mind when considering role assignment.[1]

Adjusting numbers: If you have extra students after everyone has been assigned (e.g., an odd number of students in a simulation conducted in pairs), a student showing up late for class after roles have been assigned, or other such situations, you might assign them to view the simulation as observers or improvise a role for them on the spot. For example, in the "Converging!" simulation, you can add a participant to one team as a civil rights activist. In the "Sweet Surrender" simulation, you can assign an extra student to play the role of a hospitalized patient, suffering the severe physical impact of diabetes.

2) *Role information*

Role information includes the different types of material you present to each participant for them to learn about the role they are to play and to help them play it well. This might include background information regarding the simulated situation and specific information about their own character, their role in the upcoming simulated interaction, their relationships with other roles, and more. This is generally shared in one or more of three forms:

General information: This information is 'public' in the sense that all players in the simulation have received the same information. While it might state differences of *opinion* (e.g., by stating that Country A thinks that it owns a particular territory and Country B exerts its sovereignty over the same area) the

---

[1] For more on this issue see Noam Ebner & Yael Efron, *Using Tomorrow's Headlines for Today's Training: Creating Pseudo Reality in Conflict Resolution Simulation-Games*, 21 HARV. NEGOT. J. 3, 377 (2005).

information about these opinions is shared *equally* rather than withholding information from one party while giving it to another. Often, such information is provided to all participants in a simulation to have a common foundational background against which each participant develops their own set of interests, needs, and actions. These latter can be developed by participants on their own or provided to them by the instructor via group or private information.

Group/Team Information: In simulations involving multiple teams working with and against one another, this material is provided to all the members of each team, and to them only. It will generally contain information regarding the team's constitution, aims, goals, and relationships to which members of other teams are not privy.

Private Information: This information is given out to a particular participant and contains information about their role which only they are to know. It might explain their character's personal background, goals, resources, preferences, relationships with other roles, etc.

Some simulations (such as "Converging!" in this book) involve all three types of role information. In others, (such as "Harmful tax competition: to participate or not to participate?") all players receive only general information and there is no secret information to which the entire group is not privy. Often, participants will receive general information and their own specific instructions in the form of private information.

Distribution: Role information can be distributed to students in any way that matches the course teaching methods and the preparation time required (see below). You might email students their material several days before the simulation, or hand it out on sheets of paper in class and send them off to read.

3) *Student Preparation*

Student preparation for a simulation varies. In simpler simulations, all they might need to do is read half a page of private information and give a few minutes thought to how they intend to play their role. More complex simulation might require them to read two pages of information and spend half an hour planning their actions according to a model studied in class. Still other simulations might require they put many hours into preparing for the simulation. Here are the variables affecting student preparation, its time, and its tasks:

Role information or independent research: Is the simulation self-contained, in the sense that everything a student needs to know about the situation and their role is contained in the role information? Or do students need to conduct independent research to play their roles well? For example, in a moot court simulation, students conduct independent legal research to develop the best arguments for their case. In "The United Currency Wars" simulation in this book, students must only read the general role information provided to them.

General or In-Depth Analysis? In some simulations, all students need to do is read the instructions, give the situation a few moments thought, and they are ready to begin. In others, the educational purpose requires students to engage in a more in-depth preparation process, such as by completing a preparation worksheet, applying a specific analytical model learned in class, or writing a pre-interaction brief summarizing the situation and their game plan.

Individual or Team Preparation: Some simulations set students to work on their own, with or against others. In others, students act as a team, with or against other teams. When working as a team, participants might require additional preparation time to make plans at the team level, agree on a joint strategy, distribute individual responsibilities, and the like.

No matter the preparation mode, make sure that students know precisely when and where the simulation itself will take place when supplying them with their role information. Stress that everybody must be present, prepared, and ready to begin their in-role activity at that time. Stress that absences or delays lower the odds of the simulation's educational success, their enjoyment of it, and their personal educational gain, and request their cooperation on this issue.

4) **Physical surroundings, equipment, and props**

Above, we've noted the need to verify availability of an appropriate room at the preliminary stage of deciding whether to conduct a simulation and which simulation to choose. Here, we address environmental aspects of preparing for a specific simulation.

Rooms: Some simulations require a large room, to accommodate participants' sitting around a large table or in seats placed in a large circle, or to allow for many pairs or small groups to convene separately. In some simulations, you might want to provide participants with space to convene in groups, in addition to the main convention area in the classroom. For this purpose, you may wish to arrange to use a second room or identify an adjacent hallway that serves this purpose without disturbing anyone. If you need additional seats, or for seats and tables to be configured in any particular way, arrange for this beforehand or ask students to help do this before beginning the simulation.

Equipment: Are there any maps, charts, or other documents that should be available or featured in the room? Would the simulation benefit from participants having the use of a whiteboard or flipchart? Presentation technology? If you have time while students are preparing material for the simulation, utilize it to conduct a last-minute test of all equipment.

Props for enhancing a sense of reality: To augment the sense of reality students experience in the simulation, you might add small touches conveying a sense of the real-life setting. For example, while simulating the proceedings of an international institution, you might provide participants with flag-themed name tags, placards with countries' flags printed on them, miniature flags on the table in front of the country's seats, etc. Simulating parliamentary proceedings, you may provide placards cards identifying each participant in their parliamentary role and seat them according to any real-world seating arrangements. When teachers take this kind of initiative, students will often respond with efforts of their own (particularly, if you hint that this would be appreciated!). For example, in a Model UN, students might arrive at the simulation wearing an element of the national dress of the country they are representing; for an international business negotiation or a cabinet meeting, they might dress up formally; and for a moot court, they might don judicial garb or dress according to pertinent attorney dress codes.

Phase III: Simulation Conduct

In most simulations, teachers are fairly inactive. Students are responsible for conducting the simulation they are involved in (in a one-on-one or small group simulation such as "The Colonel Chicken"); sometimes students in special roles have additional responsibility for leading entire-groups through in-simulation processes (e.g., the team leader role in the "Little Golano" simulation in this book). In fact, in many simulations the teacher's role is limited to blowing the simulation's opening and closing whistles.

In some simulations, teachers are required to take more active roles. This might be by design, such as in the "The Coffee Venture" simulation in this book, in which case specific instructions will be included in the simulation's teaching guide. Alternatively, teachers might find themselves more actively engaged in simulation as a matter of necessity. For example, in a moot court simulation, a teacher lacking the resources to empanel external experts as judges might find herself playing the judicial role.

Whether the teacher is largely active or inactive, here are some tasks teachers must generally perform in any simulation:

Presence: Teachers should largely remain present throughout the simulation. Their very presence reminds students that this is an educational experience and that their efforts matter. If the simulation involves multiple groups working independently, or one large group that occasionally breaks down into smaller caucuses, circulate among the groups. Give students their space, empowering them to lead, act, and engage with others naturally without the sense that their actions are being noted and judged. While some teachers interject questions or suggestions in sidebars or small-group meetings, others strictly maintain their stance as a fly-on-the-wall observer.

Observation: While simply being physically present has its own benefits, the main advantage of viewing the simulation is observing its dynamics, student actions and reactions, and its unfolding toward a conclusion. Such observation provides you with the material you will need to conduct a successful debrief session.

Maintaining simulation bubble: Even if students take a simulation very seriously, they might occasionally break the simulation's bubble in the sense of allowing reminders that they are involved in a simulation rather than a real-world situation to surface. This might occur due to a student becoming self-conscious or uncomfortable as they play their role, some distracting incident occurring in the real world nearby, a by-passer making a comment, etc. While this will often take a humorous turn, it can also take the form of participants making out-of-role comments regarding school (e.g., a student suddenly remembering to ask if anybody had been in a particular lesson the previous week) or closer-to-home comments regarding the course material applying to the simulation (which a real-world participant in the situation would likely not be familiar with). For the most part, the simulation bubble will be strong enough to contain these interruptions, and within a few seconds participants attention will be drawn back to reengaging with the simulated interaction. However, occasionally teachers will be required to intervene to get participants back on the simulation's track.

Responding to questions: Participants might ask teachers questions regarding their role information, the way they are expected to act, whether a specific action is allowed or not, etc. In answering questions, teachers walk a fine line between providing students with the clarity they need to participate in the simulation and directing their actions in the simulation, which might undermine its educational purposes. Whenever possible, consider redirecting students to the segment in the instructions in which the information is provided, wait for recognition to dawn on their faces, and return them to the simulation. Sometimes, however, you will need to take on the responsibility of clarifying a point or explaining something in the instructions. To this end, always review the simulation before engaging in it so you will be able to clarify or adjust details without upsetting any fundamental balances between participants.

Teacher interventions: As noted above, in some simulations teachers are highly involved in simulation management whereas in most simulations, students conduct the process themselves from beginning to end, without need for teacher guidance or prompts. However, even in those simulations in which students are expected to self-manage, teachers might choose to intervene in the simulation by adding new events or facts that affect the simulation's course. One reason to do so would be to slow down a group that is rapidly or artificially headed towards conclusion without full engagement with the issues required to achieve the simulation's educational goals. Conversely, instructors might wish to incentivize or aid a simulation group that is not making progress, whether this is due to a lack of motivation or of skill to do so. Such interventions, thereby, essentially manipulate the timeline and pace of the simulation. Finally, another reason for teachers intervening would be in order to introduce real-world or seemingly real-world occurrences into the simulation, giving participants a taste of what engaging in the simulated environment is like in the real world. For example, students simulating in the "Sweet Surrender" or the "Disposables Tax" role-plays in this book would get a sense of what it feels like to deliberate policy while real-world influences, demands, and events suddenly seep into the meeting room. In the "FlashPoint: Syria" simulation, students would get a sense of how real-world negotiation can be overtaken by events occurring on the ground.

While such externally introduced events or information might initially be categorized as 'positive' or 'negative' in the sense of their anticipated effect on participants' capacity to conclude the simulation successfully, different participants might utilize any information to achieve a variety of ends.[2]

Simulation ending: No matter how much time you have dedicated to a simulation, students might continue interacting right up until the last moment and far beyond. Ultimately, it is up to the teacher to call a halt to the simulation. This may be difficult for the teacher to do, particularly if there is a sense that students are 'almost there' in terms of concluding the simulation successfully. Still, the teacher, as the responsible adult in the room, is the one responsible for blowing the final whistle and transitioning from the simulation's enactment stage to educational debrief.

This transition is not always simple! In any simulation, and particularly in those continuing over several hours, it is difficult for participants to detach from the role they had been playing and adopt a learning stance towards themselves and their experience. Having invested so much time and energy in-role, if left to their own devices they will continue to conduct some form of negotiation even throughout the debrief process. To avoid this, allow a few minutes for freestyle relaxation and release after announcing the simulation's end. As this occurs, don't try to make any educational points, or be concerned that students making jokes about the simulation will diminish its educational impact or the gravitas of the moment. Instead, embrace the release of tension students are experiencing, and use the time to convey that the simulation is over and that participants can let things go rather than carry their in-game interaction on into the debrief session.

---

[2] For more on the introduction of such twists in simulations, see Ebner, & Efron, supra 1.

Phase IV: Debrief and further learning

Debriefing students' experience in the simulation is an essential part of its educational value. Through the debrief, you help students transform a complex array of data and interactions into knowledge that relates to their skills, studies, self-awareness and understanding. Guidance on conducting successful debrief sessions is provided elsewhere.[3] It is only mentioned here at all to provide a complete picture of the simulation-cycle. Simulations work best as an educational vehicle when teachers have a simulation's post-conduct direct learning activities in mind at the very beginning of its setup and conduct process.

In that same spirit, you might consider that a debrief session does not necessarily mark the end of the learning that will be conducted utilizing the simulation experience. You might consider squeezing some more juice out of the orange, or taking additional bites from the apple, by assigning students to engage in further learning activities beyond debrief, such as:

Writing a reflective journal on their personal simulation experience;

Writing a brief analyzing the simulation according to a specific model that went undiscussed in the class debrief; or

Engaging in a one-on-one or small group discussion of the simulation with someone in a similar role, an opposite role, or teammates, to discuss specific issues and dynamics that did not emerge in a top-level class debrief.

Alternative Simulation Formats and Uses

1) *Online simulation conduct*

This chapter, and indeed this book, has largely portrayed classroom use of simulation. Of course, many simulations can be conducted online, in a variety of ways, whether they were originally designed for online conduct or require tweaking to this end. Without getting into all for the considerations of whether and when to do so, we note that online simulation conduct can allow for simulations to occur when students cannot convene (e.g., as occurred during the COVID-19 period), students are located in different areas (e.g., in multi-international or multi-campus courses or simulations), or there is not sufficient in-class time to dedicate to the simulations.

When considering simulation conduct in this modality, there are several new issues for teachers to consider:

Interaction mode: Will the simulation be conducted synchronously or asynchronously?

Communication channel: Will the simulation be conducted via text, email, audio, or video communication? Some combination of the three?

Real-time: Will the simulation be conducted at any particular time, or according to students' preferences within a given time frame?

Conducting simulations via asynchronous text can be done in several ways. Most universities employ a learning management system (LMS) with a course area dedicated to each course. Inside this area, teachers can create a discussion forum for asynchronous participation by all parties, as well as provide private forums for groups or teams requesting to caucus among themselves. Students can interact with

---

[3] For more on debriefing simulations, see Ellen E. Deason, Yael Efron, Ranse Howell, Sanda Kaufman, Joel Lee, & Sharon Press, *Debriefing the Debrief*, EDUCATING NEGOTIATORS FOR A CONNECTED WORLD 301-332 (Rethinking Negotiation Teaching Series, volume 4, Christopher 1 Honeyman, James Coben, and Andrew Wei-Min Lee eds., 2013) available at: http://open.mitchellhamline.edu/dri_press/4/.

each other throughout the simulation by means of threaded messages. Some systems allow students to create forums on their own, in which case participants can create forums and grant access to particular others. Participants can caucus on the sidelines, if this is a desired activity in the simulation, through other channels that are often embedded within an LMS – email, videoconferencing, or instant messaging applications. Simulations, particularly those involving one-on-one or small group interactions, can also be conducted via email, with the primary mode of communication being each student clicking 're-ply all' to the last message in order to communicate with the group while preserving the communicative record below their message.

Simulations can be conducted via synchronous videoconferencing. Readily available commercial platforms such as Zoom or Webex can accommodate one-on-one interactions as well as large group discussions. When a simulation involves a large group and sub-teams, separate breakout rooms can be assigned to each group, ahead of time or *ad hoc*. Alongside the main interaction on camera, individuals can converse with one another through text-based synchronous means – either the chat offered by the videoconferencing software or other external applications.[4]

2) *Multi-session, immersive simulations*

This chapter largely discusses single-session simulations embedded within an academic course. In these activities, the simulation is a one-shot episode, a learning activity in which students apply what they have learned regarding one or more specific topics or lay experiential groundwork that will be analyzed through the perspective of a new topic. Whether the simulation takes an hour of class time or spans an entire class, it is a pinpointed experience limited in time.

Other possibilities exist for use of simulation within academic courses, in which the simulation is woven in a deep and ongoing method into the very fabric of the course. These are not intended for those courses in which experiential learning is so ingrained that students perform a different simulation every session or in every other class. Rather, these possibilities involve continuing a single simulation throughout several sessions, or throughout an entire course, with multiple developments, plot-twists, new information, and new tasks being added from one session to the next. Teachers can innovate ways to apply this educational structure in their courses; we will briefly mention three for the purposes of exemplifying what an ongoing, developing simulation activity might look like in and contribute to a course.

---

[4] For a full discussion of conducting simulations online, see David Matz & Noam Ebner, *Using role-play in online negotiation teaching* in VENTURING BEYOND THE CLASSROOM: VOLUME 2 IN THE RETHINKING NEGOTIATION TEACHING SERIES (C Honeyman, J Coben & G DiPalo, eds., 2010). Also see Noam Ebner & Sharon Press, *Pandemic Pedagogy II: Conducting simulations & role plays in online, video-based, synchronous courses* (2020) https://papers.ssrn.com/sol3/papers.cfm?abstract_id=3557303.
These papers describe online conduct of simulations in the fields of negotiation and conflict resolution; however, their suggestions are applicable to interactive educational simulations in any discipline. For an example of a detailed teaching guide providing instructions for a highly interactive simulation both in a classroom and via Zoom, see Noam Ebner & Yifat Winkler, *The Pasta Wars: a Prisoners Dilemma Simulation-Game*, 40 SIM. & GAMING 1, 134-146 (2009) https://papers.ssrn.com/sol3/papers.cfm?abstract_id=2200350. Note that the guidance provided for this simulation is likely to particularly helpful with regard to conducting Coffee Venture simulation in this book, given that it is assigned using the same foundational structure.

Multi-Class Simulations: Perhaps the simplest way to implement a single extensive educational simulation in a course is to dedicate several class sessions to a single simulation that will provide educational insights regarding a variety of course topics.[5]

Multi-Stage Simulations: Writing in the context of legal education, John Lande has suggested structuring law courses around a single, ongoing, multistage simulation.[6] Lande suggests that as students progress through a course, they simulate multiple stages of a lawyer's work on a case, within the same general fact pattern; for instance: an initial interview with a client, a negotiation with their client over a retainer agreement, the actual negotiation with the counterpart attorney, and participating in mediation with the counterpart. In their paper surveying the literature on educational simulations, Druckman and Ebner have discussed how this approach could be implemented in other disciplinary contexts.[7]

Simulation Supported Course Narrative: Ebner and Greenberg note that in traditional courses relying on simulation, teachers conduct discrete exercises into which participants 'parachute' for a brief moment, playing a role they are only superficially familiar with, in situations unrelated to each other. These simulations cease to exist, other than as lessons-learned, the moment their debrief session has ended. They recommend a new design approach to these courses, in which all course activities center around a single ongoing narrative and cast of characters. Simulations are a central activity in such a course, an important vehicle for character development and moving the narrative plot forward. Students might play the role of a character in their first salary negotiation as an intern. The character's achievements in that initial simulation then feed into the way they interact with colleagues at a decision-making meeting simulation later on in that lesson, and into the resources and character elements the character has at their disposal in a simulation conducted several weeks later, while negotiating the purchase of an apartment[8].

Debrief and Further Learning
Define Debriefing Goals

Open up the learning phase of the debrief by gathering the entire group (and, if several groups played concurrently, into a general forum comprising all the groups). Focus attention on yourself and announce the goals of the debrief. Explain that debriefing is an opportunity to transform the participants' simulation-experience into practical take-away lessons. State clearly what you hope to gain from this experience (e.g, 'Let's aim for a clear picture of how we improved our negotiation/problem-solving skills,' or 'Let's aim at summarizing the new aspect of the conflict that this simulation has brought to light.').

---

[5] See Beatty JE, Chen Y-S, Klein BD, *Games and gamification in business school courses: Experiential education that creates engagement and flow*, 19 DECISION SCIENCES JOURNAL OF INNOVATIVE EDUCATION, 170 (2021) https://doi.org/10.1111/dsji.12250 .

[6] John Lande, *Teaching students to negotiate like a lawyer*, 39 WASH. U. J. L. & POLICY 109-144 (2012); John Lande, *Suggestions for Using Multi-Stage Simulations in Law School Courses*, U. MISSOURI SCH. L. LEG. STUDIES, Research Paper No. 2013-08, 1-7 (2014).

[7] Daniel Druckman & Noam Ebner, *Games, claims, and new frames: Rethinking the use of simulation in negotiation education* 29 NEG. J. 1, 61-93 (2013).

[8] See Ebner, N. & Greenberg, E. (2020).*Designing binge-worthy courses: Pandemic pleasures and COVID-19 consequences*. NEGOTIATION JOURNAL 36(4), 535-560.

Grab Focus

Begin the debrief by asking how many groups reached agreement; ask a couple of groups for the main points of their agreements. This is done mainly to allow participants still engrossed in the game to join the group, others to vent a bit, and to stress in general the joint-but-separate experience of the groups and of each individual participant, transforming them back into one singular large learning group. For most of the remainder of the debrief, focus will be less on the outcomes and more on the process; it is helpful to touch on outcomes and set them aside right at the start.

Focus on Training Goals

Here are some suggestions for questions you may use to highlight the particular training goals you set for the simulation:

Training Goal: Mediation / Conflict Resolution Skills

Where relevant, consider asking some of these questions, focusing on how the participants playing the role of mediator handled their role. Choose questions and allow discussion according to the level of competence and confidence of the mediators, according to the their performance and according to your pre-set desired skill-set (e.g., trust-building, relationship-building, grasp of the structure of the mediation process, creativity, dealing with ethical dilemmas, confidence boosting, etc.)

- Did the mediators explain the process to the parties clearly? How did this affect the process?

- What did the mediators do to help parties get all the necessary information on the table?

- Were the mediators successful in building an atmosphere of trust around the table? How did they do this (or what might they have done, but did not do)?

- How did the mediators react in challenging situations (such as: parties interrupting each other, parties attacking each other, parties attacking the mediators, party walk-outs, etc.)?

- Do the parties feel that the mediators acted in a neutral and impartial manner? Did the mediators deal explicitly with issues of neutrality and impartiality? Can the mediators comment on ways in which they felt parties were trying to win them over to their side?

- Through what frames did the mediation process address the issues (for example: "a security issue," "an argument about borders and territory," "mistrust"' etc.)? Did this framing prove to be conducive to negotiation and settlement? Did it affect the degree to which parties were able to come to grips with the past and look ahead to the future, or transform elements of their relationship with one another?

- Did the mediators' feeling that they were familiar with the conflict (e.g., 'This has been done before' or 'A thousand mediators have failed at this conflict') affect the way they handled the case? How so?

- What do the mediators view as the largest obstacle they faced during this simulation? What were some of the tools they used to overcome it?

- Do the mediators feel they managed the process "by the book" – moving from one stage of the model they learned to the next in a conscious and controlled manner? Do they feel that the structured process they tried to manage sometimes got wrested away from them or 'hijacked' (by the parties or by circumstances)? How did they react?

- Do the parties feel that their relationship shifted at different stages of the mediation? What was the mediator's role in bringing this about (if any)?

- What did the mediators do to help parties face their problem constructively?

- Do the mediators feel their information and preparation challenged their ability to maintain neutrality? Did parties experience a sense of mediator neutrality?

- Did the conversation focus on defined problems ("the location of the wall") or did the topics widen to include different related issues? What was the mediators' role or orientation with regards to the parties' adoption of this narrower or wider focus?

- How did the process of problem solving and searching for options begin? Did the mediators take an active role in generating or evaluating options for agreement? What effect did this have on the process? What might have been done differently?

- Did the search for options (or the final agreement) focus on the elements that were very much on the table or were attempts made to expand the pie? What was the mediators' role in this?

Training Goal: Negotiation Skills

Consider asking some of these questions, focusing on the way the participants playing the conflicting parties' delegates handled their roles. Choose questions and encourage discussion according to the level of competence and confidence of the parties, according to their performance, and according to your pre-set targeted skill-set (e.g., analytical grasp of the situation, strategizing ability, trust-and relationship-building, creativity, interpersonal communication skills, ability to cope with ethical dilemmas, pie-expanding, etc.):

- How would the parties define their overall strategy, when they first walked in to the joint discussion? Help participants frame a short definition of their strategic state of mind, such as "working cooperatively" or "asking for as much as I can, and then asking for more."

- Did the parties find they adhered to this strategy throughout the negotiation? If their strategy changed, was it done consciously, or as an intuitive / instinctive shift? What triggered the change?

- Did the parties' search for options (or the final agreement) focus on elements that were very much on the table, or were attempts made to expand the pie?

- What communication tools did the parties and the mediators use throughout the discussions? Was it difficult to utilize these techniques? Why?

- Did any communication problems arise over the course of the negotiation? What was their source? How did the parties address them?

- Was an atmosphere of trust created between the parties?

- Did parties share information openly, or did they play their cards close to their chests? What behavior or circumstances proved conducive to information sharing, and what behavior or circumstances inhibited information sharing?

- Did use of particular communication tools assist trust-building?

- Do the parties feel that their relationship shifted at different stages of the mediation? How would they describe these shifts? What do they think triggered and enabled them?

- Ask participants to name particular negotiation tactics they saw other participants employ successfully.

Training Goal: Team Negotiation and Multiparty Negotiation
Forum:

- Did the forum switch between multi-way meetings and private sessions between parties and the mediators (caucusing)? Whose initiative was this? Did the conflicting parties' teams ever decide to meet bilaterally, without the mediators? Were there any other types of meetings? Were there disagreements regarding use of different forums?

- Which types of forum seemed more conducive to information sharing, collaboration or problem solving? Which were ultimately more productive? Why?

Coalitions:

- Did coalitions form between any of the parties against other parties?

- Following up on the previous question: Did coalitions form on specific issues between some of the parties, and on others between different partners? What effect (if any) did this have on the negotiations?

- Did any party feel they had to try and break up a coalition formed by two other parties?

- Did members of each team assume they were "all on the same team" going in to the negotiation? Was this perception shaken up at a later stage of the negotiation process? What effect (if any) did this have on the negotiations?

- Did any participants (besides the formal mediators, if any) feel they assumed the role of middleman, positioning themselves as the one trying pull their own team, as well as the other, to bring them closer to understanding or agreement? How did this affect the negotiations?

- Can participants identify tacit or explicit coalitions formed between two or more members of opposing teams? How did this affect the negotiations?

Process Management:

- Did the parties discuss process management rules (or reach unspoken agreements on them), such as:

1) Ground rules: What are the seating arrangements? Are interruptions permitted? Can parties consult with others?

2) Communication Rules: What order do parties speak in? How long does everybody get to express him/herself? Can parties shout at each other?

3) Decision-making rules: Who decides the final outcome? Is it decided by majority vote, or must everybody agree?

- How were these explicit or implicit dynamics or decisions affected by the multi-party/team setting of the situation, as opposed to a two party setting?

- Did one of the participants take a conspicuously leading role in the negotiations? What gave them the legitimacy to do this, in the eyes of the other participants? What did the leader use this power for? Did other participants take the lead at different points during the process? If there had been a previously dominant player – did they relinquish control or struggle to retain it?

Training Goal: Understanding of the Conflict's Nature

- What have participants learned regarding the complexity of trying to solve a conflict of the kind illustrated by the role-play (e.g., international conflict, commercial conflict, tax conflict) through negotiation? What did they learn about the specific conflict on which the role-play focused?

- Did any participant enter the simulation with a predetermined solution to the conflict, or major elements thereof? Have they changed their minds, or reconsidered the applicability of their solution, as a result of participating in the simulation?

- What do participants have to say regarding the effectiveness, the desirability and the long- and short- term effects of unilateral moves by one side to the conflict?

- Do participants view the conflict in terms of power disparity? Did this view shift during the simulation?

- Did participation in the simulation enable participants to appreciate new ideas that might be transferable to ongoing protracted conflict going on in the real world? What ideas, in particular, piqued their interest?

- Have participants encountered a newfound appreciation for a party to the conflict they might have felt (walking into the simulation) was more to blame? Or, conversely, did they find that their preconceptions on this issue were strengthened by their experience? How would they portray and explain this transformation, or lack thereof?

- If the simulation took place with several sub-groups in a class working concurrently - did different groups reach different possible solutions/agreements? What pragmatic lessons might be learned from this regarding international conflict management?

Provide for further learning activities

Trainers might assign participants a paper to write, or some other assignment, regarding their experience or particular elements thereof. In particular, teachers concerned that their students are not sufficiently familiar learning with an experiential learning model, owing to practices of their field or cultural considerations, might supplement the simulation with a more "traditional" learning and/or assessment project. Teachers can provide students with forms for self-assessment to fill out before, during, and after participating in the simulation (see sample below). Finally, trainers can administer a simulation feedback form (see sample below) in which participants make general comments regarding the simulation and its management. This form is intended for self-reflection, not necessarily for assessment. Using this periodically throughout the course allows participants to monitor their own progress. Beyond providing input vital for the trainer's growth and development, this also encourages participants to view their experience through a new critical lens, leading to new insights into their own experience and learning.

Personal Reflection Sheet
Before Game Begins

When negotiating / mediating, I feel my strongest quality or ability lies in using the following skills:

_____
_____
_____
_____
_____

The skills I would like to improve or enhance are:

_____
_____
_____
_____
_____

At Game's Mid-point

The point in the negotiation / mediation where my strongest quality or ability was best demonstrated was:

_____
_____
_____
_____
_____

I used this specific tool advance the negotiation / mediation by:

_____
_____
_____
_____
_____

Describe a point of difficulty in the negotiation / mediation. The skill or tool I might have used to advance the negotiation / mediation is:

_____
_____
_____
_____
_____

The skill / tool I would like to develop or practice during the rest of the negotiation / mediation is:

_____
_____
_____
_____
_____

Professionalism demands constant learning and improvement. Reflect on these questions – they will help take you to the next level.~

After the Game's Conclusion

The point in the negotiation / mediation where my strongest quality or ability was best demonstrated was:

_____
_____
_____
_____
_____

I used this specific tool advance the negotiation / mediation by:

_____
_____
_____
_____
_____

Describe a point of difficulty in the negotiation / mediation. The skill or tool I might have used to advance the negotiation / mediation is:

_____
_____
_____
_____

A significant insight that I gained during this role-play, regarding the practice of negotiation / mediation was:

_____
_____
_____
_____
_____

I will be be using it in my future negotiations / mediations by:

_____
_____
_____
_____
_____

Professionalism demands constant learning and improvement. Reflect on these questions – they will help take you to the next level.

Simulation-Game Feedback Sheet

We constantly wish to learn and to improve our training skills and materials. Your thoughts on the following topics will help us improve our future workshops. Please take a few minutes to answer these questions (you can expand on the opposite side of the page):

How would you say the simulation contributed to your negotiating / mediating skills?

_____
_____
_____
_____
_____

How would you say the workshop contributed to your understanding of the specific conflict and its resolution?

_____
_____
_____
_____
_____

Please comment on some of these issues, regarding the organization of the simulation:
Amount and relevance of the background material:

_____
_____
_____
_____
_____

Clarity and order of the occurrences in the simulation:

_____
_____
_____
_____
_____

Staff handling of difficulties arising during the simulation:

_____
_____
_____
_____
_____

What is your overall impression of the simulation?

_____
_____
_____
_____
_____

How can we improve this simulation in the future?

_____
_____
_____
_____
_____

Any other general / particular comments you would like to make?

_____
_____
_____
_____
_____

Who else do you think would benefit from participating in such a simulation?

_____
_____
_____
_____
_____

THE EDITORS

Dr. Yael Efron is an LL.D. graduate from the Faculty of Law at the Hebrew University, Jerusalem. She previously served as the Dean at Zefat Academic College School of Law (ZAC) and today is Dean of Social Sciences and Education and Head of the Crisis and Emergency Management Program in Ramat-Gan Academic College in Israel. Dr. Efron teaches Civil Procedure, Alternative Dispute Resolution and Family Law. She also heads the Clinical Education Program and directs the Legal-Aid Clinic at ZAC. Dr. Efron is a visiting professor of negotiation at Mitchell Hamline School of Law in Minnesota; a visiting professor at the University of Missouri LL.M. program in dispute resolution; a visiting instructor at the Osgoode Professional Development program at York University, Canada; and a visiting scholar at Masaryk University Law Faculty in the Czech Republic under the auspices of the Theodore Herzl Distinguished Chair. Dr. Efron is the recipient of the Halbert Centre for Canadian Studies Post-Doctoral Fellowship and of the Theodore Herzl Distinguished Chair Award. She has published widely on legal education, pedagogy and curriculum design, negotiation, dispute resolution and other subjects.

Professor Nellie Munin is an LL.D. graduate from the Faculty of Law at the Hebrew University, Jerusalem. She is a faculty member at Zefat Academic College School of Law (ZAC) in Israel. Previously she served as Chief Legal Advisor of the State Revenue Administration in the Israeli Ministry of Finance and as Minister of Economic Affairs in the Israeli Mission to the EU. She taught as a visiting professor in Czechia (Masaryk University, Brno Law Faculty under the auspices of the Theodore Herzl Distinguished Chair, and Palacky University, Olomouc), in Latvia (Latvia University), in Italy (Ferrara University) and in Kazakhstan (Almaty Management University), under the auspice of Israel Institute grants for international courses. She has published widely on international trade law, EU economic law, taxation and legal education.

Acknowledgements

This book is the result of the cumulative contribution of many good people over the years. First, we would like to thank Professor Noam Ebner, who participated with us in writing several of the role-plays and wrote the chapter with instructions for their execution. Professor Ebner is a prolific researcher in the field of legal education and conflict resolution pedagogy, and his articles have served and still serve as a source of inspiration for us in writing the role-plays.

We found another source of inspiration in Mr. Gideon Taran, a pedagogical expert who accompanied us when we tried out some of the exercises in class. He contributed his rich insights and experience to their improvement. At our request, he even graciously agreed to contribute the pedagogical forward to the book.

This book could not have seen the light of day if it were not for our students at Zefat Academic College School of Law, who took an active part in the role-plays detailed herein. We are full of appreciation for their willingness to experiment with this innovative and challenging learning method and to share their insights from it with us. We also wish to thank Professor Aharon Kellerman, former president of Zefat Academic College, who gave his blessing for the establishment of The Center for Legal Didactics, and to the heads of the Zefat Academic College School of Law throughout the years, who allowed us to give free rein to our innovative ideas and their implementation in our classrooms.

We were able to accompany our effort with evaluation studies which allowed us to gather broad insights regarding legal education in general and role-playing games in particular. Our studies were made possible through, among other things, the generous funding of The Research Center for the Study of Cultures in the Galilee at Zefat Academic College. We thank Mirit Mehdkar and Shlomit Ariel for their assistance in the research.

Our beloved families also deserve our gratitude for their constant support.

Warm thanks to DRI Press and the Dispute Resolution Institute at Mitchell Hamline School of Law, headed by Professor Sharon Press, for agreeing to publish this book as part of its growing repository of skill building resources. Special thanks to the copy editor, Lianne Pinchuk, and the design editor, Erik Christopher, for their pleasant and kind support in the editing process and the production.

Finally, we would like to thank our colleagues, the teachers, who dare from time to time to have fun with our innovative teaching ideas and to experiment with our pedagogic proposals. The feedback they provide us encourages us to continue creating and expanding the repertoire offered to our colleagues. We appreciate any feedback for improvement of the exercises. We extend our invitation to other lecturers and teachers from all fields, especially those that are not covered in this book. If you are interested in participating in creating or applying role-playing games in your field, please contact us. We thank you in advance for any such cooperation.

BIBLIOGRAPHY

Books and Dissertations

Jeanne M. Brett, Negotiation Globally (2nd ed., 2007).

P. Christopher Earley & Soon Ang, Cultural Intelligence: Individual Interactions Across Cultures (2003).

Roger Fisher & William Ury, Getting to Yes: Negotiating Agreement Without Giving In 45 (2011).

Geert Hofstede, Culture's Consequences: International Differences in Work-Related Values (1984).

Culture, Leadership, and Organizations: The GLOBE Study of 62 societies (Robert J. House, Paul J. Hanges, Mansour Javidan, Peter W. Dorfman, & Vipin Gupta, eds, 2004).

Robert Kreitner, Angelo Kinicki & Nina Cole, Fundamentals of Organizational Behavior 154 (2007).

Michelle LeBaron, Bridging Cultural Conflicts: A New Approach to a Changing World (2003).

Michelle LeBaron & Venashry Pillay, Conflict Across Culture: A Unique Experience of Bridging Differences (2006).

Menachem Mautner, On Legal Education (2002).

Bernard S. Mayer, the Conflict Paradox: Seven Dilemmas at the Core of Disputes (2015).

Mark Hungerford Salisbury, The Effect of Study Abroad on Intercultural Competence Among Undergraduate College Students, (Ph.D. Dissertation, University of Iowa) (2011) https://iro.uiowa.edu/esploro/outputs/doctoral/The-effect-of-study-abroad-on/9983777141002771?institution=01IOWA_INST.

Austin Sarat, Matthew Anderson & Cathrine O. Frank, Law and the Humanities: An Introduction (2009).

Lisa Schirch, Exploring the Role of Ritual in Conflict Transformation (1997) (unpublished Ph.D. dissertation, George Mason University) (on file with author).

Tamar Shapira, Blocking and Empowerment in the Educational and Public Spheres: Women in the Arab Education System in Israel (2006) (unpublished Ph.D. dissertation, Haifa University Israel) (on file with author) http://in.bgu.ac.il/icqm/DocLib1/%D7%AA%D7%9E%D7%A8- %D7%A9%D7%A4%D7%99%D7%A8%D7%90.pdf.

WILLIAM M. SULLIVAN ET. AL., EDUCATING LAWYERS: PREPARATION FOR THE PROFESSION OF LAW (2007).

RUSSELL B. SUNSHINE, NEGOTIATING FOR INTERNATIONAL DEVELOPMENT: A PRACTITIONER'S HANDBOOK 214 (1990).

RICHARD SUSSKIND, TOMORROW'S LAWYERS: AN INTRODUCTION TO YOUR FUTURE (2017).

DAVID C. THOMAS ET. AL., CULTURAL INTELLIGENCE: SURVIVING AND THRIVING IN THE GLOBAL VILLAGE (2017).

LEIGH L. THOMPSON, THE MIND AND HEART OF THE NEGOTIATOR, 5TH EDITION (2011).

FONS TROMPENAARS & CHARLES HAMPDEN TURNER, RIDING THE WAVES OF CULTURE: UNDERSTANDING CULTURAL DIVERSITY IN BUSINESS (1998).

Articles and Book Chapters

Nadja Alexander & Michelle LeBaron, *Death of the Role-Play*, in RETHINKING NEGOTIATION TEACHING: INNOVATIONS FOR CONTEXT AND CULTURES 29, 179 (Christopher Honeyman, James Coben & Giuseppe De Palo eds., 2009).

American Public Health Association, *Impact of the Berkeley Excise Tax on Sugar-Sweetened Beverage Consumption - Abstract* (2016).

Piomelli Ascanio, *Cross-Cultural Lawyering by the Book: The Latest Clinical Texts and a Sketch of a Future Agenda*, 4 HASTINGS RACE & POV. J. 131-179 (2006).

Azam Rifaat, *The Interpretation of Tax Law: True Tax and Human Rights in the Supreme Court Ruling* 18 MISHPAT VE'ASAKIM [Hebrew] 401 (2014) https://papers.ssrn.com/sol3/papers.cfm?abstract_id=2864397.

Aharon Barak, *Some Reflections on the Israeli Legal System and Its Judiciary*, 6 ELECTRONIC J. COMP. L. 1 (2002) http://www.ejcl.org/61/art61-1.html.

Daphne Barak-Erez, *The National Security Constitution and the Israeli Condition*, in ISRAELI CONSTITUTION IN THE MAKING 429 (Gideon Sapir, Daphne Barak-Erez & Aharon Barak eds., 2013).

Joy E. Beatty, Yi-Su Chen & Barbara D. Klein, *Games and gamification in business school courses: Experiential education that creates engagement and flow*, 19 DECISION SCIENCES JOURNAL OF INNOVATIVE EDUCATION, 170 (2021) https://doi.org/10.1111/dsji.12250

Phyllis E. Bernard, *Finding Common Ground in the Soil of Culture* in RETHINKING NEGOTIATION TEACHING: INNOVATIONS FOR CONTEXT AND CULTURES 29 (Christopher Honeyman, James Coben & Giuseppe De Palo eds., 2009).

John Brondolo, *Collecting taxes during an economic crisis: Challenges and policy options*, IMF FISCAL AFFAIRS DEPARTMENT (2009), http://www.imf.org/external/pubs/ft/spn/2009/spn0917.pdf.

Susan Bryant & Jean Koh Peters, *The Five Habits of Cross Cultural Lawyering*, in RACE, CULTURE, PSYCHOLOGY AND LAW 47 (Kimberly Barrett & William George eds., 2005).

Tomer Brodie, *It will sell you space, the golden field: State sovereignty and international economic law*, ISRAEL DEMOCRACY INSTITUTE [Hebrew] (2010) https://www.idi.org.il/parliaments/7751/8170.

Hongbin Cai & Qiao Liu, *Competition and corporate tax avoidance: Evidence from Chinese industrial firms*, 119 Econ. J. 764–795 (2009).

Debra Chopp, *Addressing Cultural Bias in the Legal Profession*, 41 N.Y.U. Rev. L. & Soc. Change 367, 367 (2017).

Jerome A. Cohen, Settling *International Business Disputes with China: Then and Now*, 47 CORNELL INTERNATIONAL LAW JOURNAL 555 (2014). Available at: http://www.lawschool.cornell.edu/research/ILJ/upload/Cohen-final.pdf

Alexandra Crampton & Melissa Manwaring, *Reality and Artifice in Teaching Negotiation: The Variable Benefits of 'Keeping it Real' in Simulations*, 2 TEACH. NEG. 1 (2008) http://archive.constantcontact.com/fs079/1101638633053/archive/1102208945307.html.

Ellen E. Deason et. al., *Debriefing the Debrief*, EDUCATING NEGOTIATORS FOR A CONNECTED WORLD: VOLUME 4 IN RETHINKING NEGOTIATION TEACHING SERIES (Christopher Honeyman, James Coben, & Andrew Wei-Min Lee eds., 2013) http://open.mitchellhamline.edu/dri_press/4/.

Susan DeJarnatt & Mark Rahdert, *Preparing for Globalized Law Practice: The Need to Include International and Comparative Law in the Legal Writing Curriculum*, 17 J. LEG. WRI. INST. (2011).

Glauco De Vita, *Learning Styles, Culture and Inclusive Interaction in the Multicultural Classroom: A Business and Management Perspective*, 38 INNOVATIONS EDU. & TEACH. INT'L 2, 165 (2001).

Daniel Druckman & Noam Ebner, *Onstage or Behind the Scenes? Relative Learning Benefits of Simulation Role-Play and Design*, 39 SIM. & GAMING 4, 465 (2008).

Daniel Druckman & Noam Ebner, *Games, claims, and new frames: Rethinking the use of simulation in negotiation education* 29 NEG. J. 1, 61-93 (2013).

Noam Ebner, *Negotiation is Changing*, 99 J. DISPUTE RES. 1 (2017).

Noam Ebner & Sharon Press, Pandemic Pedagogy II: Conducting simulations & role plays in online, video-based, synchronous courses (2020) https://papers.ssrn.com/sol3/papers.cfm?abstract_id=3557303.

Noam Ebner & Yael Efron, *Using Tomorrow's Headlines for Today's Training: Creating Pseudo Reality in Conflict Resolution Simulation-Games*, 21 HARV. NEGOT. J. 3, 377 (2005).

Noam Ebner & Yifat Winkler, *The Pasta Wars: a Prisoners Dilemma Simulation-Game*, 40 SIM. & GAMING 1, 134-146 (2009) https://papers.ssrn.com/sol3/papers.cfm?abstract_id=2200350.

Noam Ebner & Kimberlee K. Kovack, *Simulation 2.0: The Resurrection* in VENTURING BEYOND THE CLASSROOM: VOLUME 2 IN THE RETHINKING NEGOTIATION TEACHING SERIES (C. Honeyman, J. Coben & G. DiPalo eds, 2010) http://ssrn.com/abstract=1916794.

Yael Efron, *Legal Education in Israel: Where Is It Headed?*, 9 ALEI MISHPAT [Hebrew, Law Review of the Academic Center of Law & Business] 45 (2010).

Yael Efron, *Clinical Legal Education in Israel* in CLINICAL LEGAL EDUCATION IN ASIA: ACCESSING JUSTICE FOR THE UNDERPRIVILEGED 91 (Shuvro Prosun Sarker ed., 2015).

Yael Efron, *What is Learned in Clinical Learning?*, 29 CLINICAL L. REV. 259 (2023).

Yael Efron, *The Pentalectic Sphere as Means for Questioning Legal Education – Towards a Paradigm Shift*, 9 ARIZONA SUM. L. REV. 285 (2016).

Yael Efron & Nellie Munin, *Role Plays Bring Theory to life in a Multicultural Learning Environment*, 66 J. LEG. EDU. 2, 309 (2017).

Yael Efron & Yaron Silverstein, *Legal Education as a Means for Social Ethnic and Inter-Ethnic Change: The Case of Arab Law Students in Zefat College*, 19 HAMISHPAT [Hebrew, Colman L. Rev.] 331 (2014).

Yael Efron & Yaron Silverstein, *Law Students as Agents of Change*, 6 Ma'asei Mishpat [Hebrew, Tel Aviv Univ. J. for Soc. Change] 105 (2014).

Ehud Eran, *FES Southern Perspective: Israel's Strategic Interests in the Eastern Mediterranean*, Fes Peace & Security (2021) http://library.fes.de/pdf-files/bueros/israel/17835.pdf.

María G. Fábregas Janeiro, Ricardo López Fabre, & José Pablo Nuño de la Parra, *Building Intercultural Competence Through Intercultural Competency Certification of Undergraduate Students*, 10 J. Int'l Edu. Research 1, 15-22 (2014).

James Faulconbridge & Daniel Muzino, *Legal Education, Globalization and Cultures of Professional Practice*, Georgetown J. Leg. Ethics 1335-1359 (2009).

Graham Ferris, *The Legal Educational Continuum That Is Visible Through A Glass Dewey*, 43 L. Teacher 2, 102-113 (2009).

Shigeru Fujita & Giuseppe Moscarini, *Recall and unemployment*, 107 Am. Econ. Rev. 12, 3875-3916 (2017) http://dx.doi.org/10.1257/aer.20131496.

Roger Gomm et. al., *Case Study and Generalization*, in Case Study Method: Key Issues, Key Texts 98 (Roger Gomm, Martyn Hammersley & Peter Foster, eds., 2000).

John L. Graham & N. Mark Lam, *The Chinese Negotiation*, Harv. Business Rev. (2003) https://hbr.org/2003/10/the-chinese-negotiation?autocomplete=true.

Phil Hodkinson & Heather Hodkinson, *The Strengths and Limitations of Case Study Research* 11 (2001), https://www.academia.edu/31677978/The_Strengths_and_Limitations_of_Case_Study_Research.

Jan L. Jacobowitz, *Lawyers Beware! You Are What You Post---The Case for Integrating Cultural Competency, Legal Ethics, and Social Media* 17 Sci. & Tech. L. Rev. 4, 541-580 (2014) https://papers.ssrn.com/sol3/papers.cfm?abstract_id=2514678.

Kimberlee K. Kovach, *Culture, Cognition and Learning Preferences*, in Rethinking Negotiation Teaching: Innovations for Context and Cultures 29, 343 (Christopher Honeyman, James Coben & Giuseppe De Palo eds., 2009).

John Lande, *Teaching students to negotiate like a lawyer*, 39 Wash. U. J. L. & Policy 109-144 (2012).

John Lande, *Suggestions for Using Multi-Stage Simulations in Law School Courses*, U. Missouri Sch. L. Leg. Studies, Research Paper No. 2013-08, 1-7 (2014).

John Lande & Jean R. Sternlight, *The Potential Contribution of ADR to an Integrated Curriculum: Preparing Law Students for Real World Lawyering*, 25 Ohio St. J. On Disp. Resol. 247, 251–52 (2010).

Betty Leask, *Using Formal and Informal Curricula to Improve Interactions Between Home and International Students*, 13 J. Studies Int'l Edu. 2, 205-221 (2009).

Michelle LeBaron, *Transforming Cultural Conflict in an Age of Complexity*, in Berghof Handbook for Conflict Transformation 2 (2001), https://edoc.vifapol.de/opus/volltexte/2011/2578/.

Tomaz Lesnik et. al., *Recession and tax compliance – The case of Slovenia*, 25 Inzinerine EkonomikaEngineering Econ. 2, 130, (2014).

Michael W Long et. al., *Cost effectiveness of Sugar-Sweetened Beverages Excise Tax in the U.S.*, 49 am. J. preventive med. 1 (2015) https://www.sciencedirect.com/science/article/abs/pii/S0749379715000963?via%3Dihub.

Zhenzhong Ma & Alfred Jaeger, *Getting to Yes in China: Exploring Personality Effects in Chinese Negotiation Styles*, 14 GROUP DECISION & NEGOTIATION, 415-437 (2005) https://link.springer.com/article/10.1007/s10726-005-1403-3.

David Matz & Noam Ebner, *Using role-play in online negotiation teaching* in VENTURING BEYOND THE CLASSROOM: VOLUME 2 IN THE RETHINKING NEGOTIATION TEACHING SERIES (C Honeyman, J Coben & G DiPalo, eds., 2010) https://papers.ssrn.com/sol3/papers.cfm?abstract_id=1916792.

Menachem Mautner, *Three Approaches to Law and Culture*, 96 CORNELL L. REV. 839 (2011).

Gabriel Mitchel, *The Eastern Mediterranean Gas Forum: Cooperation in the Shadow of Competition*, MITVIM (2020) https://tinyurl.com/2k3a6meh.

Andrew Molinsky, *A Situational Approach For Assessing and Teaching Acculturation*, 34 J. MAN. EDU. 5, 723-745 (2010).

Nellie Munin, *Do The New Peace Agreements Between Israel and the Gulf States Set a "Honey Trap" for Israel?*, 4 BRATISLAVA L. REV. 2, 95-110, (2020).

Nellie Munin, *With a Little Help of my Friends - Examining the Logic behind Israel-Jordan-UAE Water for Electricity Deal*, 9 ATHENS J. MED. STUDIES 1 (2023).

Nellie Munin & Karnit Malka-Tiv, *Tax Obedience in Corona Times*, 13 J. MULTIDISCIPLINARY RESEARCH 2 (2021).

Nellie Munin & Karnit Malka-Tiv, *Tax Obedience in Corona Times*, IUP 16 J. GOV. & PUBLIC POL. 4, 46-68 (2022).

Ian S. Mutchnick, Cherly A. Moyer, & David T. Stern, *Expanding the Boundaries of Medical Education: Evidence for Cross-Cultural Exchanges*, 78 ACADEMIC MED. 10, S1-S5 (2003).

OECD Environment Directorate et. al., *Preventing single-use plastic waste: implications of different policy approaches*, OECD (2021) https://www.oecd.org/content/dam/oecd/en/publications/reports/2021/10/preventing-single-use-plastic-waste_5bb4030a/c62069e7-en.pdf.

Rebecca Lindsey Parsons, *The Effects of an Internationalized University Experience on Domestic Students in the United States and Australia*, 14 J. STUDIES INT'L EDU. 4, 313-334 (2010).

Merav Peleg-Gabay, *Taxation of Soft Drinks for Health Reasons*, KNESSET RESEARCH AND INFORMATION CENTER [Hebrew] (2021) https://tinyurl.com/48pr3sj5.

David Perkins, *What is understanding?* in TEACHING FOR UNDERSTANDING: LINKING RESEARCH WITH PRACTICE 39–57 (Martha Stone Wiske ed., 1998).

Thomas Pettigrew et. al., *Recent Advances in Intergroup Contact Theory*, 35 INT'L J. INTERCULTURAL REL. 3, 271-280 (2011).

Galia Press Barnathan, *The Neglected Dimension of Commercial Liberalism: Economic Cooperation and Transition of Peace*, 43 J. PEACE RESEARCH 3, 261-278 (2006).

Vassilis T. Rapanos, *The Effects of Environmental Taxes on Income Distribution*, 11(3) EUROPEAN J. POL. ECON. 487 (1995).

Noya Rimalt, *Legal Education: Between Theory and Practice*, 24 TEL AVIV U. L. REV. 81, 129 (2001).

Leonard L. Riskin, *The Contemplative Lawyer: On the Potential Contributions of Mindfulness Meditation to Law Students, Lawyers, and their Clients*, 7 HARV. NEGOT. L. REV. 1, 17 (2002).

Antoinette Sedillo López, *Making and Breaking Habits: Teaching (and Learning) Cultural Context, Self-Awareness, and intercultural Communication Through Case Supervision in a Client-Service Legal Clinic*, WASHINGTON U. J. L. & POL. 28, 37-68 (2008).

Marci Seville, *Chinese Soup, Good Horses, and Other Narratives: Practicing Cross-Cultural Competence before We Preach* in VULNERABLE POPULATIONS AND TRANSFORMATIVE LAW TEACHING: A CRITICAL READER 277 (2011).

Sharma Madhav & Loren B. Jung, *How Cross-Cultural Social Participation Affects the International Attitudes of U.S. Students*, 9 INT'L J. INTERCULTURAL REL. 4, 377-387 (1985).

Carole Silver, *Getting Real About Globalization and Legal Education: Potential and Perspectives for the U.S.*, 24 STANFORD L. & POL. REV. 2, 457-501 (2013).

Yaron Silverstein & Yael Efron, *Law Students as Agents of Social Change–Moral Values and Attitudes in Zefat College School of Law*, 6 MA'ASEI MISHPAT [Hebrew, Tel Aviv Univ. J. for Soc. Change] 105, 108 (2014).

Shiri Specter-Ben Ari, *Taxation of disposable plastic utensils*, KNESSET RESEARCH AND INFORMATION CENTER [Hebrew] (2021) https://tinyurl.com/mrxp6y2j.

David Sugarman, *Beyond Ignorance and Complacency: Robert Stevens' Journey Through Lawyers and the Courts*, 16 INT'L J. OF LEG. PROF. 10 (2009).

Sherry Sullivan & Howard S. Tu, *Developing Globally Competent Students: A Review and Recommendations*, 19 J. MAN. EDU. 4, 473-493 (1995).

Charles Taylor, *The Politics of Recognition* in MULTICULTURALISM: EXAMINING THE POLITICS OF RECOGNITION 25-73 (Amy Gutman ed., 1994).

Laurel S. Terry, *U.S. Legal Ethics: The Coming of Age of Global and Comparative Perspectives*, 4 WASHINGTON U. GLOBAL STUDIES L. REV. 3, 463-533 (2005).

Paul R. Tremblay, *Interviewing and Counseling Across Cultures: Heuristics and Biases*, 9 CLINICAL L. REV. 1, 373-416 (2002).

Carina Weng, *Multicultural Lawyering: Teaching Psychology To Develop Cultural Self-awareness*, 11 CLINICAL L. REV., PAPER NO. 823: 369-403 (2005).

Stephen Wizner, *The Law School Clinic: Legal Education in the Interests of Justice*, 70 FORDHAM L. REV. 1929, 1934 (2002).

Neta Ziv, *Legal Education and Social Responsibility: On the Link Between the Law Faculty and the Community in Which It Is Placed*, 25 THEORETICAL INQUIRIES IN L. 2, 385 (2001).

Laws

Bar Association Law, 5721-1961, § 25(1), 178 [Hebrew].

Income Tax Ordinance, 5721-1961 [Hebrew].

Israeli Customs Tariff Order, Purchase Tax on Soft Drinks (Amendment No. 4), 2021 [Hebrew] https://tinyurl.com/2fkbd6sn.

Israeli Customs tariff order and exemptions and purchase tax on goods (Amendment No. 8), 2022 [Hebrew] https://bit.ly/3FUkKr0.

International Agreements

Chemical Weapon Convention, 1974 U.N.T.S. 45 (1992).

Israel-Palestine Liberation Organization: Declaration of Principles on Interim Self Government Arrangements ["Oslo I" agreement], 32 I.L.M. 1525 (1993).

Israel-Palestine Liberation Organization: Interim Agreement on the West Bank and the Gaza Strip ["Oslo II" agreement], 36 I.L.M. 551 (1997).

Peace Treaty between Israel and Egypt (1979) https://www.gov.il/en/pages/israel-egypt-peace-treaty.

Peace Treaty between Israel and Jordan (1994) https://www.gov.il/en/pages/israel-jordan-peace-treaty.

United States, Mexico, Canada (USMCA) Agreement (2020) https://ustr.gov/trade-agreements/free-trade-agreements/united-states-mexico-canada-agreement.

Resolutions, Declarations & Recommendations

Israeli Higher Education Commission Compilation of Main Resolution 2002-2007 [Hebrew] (1997) https://tinyurl.com/3kbnvnd4.

Israeli Government Decision No. 263 regarding the promotion of a healthy lifestyle [Hebrew] (2021) https://www.gov.il/he/departments/policies/dec263_2021.

The State of Israel's Declaration of Independence (1948).

The Teaching of Public and Private International Law, INSTITUT DE DROIT INTERNATIONAL [French, The Inst. of Int'l Law] 1 (1997), https://www.idi-iil.org/app/uploads/2017/06/1997_str_01_en.pdf.

UN General Assembly Res. 181 (II) (1947).

UN Partition Plan–Resolution 181 (1947), ISRAEL MINISTRY OF FOREIGN AFFAIRS, https://www.gov.il/en/pages/1947-un-partition-plan.

Online Sources

A comprehensive and updated report on the new purchase tax on disposable plastic utensils, TEL AVIV AND CENTRAL TRADE CHAMBER [Hebrew] https://www.chamber.org.il/foreigntrade/1109/1111/125309/.

Berkeley Soda Tax Campaign, ECOLOGY CENTER https://ecologycenter.org/berkeley-soda-tax-campaign/.

Comparative information on the deposit law on beverage containers, ISRAELI CONSUMERS COUNCIL (1999) https://www.consumers.org.il/category/deposit-law-general.

Noam Ebner & Yael Efron, *Converging!*, SYRACUSE UNIVERSITY (2007) https://www.maxwell.syr.edu/research/article/converging!.

Noam Ebner & Yael Efron, *Little Golano: An International Conflict Management Simulation*, SYRACUSE UNIVERSITY (2011) https://www.maxwell.syr.edu/research/article/little-golano.

Noam Ebner, Yael Efron & Nellie Munin, *Flashpoint: Syria, 2014—An International Conflict Management Simulation* (2014) http://dx.doi.org/10.2139/ssrn.2476968.

Frequently Asked Questions about the taxation of disposable plastic utensils, ISRAEL MINISTRY OF ENVIRONMENTAL PROTECTION [Hebrew] https://www.gov.il/he/departments/faq/why_pay_more.

Barbara Gray, Peter T. Coleman & Linda L. Putnam, *Introduction: Intractable Conflict: New Perspectives on the Causes and Conditions for Change*, 50 AM. BEHAV. SCIENTIST 1415 (2007).

Heather Horn, *Is Eastern Europe Any More Xenophobic Than Western Europe?: Investigating a Stereotype of the Refugee Crisis*, THE ATLANTIC (2015) https://www.theatlantic.com/international/archive/2015/10/xenophobia-eastern-europe-refugees/410800/.

Israeli Worldview, IOR (2018) http://www.iorworld.com/israel-pages-789.php.

Osnat Lautman, *The Positive Attitude Toward Failure in the Culture of Israeli Innovation*, OLM Consulting (2016), available at: https://olm-consulting.com/positive-attitude-toward-failure-culture-israeli-innovation/

Deborah Lau, *The Chinese Tradition Trap – Failure is Not an Option*, Reprogramming Directive (2010). https://deborahlau.com/2010/04/chinese-tradition-trap/

Christina Martini & David Susler, *Inside Out: Going Global Should Be for Everyone*, Chicago Lawyer Magazine (2011) https://www.lawyerport.com/chicagolawyer/inside-out-20111010#/&hl=%7B%22author%22%3A%5B%22martini%22%5D%7D.

Andrea Masullo, The Importance of Diversity and Multiculturalism in the Classroom! Retrieved from Andrea Masullo's, Professional Art Education Portfolio (2013).

Preliminary analysis of trends in the purchase of sugary drinks following the imposition of a tax on them, Bank of Israel [Hebrew] (2022) https://tinyurl.com/2x7sxua3.

Gianni Pittella, *Populism, Racism and Xenophobia Have Infected Europe*, euractive (2016) https://www.euractiv.com/section/global-europe/opinion/populism-racism-and-xenophobia-have-infected-europe/.

William Poundstone, Prisoner's Dilemma (Anchor Books 1992).

Presidential Workshop on Globalizing the Curriculum at the 2013 AALS Annual Meeting, Association of American Law Schools (2012).

Revenue statistics in Latin America and the Caribbean, OECD, (2021), 29-59, https://www.oecd.org/en/publications/revenue-statistics-in-latin-america-and-the-caribbean-2021_96ce5287-en-es.html.

Eduard Soler, *The EU and Eastern Mediterranean: How to Deal with Turkey*, Barcelona Centre for International Affairs (2021) https://www.cidob.org/en/publications/eu-and-eastern-mediterranean-how-deal-turkey.

Trade set to plunge as COVID-19 pandemic upends global economy, WTO (2020) https://www.wto.org/english/news_e/pres20_e/pr855_e.htm.

Trade falls steeply in the first half of 2020, WTO (2020) https://www.wto.org/english/news_e/pres20_e/pr858_e.htm.

Translating and the Law: Legal Language, The Economist (2012) https://www.economist.com/business/2012/11/10/legal-language.

WHO calls on countries to tax sugar-sweetened beverages to save lives, WHO (2022) https://www.who.int/news/item/13-12-2022-who-calls-on-countries-to-tax-sugar-sweetened-beverages-to-save-lives.

www.ingramcontent.com/pod-product-compliance
Lightning Source LLC
LaVergne TN
LVHW061253060426
835507LV00020B/2306